SAFARI

PATRICK DE WILDE

Flammarion

For Swann, Clémence ... and other animals.

CONTENTS

INTRODUCTION

Imagine. The sun is setting in a crimson blaze. Tired but happy, you are relaxing in a canvas or wicker lounger after a long, hot day. The flickering flames of the campfire set you dreaming as you listen to the tall stories of the rangers who vie to outdo each other with their tales of bravery. A few feet away, under an elegant awning, the table is set with a creamy linen tablecloth, the finest porcelain, silverware, and crystal goblets. The camp is guarded by slender tribesmen armed with spears. The tents are a short distance away. The path is lit by old-fashioned oil lamps hanging from the acacia trees. Beyond, the magnificent savanna stretches as far as the eye can see. As night falls, the stars come out one by one until the inky black sky is thickly clustered with pinpoints of light. The camp is a tiny dot in the immensity of the plain. Utter silence reigns, interrupted only by the occasional roar of a lion. The sound carries for miles in the still air.

A safari is more than just a holiday. It is a once-in-a-lifetime experience, a way for people caught up in the non-stop pressures of modern life to take a step back and rediscover a part of themselves they have lost touch with. Safaris have taken on an almost mystical, spiritual dimension. They strip away all the unnecessary stresses of life and bring us to the stark realization that in a hostile environment, all the trappings of civilization are useless to protect us. Nowadays, safaris are about watching animals rather than hunting them. In the valleys, mountains, forests, plains, lakes, and deserts of Africa, we rediscover the life our ancestors led tens of thousands of years ago—but with the knowledge that the comfort of the camp awaits when we return exhausted in the evening.

These days, vacation companies offer safari adventures in many parts of the world—not just in Africa—such as Australia, Central America, and the Central Asian republics: everywhere where nature is still red in tooth and claw, where tourists can experience true wilderness within relatively easy reach of international airports. But Africa will always be the home of the safari. This is where the very concept of the safari was born, inspired by the landscapes, the flora and fauna, the culture and climate of Africa. Only Africa, the cradle of humankind, could inspire in modern man the wish to rediscover the natural world, to explore its mysteries, first as a source of great wealth to be plundered, then later as a magnificent record of the common history of humanity.

It is misleading to talk of safaris as if the experience were the same throughout Africa. Tourists will come away with very different encounters with Africa depending on which country they visit. Safaris offer a wealth of complex and varied experiences. A safari in Kenya is nothing like a safari in Zimbabwe, or Namibia, or South Africa. There are so many factors that can vary, from the very nature of the landscape—from arid savanna to lush rainforest—to the skill and dedication of the rangers and the government's attitude towards the tourist industry, which can be more or less welcoming. Of course, each country, even each game reserve, has its own character, its own star attractions, and its own style of lodges.

Some tourists now go on safari expecting to see wildlife in the same way they might visit the pyramids in Egypt or the temples of Cambodia, ticking them off on a mental list as they travel. This is to miss the point of the safari experience. To get the most out of a safari, you must tune your mind to be in awe of the magnificence of the ephemeral spectacle that nature provides. Each day is different. The game reserves are constantly changing as the herds of animals move around the park. No two visitors will ever have quite the same experience. It is a real privilege to see the animals of Africa in their natural habitat—a privilege that demands patience and a certain degree of humility. There are no guarantees with a safari. You may be lucky and see a lioness bringing down a wildebeest—or you may see nothing but common impalas. What is certain, however, is that it is preferable to travel alone or as part of a small group, as much of the romance of the safari is lost if every time the radio directs your minibus to somewhere you can find rare animals, the place is already crowded with vehicles. Similarly, a week spent in a hotel with all modern conveniences is a far cry from the romance of a night under canvas in a remote corner of the bush. Such moments of harmony with the natural world are rare and precious. They can make you forget the very existence of your life back in civilization, the bustle of modern cities, the stress, and the noise. All that sloughs away in the bright light of the African savanna. Nothing makes you feel alive like waking in the warm light of dawn and seeing animals drinking at the watering hole outside your tent, or coming face to face with a wild creature, your eyes locking for a fleeting second before it skitters off into the bush. Nature is a place for quiet contemplation. To understand its secrets, you must free yourself of preconceptions and open your mind to all forms of beauty—the subtle gray-green of lichen growing on a fallen tree trunk, the graceful curves of an oryx's horns. Sadly, much of the beauty of the African landscape is under constant threat, although people are beginning to realize more and more that the earth and its bountiful resources are finite. While big game hunting is now strictly controlled and licensed, there are still large numbers of unscrupulous poachers eager to earn a few dollars on the black market by snuffing out the life of a beautiful and precious creature. While the image of the hunter shooting down a rampaging elephant or angry lion about to pounce to save his own life has proved an enduring one, these days the hunters are extremely well equipped and often shoot down animals completely unaware of their presence using powerful rifles from inside their vehicles, not even leaving the creature a sporting chance to get away.

Ancient African legends handed down from generation to generation tell strange tales that indicate that traditional folk culture was well aware of the importance of living in harmony with the natural habitat long before the Western world awoke to the necessity of protecting the environment. The tales tell of shamans who warned hunters who killed too much game that the spirit that watched over the plains would wreak dreadful revenge on them. They told that every animal the hunter killed would take away part of his soul. Any hunter who killed for pleasure or blood lust would pay a terrible price.

Fortunately, in recent years, a higher level of environmental awareness has led to a major change in the way Western societies look at animals. Scientists have come to grasp the importance of observing animals in their natural environment as a way of understanding the structure and hierarchy of the group. The importance of observing animal behavior in the wild was noted as early as 1762 by the philosopher Charles-Georges Le Roy who wrote a series of *Philosophical Letters on Animals,* claiming that animals share certain traits with humans, such as communication using a form of language. However, this theory was neglected in favor of the notion developed by Descartes in 1637 of the animal as a form of machine. This theory was championed by Malebranche in 1674 and then by the great naturalist Buffon in 1753. It would have a profound and lasting impact on scientific thinking for the next three centuries. Despite alternative theories put forward by naturalists and thinkers such as Alfred Espinas, Jean-Baptiste Lamarck, Douglas Spalding, George John Romanes, Lloyd Morgan, and Julian Huxley, Descartes's theory dominated thinking until the dawn of the twentieth century, when Oscar Heinroth challenged the simplistic theories put forward in Descartes's *Discourse on Method* with his work on the phylogenesis of characteristics, which underlined the importance of cognitive observation and gave rise to the new discipline of ethology—the study of animal behavior in the natural environment. Among the founding fathers of modern ethology are the Nobel Prize winners Konrad Lorenz, Niko Tinbergen, and Karl von Frisch. Many women have also contributed considerable bodies of research to the field, turning ethology into a major new discipline and changing the way we look at animals forever. Ethology owes much to the work done by Joy Adamson on lions, Betty Leslie Melville on giraffes, Ala Sussens on leopards, Patty Wilson on hyenas, Barbara Travers on rhinos, Jeanne Altman on baboons, Sophie de Wilde on sea lions, Dian Fossey on gorillas, and Jane Goodall on chimpanzees.

To find and collate the precious data that constitutes the backbone of their research, these men and women devoted their lives to observing animals in the wild. Several of them paid for their dedication with their lives. Safaris, which share the same goals as ethology—the study of animals in their natural habitat—equally demand much time and patience. Contrary to what wildlife documentaries might lead tourists to expect, lions do not spend all day hunting, monkeys often spend hours hiding in trees rather than playing about for the camera, and hippos rarely fight. It can take several months of preparation to obtain just a few excellent shots or a couple of minutes of screen time. To capture on film the most exciting moments of life on the savanna, you must be prepared to wait, and wait, and wait. The only sure way of being there to shoot the moment of drama is to be constantly alert, curious, and ready to move at a moment's notice. This holds true for safaris, too. You need patience, perseverance—and a healthy dose of luck.

Given the time it takes to observe animals in their natural habitat, it is best to make a very early start—preferably before sunrise, around five in the morning, when every sound, every footprint, every scent becomes a clue to be followed by the ranger. The game drive begins in an all-terrain vehicle that is designed for endurance rather than comfort. The roads in the game parks are often little more than deeply rutted dirt tracks, and breaking down here would be extremely dangerous. We drive around until late morning, when the light becomes too glaring and the sun too hot to continue. We stop for a well-deserved siesta before continuing in mid-afternoon. We return to the camp as night falls, relaxing with a glass of brandy or wine as the sun sets, watching the golden rays of the dying sun pour over the landscape like honey. If nighttime drives are allowed, we go for another drive, the vehicle's powerful projectors picking out civets, genets, porcupines, leopards, and serval cats. The rhythm of life on the savanna follows the sun. Few animals are out and about during the heat of midday, but as evening falls, the animals awaken and often head for the watering holes.

The safari experience is all about discovering the natural environment and the animals that live there. It is perhaps understandable that most people wish to see the "Big Five"—elephants, buffaloes, rhinos, leopards, and lions—but it is a shame that so many guides encourage this, rather than pointing out the fascinating secrets of some of the smaller animals—mongoose, meerkats, birds—that are just as interesting from a scientific point of view.

Because safaris are all about rediscovering simple, natural pleasures, a number of other factors also contribute to their success, including the accommodation. This is where the game lodge comes in. Game lodges are a cross between a hotel, a holiday villa, and a cottage. They are generally built in the heart of the bush, using local materials and environmentally friendly techniques. Lodges represent more than just tourist accommodation. They symbolize a vision of man's place in the natural world, living in harmony with it rather than imposing his will. In many camps, there is no barrier between the tents and the savanna and it is not uncommon to wake up to find wild animal tracks all around the tent. Each camp makes it a point of honor to welcome guests warmly. The rangers are always willing to point out interesting natural features, and it is delightful to share a meal with your fellow travelers under the stars, finishing the evening round the campfire before returning to your tent, the path bathed in the soft glow of the oil lamps hanging from the acacias. The camp is often staffed by local tribesmen who dance and play traditional music late into the night. This must be one of the most serene and peaceful ways to spend an evening.

Tourist accommodation in most of southern Africa has made spectacular progress in the past ten years or so. A decade ago, the camps were very basic, and the only visitors were those who saw roughing it

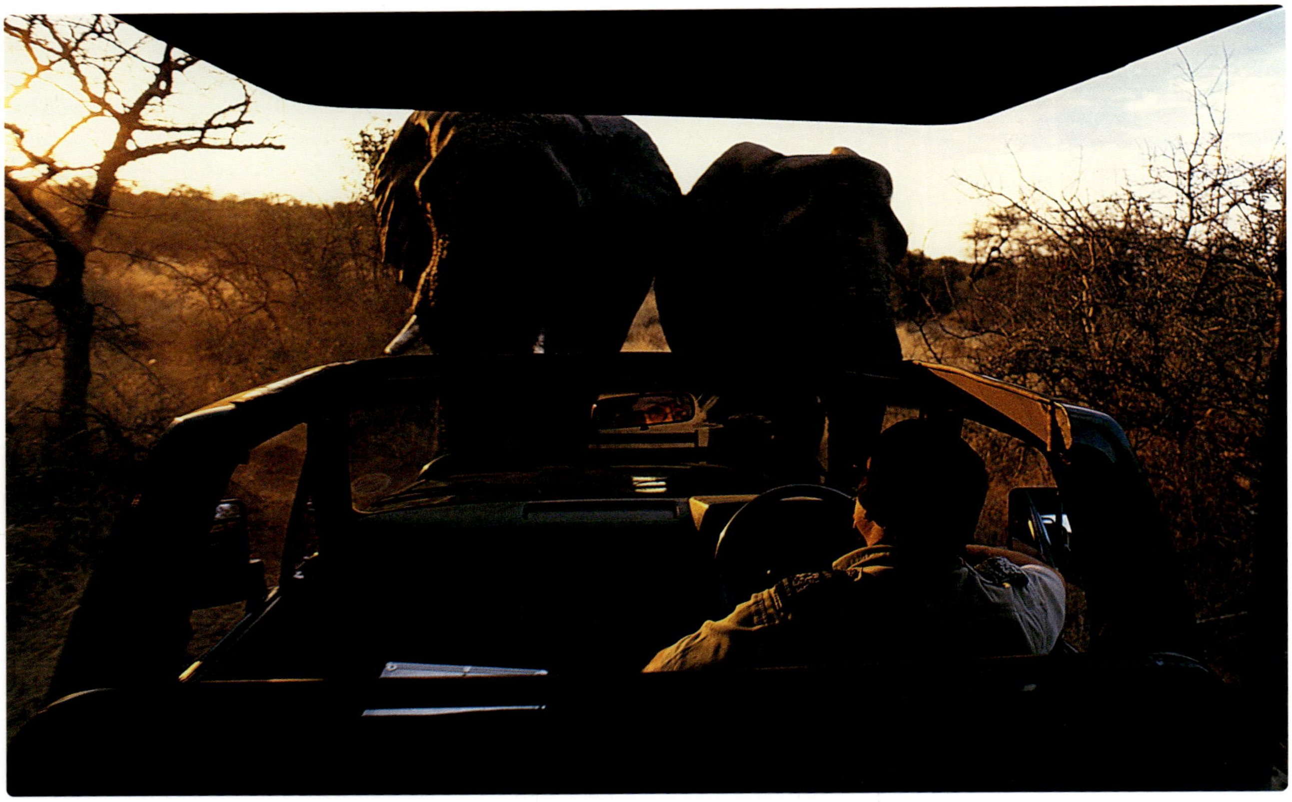

Snapshots are often emotion-packed. The Kruger elephants sometimes prove to be quite mischievous. Deliberately blocking our route, these giants attacked our vehicle and then scrupulously inspected its interior.

as part of the authentic safari experience. Nowadays, tastes have changed and the increasing popularity of safaris among travelers—particularly from North America—has led to vastly improved standards of comfort. Luxury is not too strong a word for some camps. The sense of utter freedom enjoyed by the pioneers of safaris in the region can still be enjoyed, but at a price. Now that safaris have become so popular, the industry is a major source of foreign revenue for many countries in southern Africa. The first game camps to latch onto the international tourist trade, many of them in Kenya, have turned into what could almost be called theme parks. It is true that running a safari is a far more profitable venture than farming. An entire industry has sprung up breeding and selling wild animals. A black rhino costs around seventy-five thousand dollars, a buffalo thirty thousand, a white rhino twenty-six thousand, a lion three thousand, and a zebra just three hundred. The wilderness that once covered much of Africa has been nibbled away by farmland, towns, and villages. The great annual migrations, necessary for the survival of many species of antelope in particular, are now faced with the additional dangers of barbed-wire or electric fences strung across what used to be open savanna but is now privately owned farmland. The animals are forced to abandon their migratory habits and stay in one place, which they then strip bare of all plant life as they try to ward off starvation. In order to rectify the dangerous imbalance in the ecosystem that such changes create, the authorities are now making serious efforts to control animal populations—something that nature has been doing perfectly for countless millennia. Elephants are the first victims of this policy, because they are often accused of rooting up saplings with their tusks and thus contributing to deforestation. However, it is equally the case that elephants play a vital role in maintaining the ecosystem of the savanna by opening up stretches of the plains for other herbivores and by spreading seeds in their dung. The problem of deforestation owes much more to arsonists and unregulated slash-and-burn farming techniques.

This issue was addressed by Ron Thomson in his 1986 book *On Wildlife Conservation*. He wrote that in the future, as a result of the increasing human population, wildlife would no longer be afforded a place unless it could be seen to have economic benefits. Ironically, given that vacationers are a vital source of foreign revenue, tourism has come to play an increasingly important role in environmental protection. After all, the tourists will stop coming if there are no more animals to see. This is the challenge faced by all the countries of southern and eastern Africa who now grasp the importance of safeguarding these fragile ecosystems.

The wealth of the untamed wildernesses of Kenya, Tanzania, South Africa, Namibia, Botswana, Zambia, and Zimbabwe cannot be measured in terms of revenue and balance sheets. No great monuments bear witness to the memory of our earliest ancestors. All there is to remind us that this is where humanity originated are the trees, the plains of waving grass, the tribal legends and amulets that are worn to appease the angry spirits, the stones placed on the otherwise unmarked graves of their forebears, the brushwood fires to ward off attacks by hungry lions. Africa does not build monuments. It lives in a permanent, luminous present. As Olive Schreiner wrote in the second chapter of her 1883 novel *The Story of an African Farm*:

> Always in the present; letting each day glide, bringing its own labour, and its own beauty; the gradual lighting up of the hills, night and the stars, firelight and the coals! To live on so, calmly, far from the paths of men; and to look at the lives of clouds and insects; to look deep into the heart of flowers, and see how lovingly the pistil and the stamens nestle there together; and to see in the thorn-pods how the little seeds suck their life through the delicate curled-up string, and how the little embryo sleeps inside! Well, how well, to sit so on one side taking no part in the world's life; but when great men blossom into books looking into those flowers also, to see how the world of men too opens beautifully, leaf after leaf. Ah! life is delicious; well to live long, and see the darkness breaking, and the day coming! The day when soul shall not thrust back soul that would come to it; when men shall not be driven to seek solitude because of the crying-out of their hearts for love and sympathy. Well to live long and see the new time breaking. Well to live long; life is sweet, sweet, sweet!

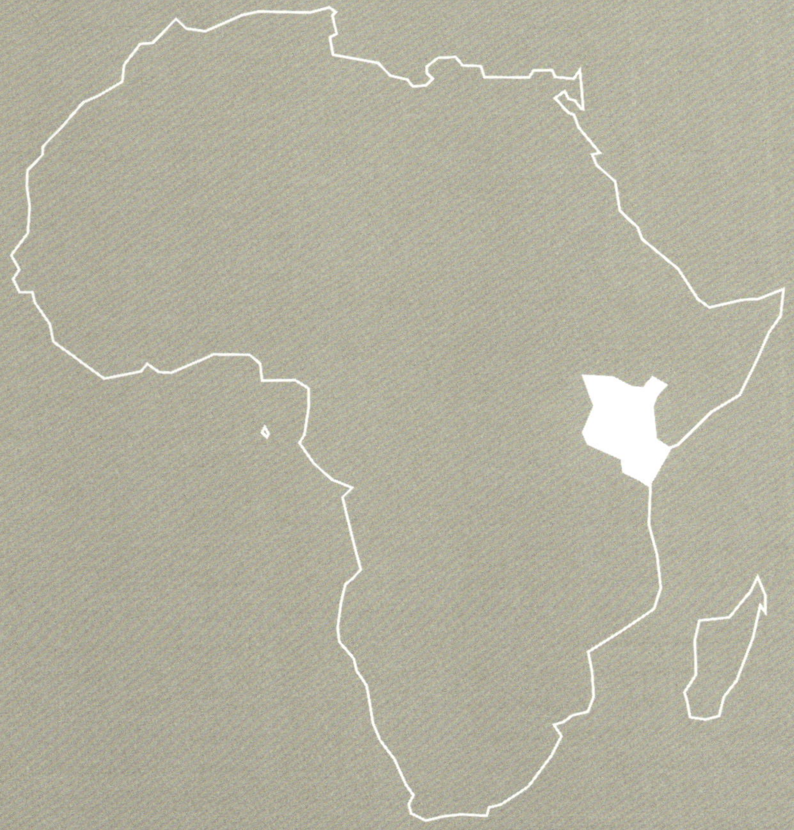

CHAPTER ONE

KENYA

THE ATMOSPHERE IS SO CLEAR THE AIR ALMOST SEEMS TO SPARKLE, GIVING THE SCENERY A FAIRYLIKE CHARM, PARTICULARLY IN THE VICINITY OF THE GREAT SALT PANS OF THE VAST LAKE THAT DRIED OUT COUNTLESS THOUSANDS OF YEARS AGO. THE WINDS SWEEP UP A HAZE OF SHIMMERING WHITE DUST, WHILE MIRAGES SEEM TO HANG IN THE SKY.

There they are, just a few feet away. Their bulk is unwieldy and yet somehow deeply moving. I watch in awe as they gracefully tear up clumps of grass with their trunks and swing them into their mouths. In the background, Mount Kilimanjaro stands proud and stark against the pale sky. There is something infinitely soothing about watching a family of elephants peacefully feeding, the mothers shepherding the infants and watching out for danger. These placid giants have been hunted by men for centuries, and have much to teach us about courage, dignity, and loyalty. The animal kingdom still has so much for us to discover.

Kenya is surely one of the most spectacular countries on earth. Its breathtaking landscapes are the perfect place to begin a safari—and in fact, this is where safaris were invented. The word itself comes from the Swahili *safora*, meaning journey. The term "safari" was first used for the great hunting expeditions recorded in engravings that graced the drawing rooms of our great-great-great-grandfathers. The word took on its current meaning in the mid-twentieth century, when tourists, mainly from Britain and America, began to visit East Africa for its fabulously diverse wildlife, inspired by heroic tales of bravery in the bush that now read like relics of a lost world, the days of colonialism and the British Empire. Kenya, the foremost tourist destination in sub-Saharan Africa, has a long tradition of tourism and the infrastructure is therefore generally well-developed, if somewhat run down in places. The country offers some of the most awe-inspiring scenery in all Africa—families of elephants feeding against the backdrop of the everlasting snows on Mount Kenya, countless thousands of wildebeest thundering across the arid savanna, and luxuriously appointed game lodges such as Little Governor's or Finch-Hatton's camp, where you half expect to see Karen Blixen emerging from the early morning mists.

Kenya sits astride the equator. The land essentially consists of vast high-altitude plains that came into existence when the pre-Cambrian rocks eroded, eight hundred million years ago, when oceans covered the surface of the globe. The plateaus rise progressively from the Indian Ocean to the deep tear in the earth's surface known as the Rift Valley. This gigantic rift, which splits the African continent from the Red Sea down to the Mozambique Channel, has led to the formation of a magnificent series of lakes scattered down the eastern side of the continent like a pearl necklace. These lakes—Turkana, Baringo, Bogoria, Nakuru, Naivasha, Magadi—are home to a wealth and diversity of wildlife that is almost without parallel. A number of ancient volcanoes, their flanks etched deep by glaciers, dominate the high plateaus. Mount Kenya attains an altitude of 17,060 feet (5,199 meters), while Kilimanjaro (just over the Tanzanian border) is the highest peak in Africa at 19,340 feet (5,895 meters). The country has a population of 31,540,000 inhabitants and a total area of 224,100 square miles (580,370 square kilometers), giving a relatively high population density of 140 people per square mile (55 per square kilometer). While the facts seem to belie the image of the vast tracts of open savanna as seen in films such as Sydney Pollack's superb *Out of Africa*, the home of the safari still has vast swathes of unspoiled land, much of it preserved as national parks.

The Amboseli National Park, the setting of Hemingway's *The Snows of Kilimanjaro*, is perhaps the most grandiose. Maybe it is the fact that it lies at the foot of the imposing snow-capped peak that makes it so different from the other game parks. The brooding presence of the mountain is inescapable. The park offers unparalleled views of the peak. The quality of light, too, is remarkable. The atmosphere is so clear the air almost seems to sparkle, giving the scenery a fairylike charm, particularly in the vicinity of the great salt pans of the vast lake that dried out countless thousands of years ago. The winds sweep up a haze of shimmering white dust, while mirages seem to hang in the sky. The elephants lead the way to the lush marshlands where the ground gently steams in the morning sun. The park is home to over a thousand elephants, who every morning wind their way down the ancestral paths to the marshes of Ol Okenya and Ol Tukai, sharing the watering holes with zebras, wildebeest, buffaloes, gazelles, and hippopotamuses. The elephants near Nahelog, Kimane, and Chyulu in the West Tsavo region are becoming increasingly hemmed in by the spread of shantytowns and the fields where the locals cultivate their meager crops. The elephants are now trapped in an ecosystem which cannot sustain them all year round. Their future is bleak: they will either be moved elsewhere or, more likely, culled. The conservationist Cynthia Moss and the bush pilot Alex Peltier have been campaigning to have the migration trails reopened. Sadly, their voices seem destined to remain unheard as the Kikuyu government continues to support the ever-increasing numbers of Masai who are choosing to abandon their traditional nomadic lifestyle and settle down as farmers. Their campaign has, however, taught the local tribes that wildlife is in fact their

PRECEDING PAGES:
Although Mount Kilimanjaro is in Tanzania, the most magnificent view is from the Amboseli National Park on the Kenyan side of the border. The awe-inspiring mountain, sacred to the Masai, is home to over a thousand elephants.

FACING PAGE:
Adult rhinoceroses have no natural predators. Even lions are scared off by their bulk. Their horns are a fearsome weapon that means they can graze in peace without risk of attack.

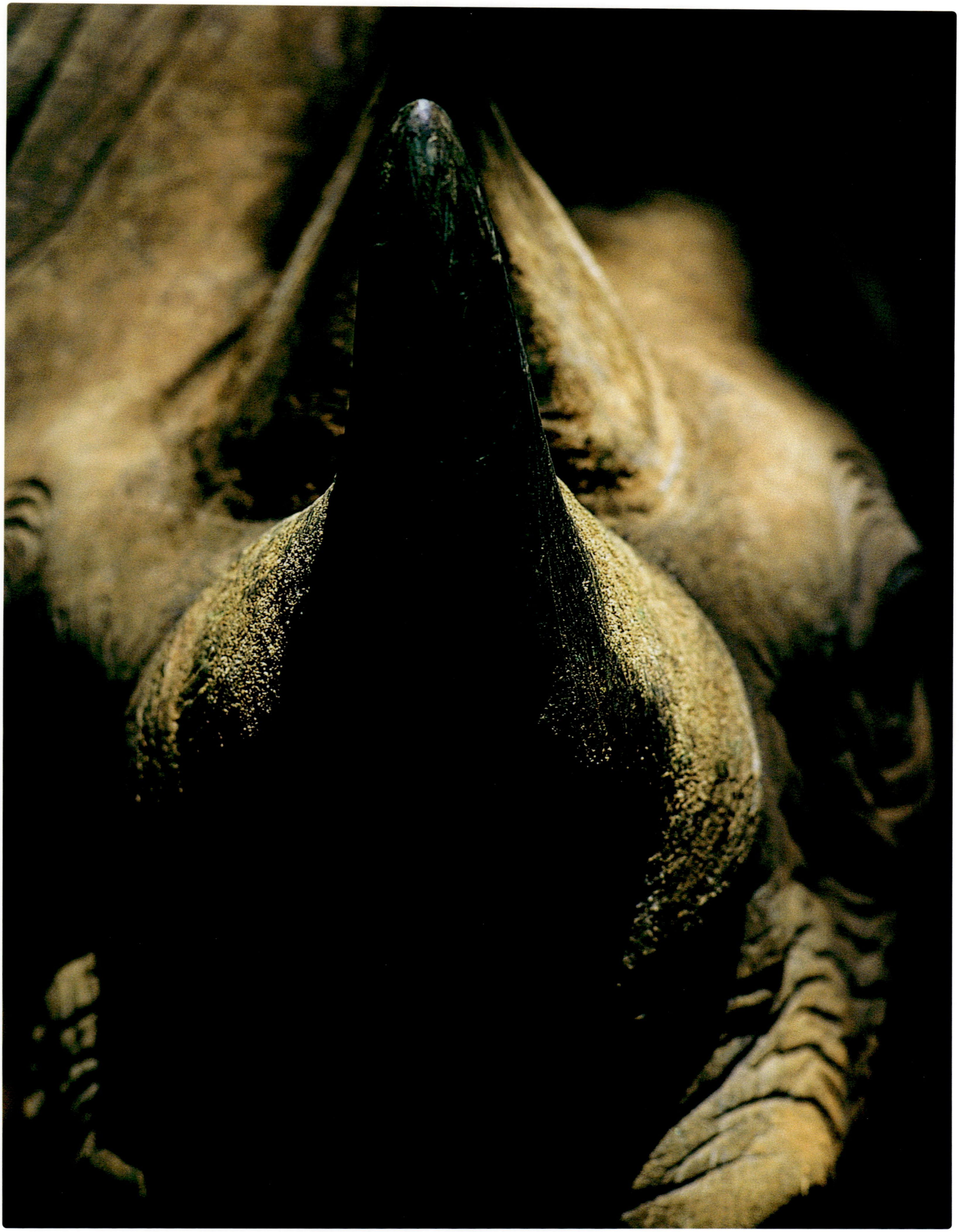

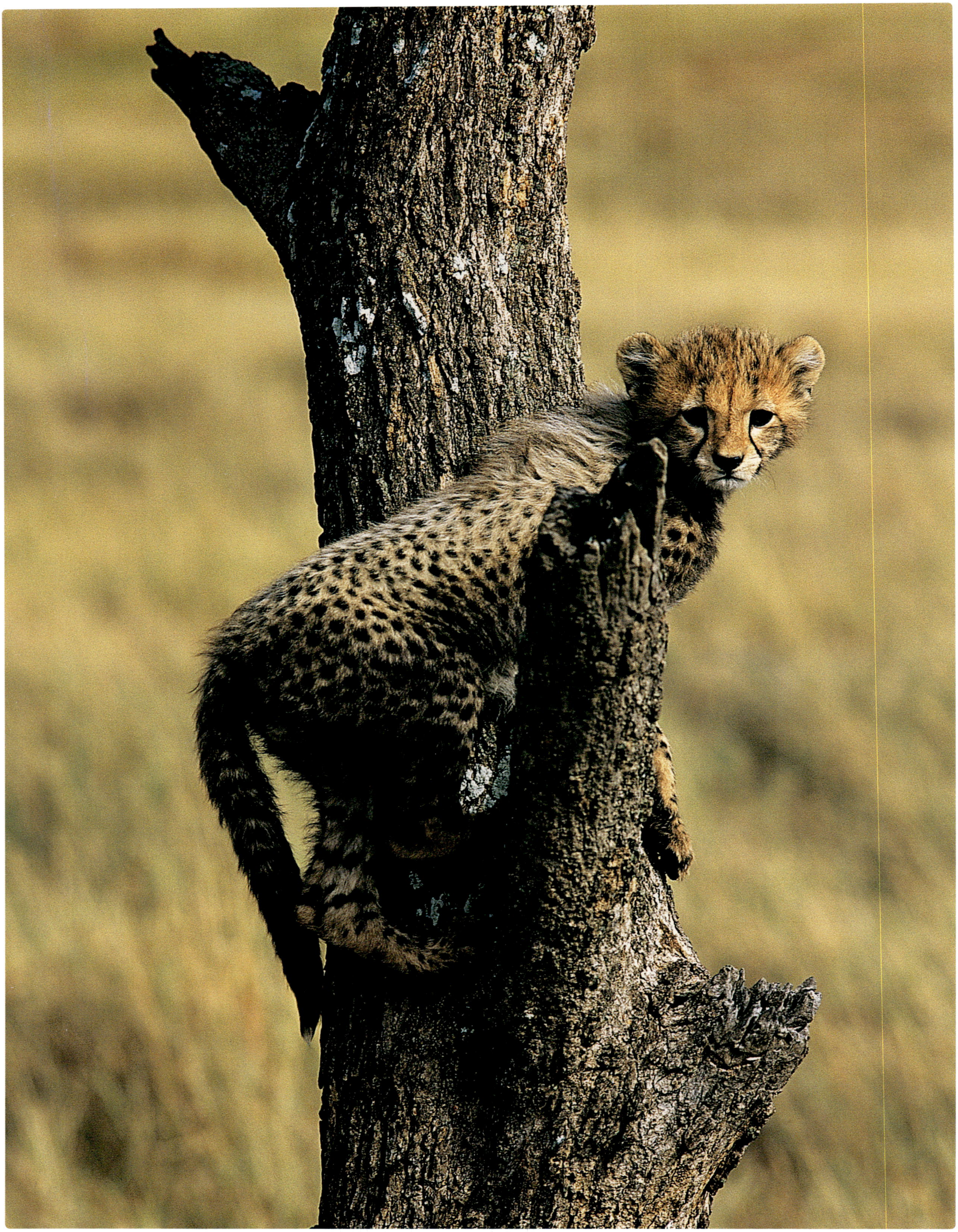

greatest asset. The locals have even created their own nature reserve, Kimana, which has the most beautiful views of Kilimanjaro and a wealth of giraffes, buffaloes, elephants, lions, and leopards to attract tourists. While the national parks like Amboseli are run by a government agency and generally do not allow the locals to live within the park's boundaries, the national game reserves are managed locally and the rules are applied much less stringently.

The Masai Mara national game reserve is unique. Its 695 square miles (1,800 square kilometers) offer a wealth of safari experiences, from traditional game lodges to hot-air ballooning. Flying low over the savanna at daybreak is truly a once-in-a-lifetime experience. You can easily imagine that the Garden of Eden looked like this superb landscape of hills, valleys, and plains dotted with acacias. From August to October, the park is crisscrossed by vast herds of zebras and wildebeest that come to feed on the rich grasslands of the savanna. The migrations are at their most spectacular when the herds arrive on the banks of the crocodile-infested Mara River. The antelopes rush headlong into the foaming waters. Many do not make it to the other side, falling prey to hungry jaws or simply drowning in the crush. Although the wildlife is abundant throughout the park, the southern half is very different from the north. Generally speaking, the southern half is much more popular with the minibus tours that regularly call for tourists at the numerous hotels. In the northern half of the park, the camps are smaller and fewer, and most of the vehicles are 4x4s. One reason why the Masai Mara is so popular is because many of the big cats are active during the day. Many of the other species roaming free here—zebras, wildebeest, gazelles, impala, giraffes—are less spectacular, but just as interesting. It is perfectly possible to see such animals beyond the administrative limits of the park, particularly in the north, towards the Oloololo escarpment and the plains of Miti Mbili. There are a number of superb game lodges that are perfect as bases for a safari, including the Intrepid, Governor's Lodge, the Mara Safari Club, Kichwa Tembo, and—for the wealthiest clients—the Bateleur, Ilmoran, and Explora.

Unlike Amboseli and the Masai Mara, Tsavo National Park only unveils its charms to the most persevering visitors, those purists who are willing to spend time seeking out the secret life hidden in the depths of the forests and isolated in pockets on the arid plains. The region has lost a great deal of its wildlife, first to professional big game hunters and more recently to poachers who have caused immense damage. Animal numbers in the park dropped steadily for years until in 1977 the government decided to take matters in hand, declaring war on the poachers. However, the numbers of rhinoceros and elephant have fallen even further. The best way to see wildlife in Tsavo is not to drive aimlessly on the dusty tracks, but to wait at the watering holes for it to come to you. The park is divided into two administrative areas separated by the famous Mombasa-Kisumu railroad that links the city on the Indian Ocean to the town near the Ugandan border. The railroad, completed in the early years of the twentieth century, is notorious for the numbers of workers who fell victim to man-eating lions and to the no less deadly mosquito while building it. The arid eastern plains of the park stretch over 4,200 square miles (eleven thousand square kilometers). Here, tourists are few and far between, although the Kanderi marshlands, fed by the waters of the Voi River, attract huge herds of buffaloes, elephants, zebras, and elands. Recently, a project to reintroduce the black rhinoceros has been launched in Galdessa. The Galdessa camp has eight superb tents that are popular with a certain well-heeled clientele. The western part of Tsavo covers 3,282 square miles (8,500 square kilometers). It has a number of well-known tourist attractions such as Mzina Springs, where an observation room allows visitors to watch hippopotamuses underwater, and the forbidding, rock-strewn landscape of the Chaimu lava flow. However, tourists would be well advised to avoid traveling alone in certain areas of the park, particularly near the Tanzanian border. In a few areas, visitors are escorted under the protection of the Kenyan army. Yet Tsavo also has the most elegant of Kenya's game lodges. The Finch-Hatton Lodge is like something straight out of a novel. It is a superb colonial-style mansion full of antique crystal and silver. The walls are hung with paintings by the writer Karen Blixen. Visitors can sleep in one of the spacious raised huts facing a small lake where hippopotamuses grunt and wallow. Some of the best camps, like this one, are completely unfenced. This means it is best to call on the services of a guide to return to the huts. Coming face to face with an elephant may be more frightening than truly life-threatening, but bumping into a lion—as I did—is another matter.

THE MASAI MARA NATIONAL GAME RESERVE IS UNIQUE. ITS 695 SQUARE MILES (1,800 SQUARE KILOMETERS) OFFER A WEALTH OF SAFARI EXPERIENCES, FROM TRADITIONAL GAME LODGES TO HOT-AIR BALLOONING.

Some 220 miles (350 kilometers) to the north of Nairobi is a cluster of three game reserves—Samburu, Buffalo, and the less well known but equally remarkable Shaba. Together, the three reserves cover 325 square miles (844 square kilometers), fed by the waters of the Uaso Nyiro River. The rolling hills are covered in doum

FACING PAGE:
Watching young cheetahs at play is great fun. They have a marked liking for testing their skills, often getting into difficult situations and having to be rescued by a patient mother.

THE FRIENDLINESS OF THE PEOPLE MAKES THE COUNTRY A WONDERFUL PLACE TO VISIT. AND WATCHING THE ANTELOPES STEPPING DELICATELY PAST THE ELEPHANTS TO DRINK FROM A WATERING HOLE AS THE SUN SETS OVER THE SAVANNA IS A TRULY MAGICAL EXPERIENCE.

palms, tamarind trees, and acacias, offering a last oasis of greenery before the arid sands of the desert, where incursions by small groups of rebels make the area out of bounds for tourists. Samburu, Buffalo, and Shaba are the best places to see dik-diks, cheetahs, elephants, gerenuk, reticulated giraffes, and the now rare Grevy's zebra. There are also leopards, but these are timid creatures, and often the only way to know one has been spotted is by the tangle of minibuses as visitors crane to catch a glimpse of the spotted coat. The Samburu people are more welcoming than their Masai cousins. They live in a vast area stretching from Isiolo to Loyangalani. Larsen's Camp is basic yet elegant, the perfect base for a safari adventure. It is in a fantastic site on the riverbank, making it a great place to spot wildlife coming to drink.

Between Samburu and Nairobi, right on the equator, Mount Kenya is increasingly popular with visitors. It is relatively easy to climb, making an ideal four-day excursion from Naro Moru. The lakes of Naivasha, Baringo, Nakuru, and Bogoria are excellent for bird-watching. Nakuru and Bogoria in particular are home to huge flocks of flamingos.

The Nairobi game park was founded in 1946. It offers extremely easy access and large numbers of buffaloes, giraffes, baboons, cheetahs, and rhinoceroses. It is striking to see such exotic wildlife against the backdrop of a major city.

Kenya is a large country with vast, sweeping stretches of open grassland where many species roam free, but the country's tourist industry is in danger of being too successful for its own good. All the specialist guides agree that there are too many minibuses and too many hotels, and that the ever-increasing numbers of visitors is having a negative effect on the environment, not to mention the quality of the safari experience. No one wants their photograph of a lion to have a cluster of minibuses in the background. Scientists report that cheetahs are changing their hunting patterns and that leopards are increasingly stressed by the human presence. It is undeniable that the hordes of tourists have had an impact on the cheetahs of the Masai Mara, for instance, which are now forced to hunt between midday and two in the afternoon—the hottest hours of the day, when the tourists are enjoying a siesta back in their air-conditioned hotels. There is also much evidence to show that the big cats are becoming over-accustomed to the presence of tourists, even incorporating them into their hunting techniques. In the Paradise Mara Camp, a popular destination for wildlife photographers and documentary makers, the cheetahs now often leap onto the hoods of the 4x4s, using them as a lookout post just as they would an anthill. Lionesses have likewise learned to slink along, hidden from view by the body of the vehicle, before charging out and attacking their prey. Of course, animals have always adapted their behavior to their circumstances, but these changes in hunting techniques seem somehow symptomatic of man's often negative impact on his environment.

While modern technology has taken much of the romance out of the safari, in some ways it has made it easier to see the animals. A few years ago, there was no guarantee of seeing some of the rarer species even after many hours' drive in the heat and dust. Today, whenever a rare animal, or a big cat closing in for the kill, is spotted, the guides instantly radio the find to each other and the vehicles flock to the spot within minutes. The question is not whether you will be fortunate enough to see some animals, but whether your diver will manage to jockey your minibus into a good position. A spot close to the kill is worth a good-sized gratuity to the driver. Bribes and backhanders are something of a way of life here. The tourist industry has suffered from the lack of a concerted policy of development and planning control, while the government has been dogged by accusations of corruption. The country's image has also been tarnished by political troubles, tribal conflicts, and a high urban crime rate. In the presidential elections of December 27, 2002, the Kenyans voted in a new leader, Mwai Kibaki of the National Rainbow Coalition, after twenty-four years of corrupt and authoritarian rule by the KANU (Kenya African National Union) party under Daniel Arap Moi. Visitor numbers have been dropping for some years—a serious blow in a country where tourism represents the largest source of foreign income. In a bid to reverse the slide, the government launched a new campaign in early 2004, designed to attract wealthy tourists back to the country. However, this seems unlikely to yield results straight away, particularly as Kenya now faces competition from Tanzania and the countries of southern Africa.

Yet despite all its current difficulties, Kenya is still the country people associate with safaris and spectacular wildlife. The friendliness of the people makes the country a wonderful place to visit. And watching the antelopes stepping delicately past the elephants to drink from a watering hole as the sun sets over the savanna is a truly magical experience.

FACING PAGE:
The Masai Mara reserve is popular with visitors who come to see the magnificent wildlife. The lands round the Paradise Mara Lodge are particularly well known as a place to spot big cats. I once counted twenty-six lions round a buffalo kill.

FOLLOWING PAGES:
The start of the dry season in Tanzania heralds the arrival of one and a half million herbivores across the border, fleeing the drought. The wildebeest blindly follow the migrating group, often blundering straight into the jaws of their predators.

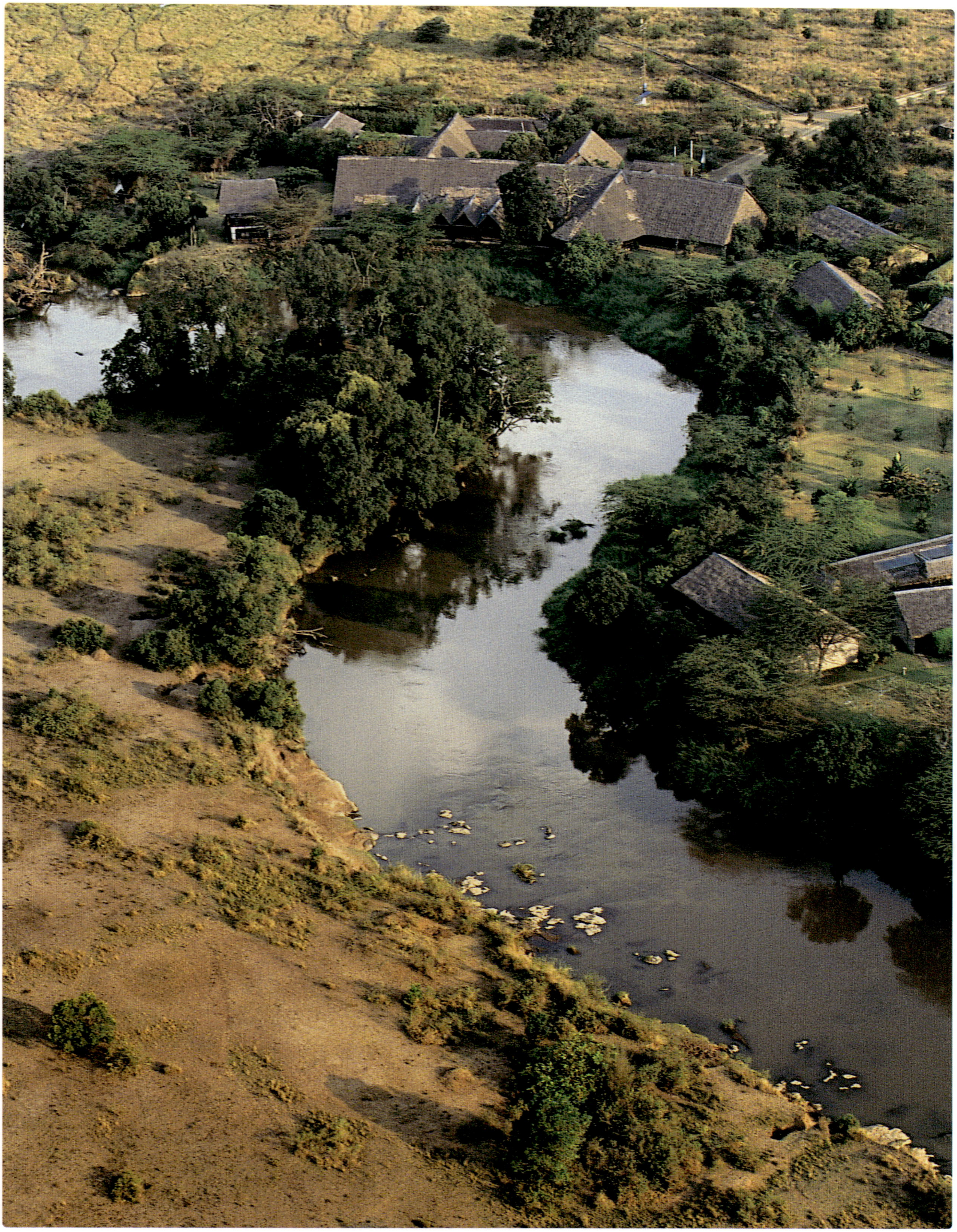

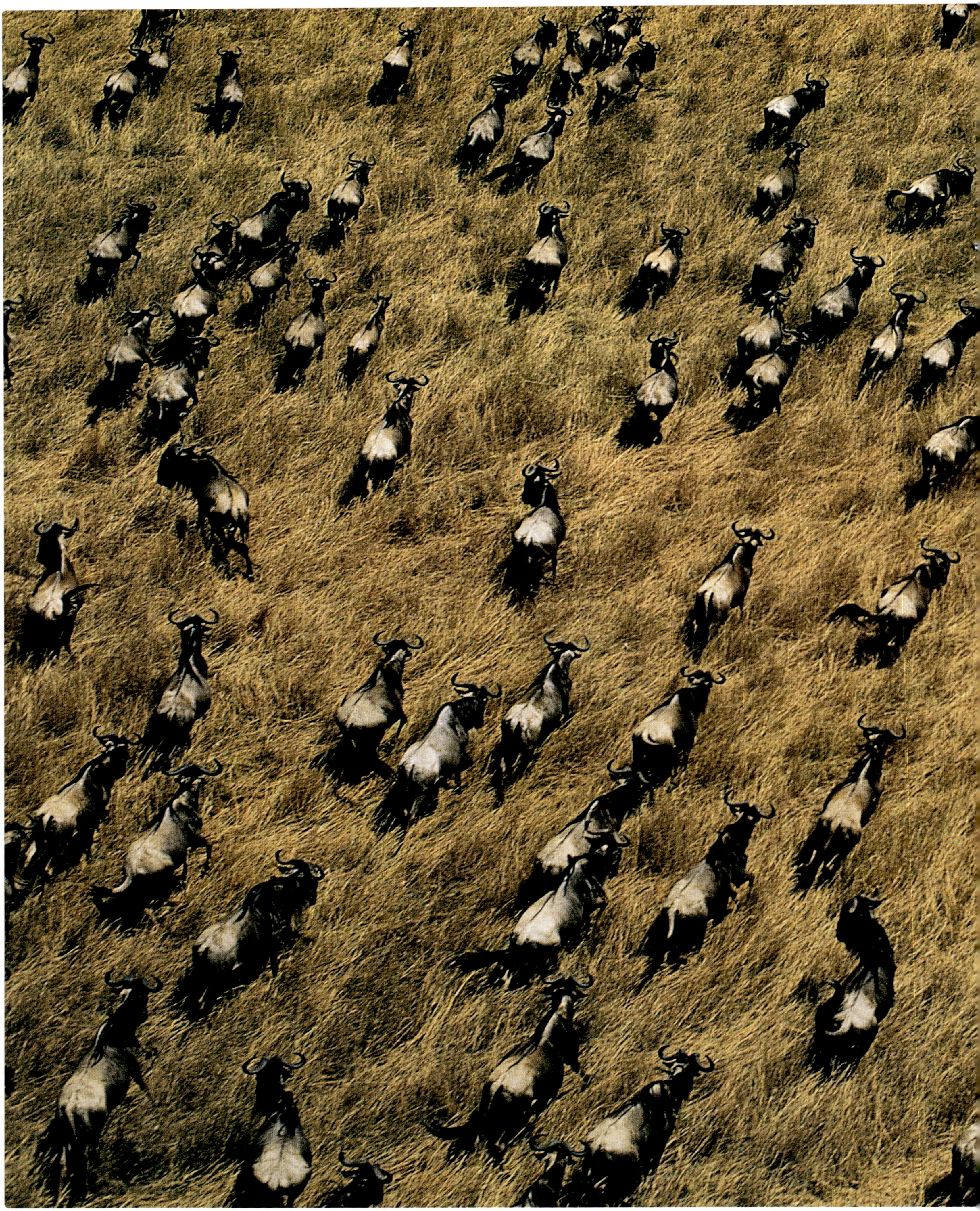

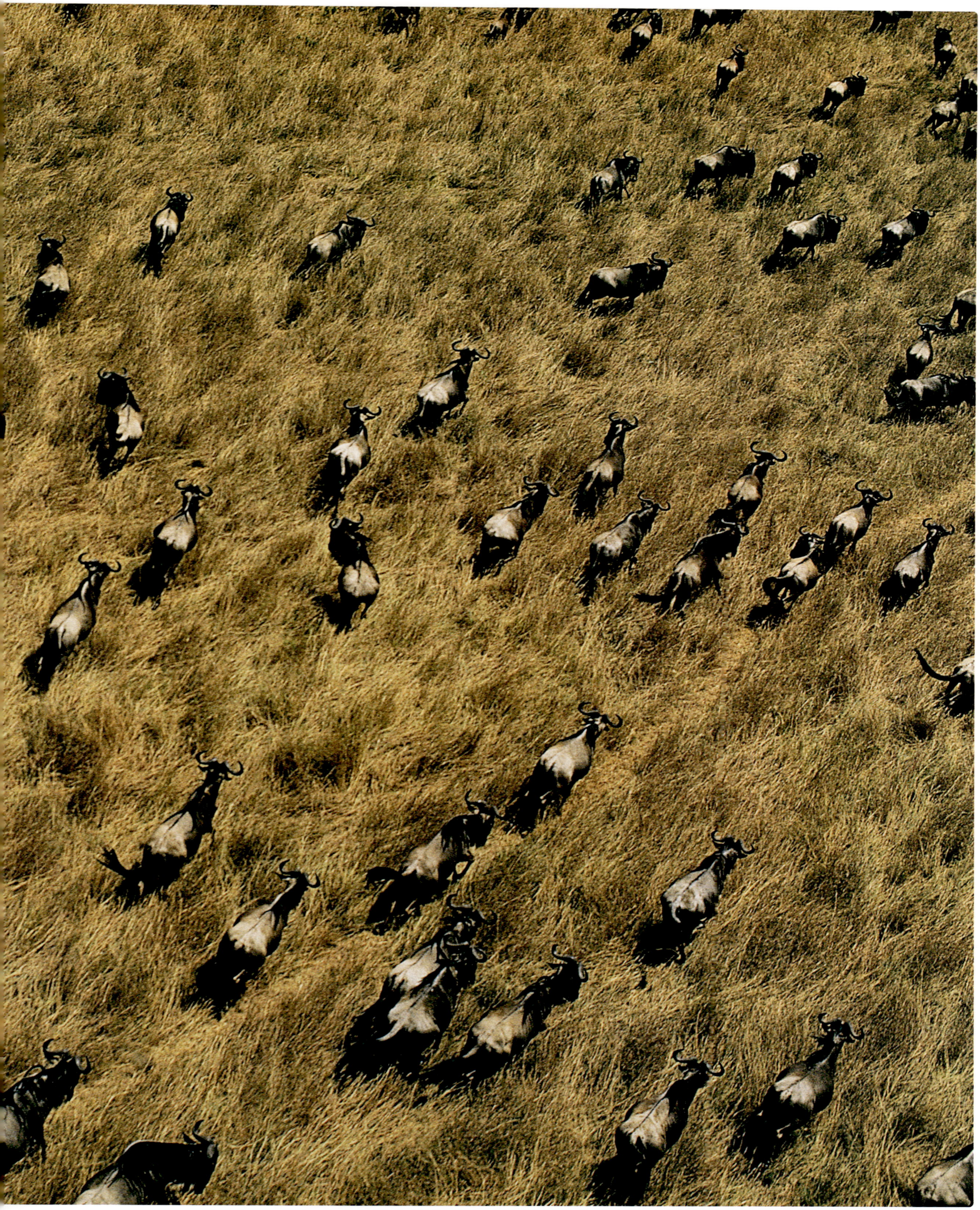

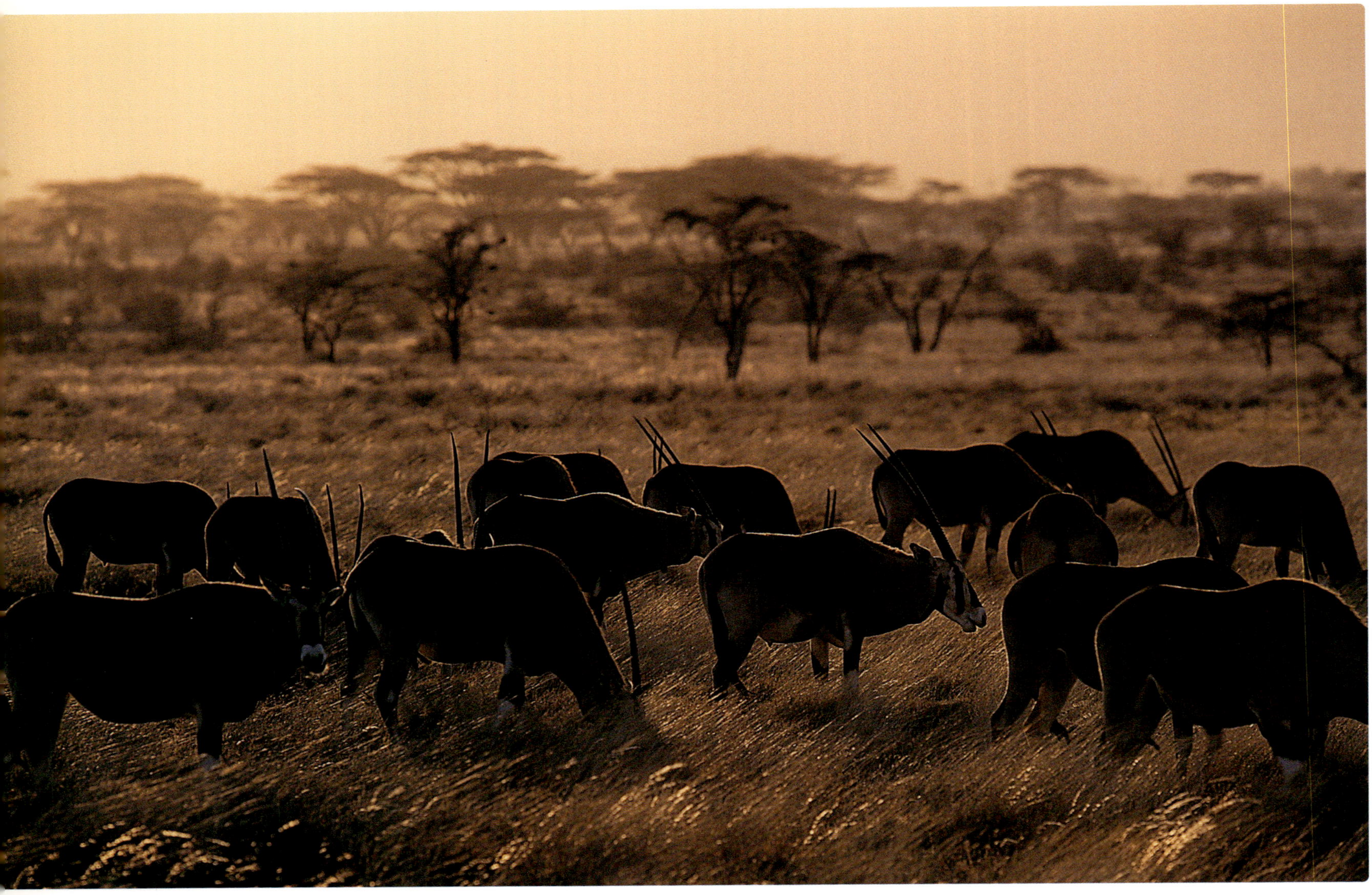

Dusk is always the best time to observe the various species of antelope. The big cats have also learned to attack as the light fails. The antelopes huddle together for protection. Any stragglers are vulnerable.

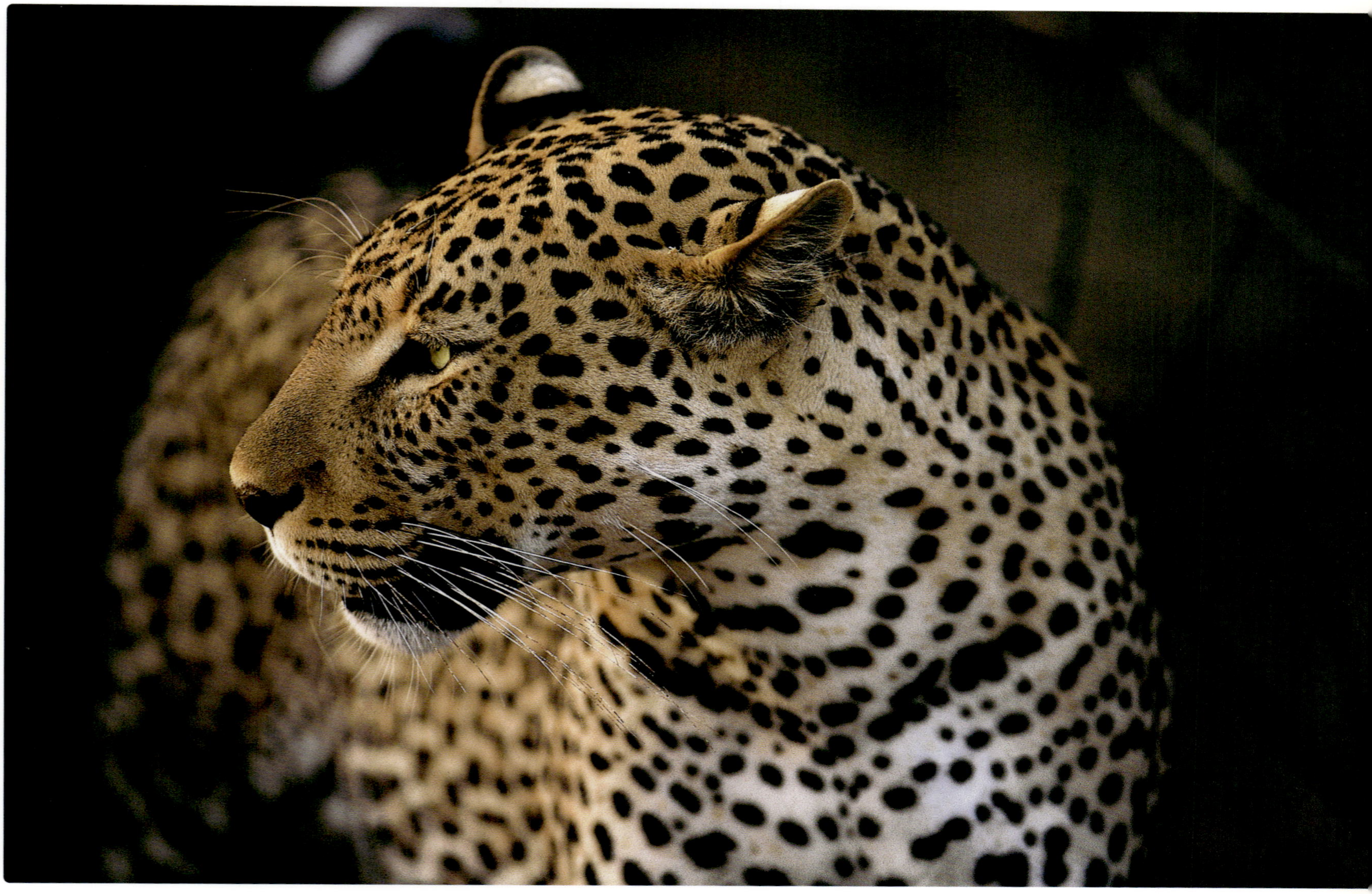

Leopards hunt at night. I came across this magnificent beast by chance, early one morning in Shaba. It had just killed a gazelle and was carrying it up to a high branch to prevent it from being stolen by lions.

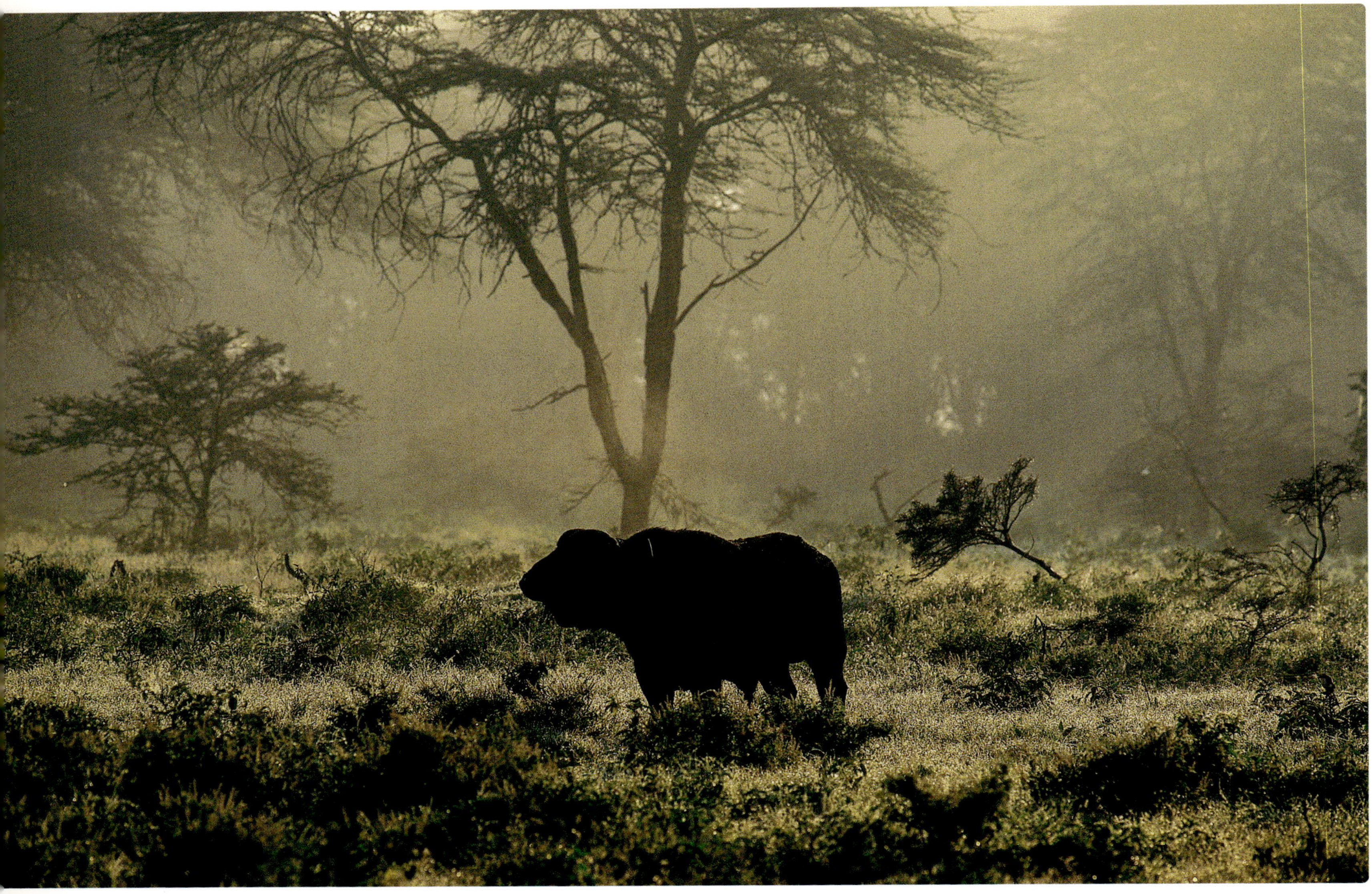

Although the buffalo appears peaceful, it is in fact one of the animals rangers fear most. During the dry season, the old males live apart from the herd, until the rutting season begins. They are vulnerable and thus liable to behave unpredictably.

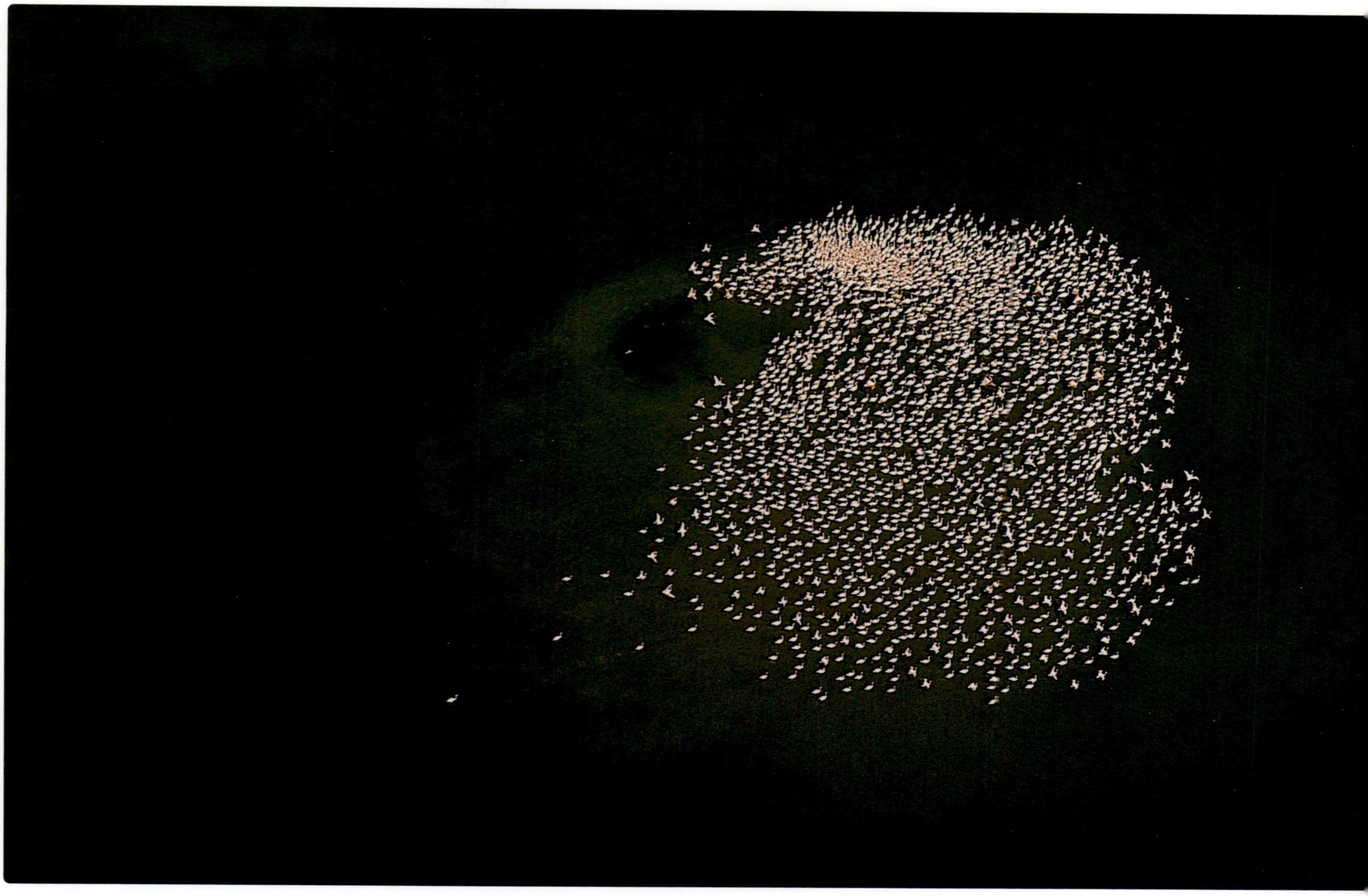

There are two species of flamingo—greater and lesser. Birds living on Lake Nakuru have suffered a great deal from nitrate pollution. Nowadays, more birds are to be found on Lake Elementaita.

FOLLOWING PAGES:
The Samburu Park is home to large herds of Grevy's zebras. This is one of three species of zebra, the other two being common zebras and mountain zebras. The males often fight over their harems, using their hooves and teeth as weapons.

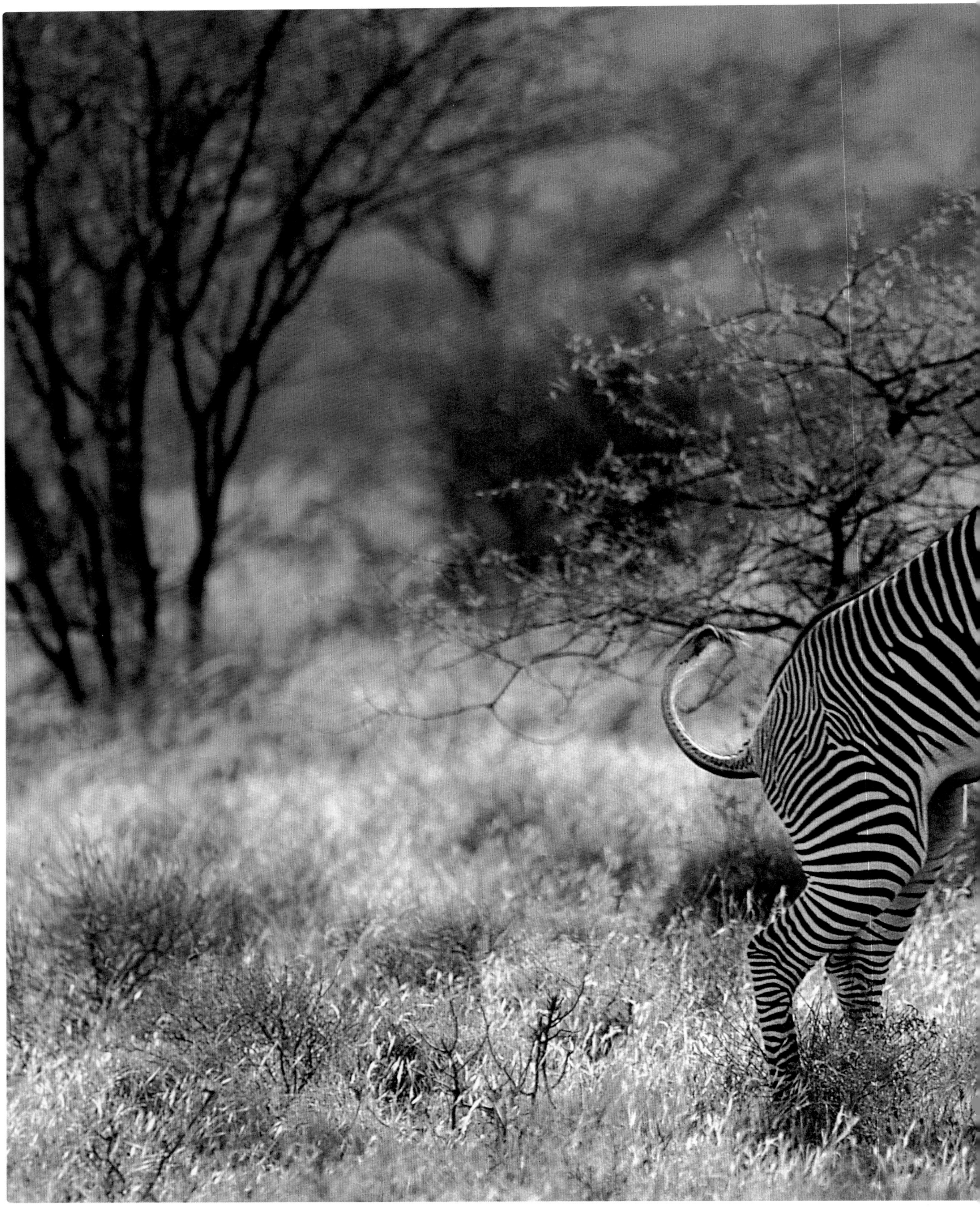

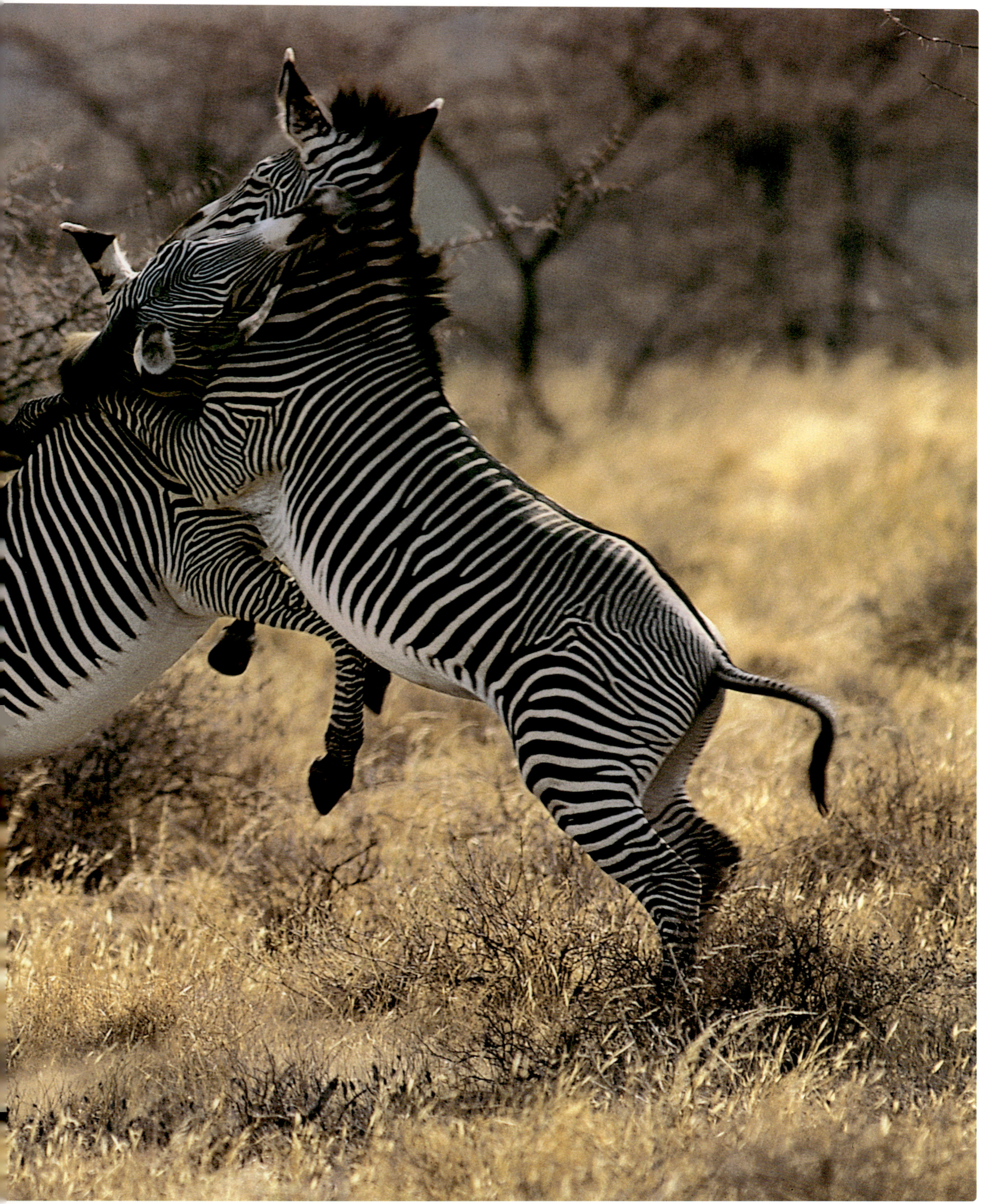

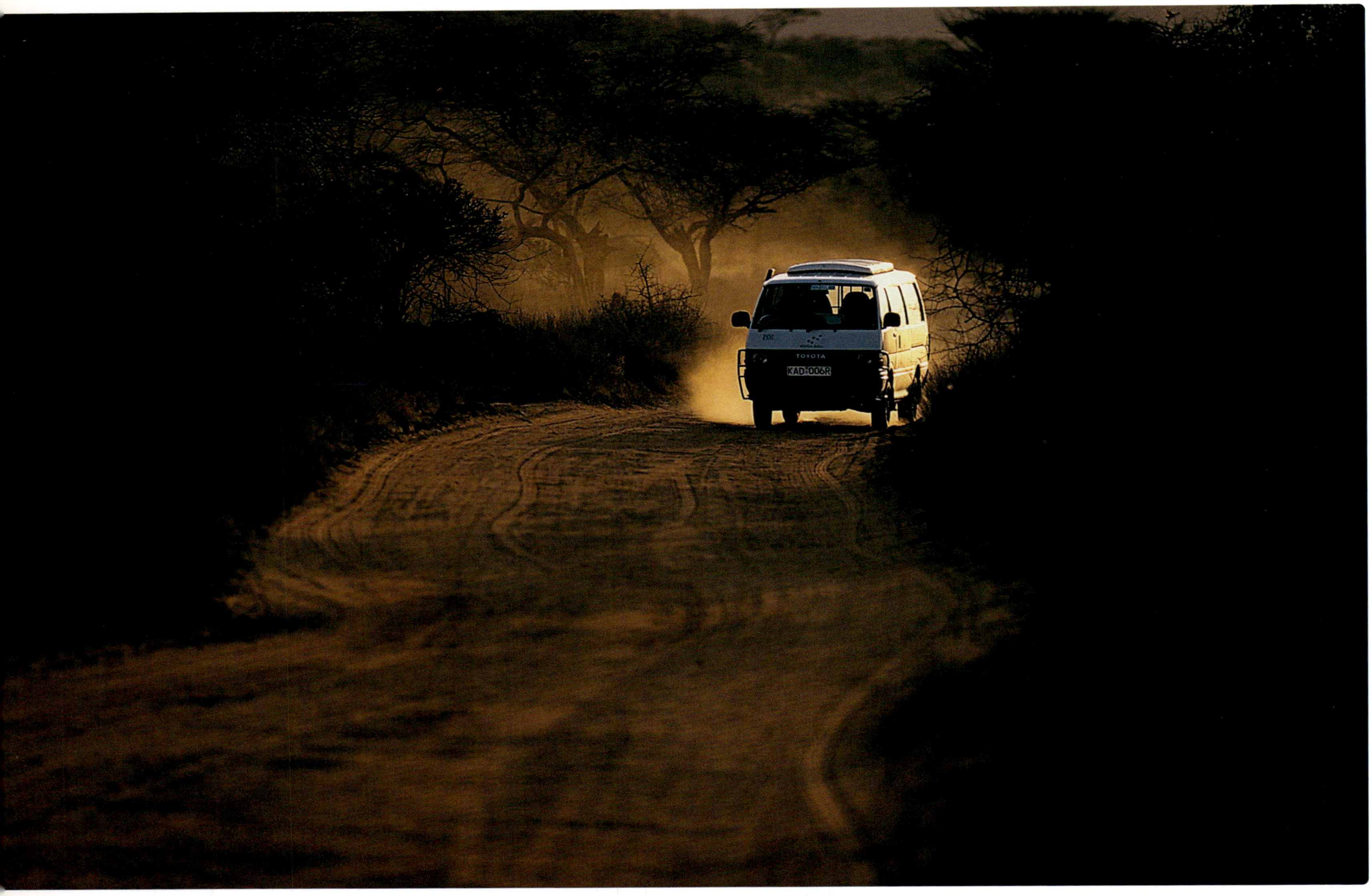

Minibuses are a common sight in Kenya's national parks. Although safari purists dislike them, they do allow far greater numbers of people to see Kenya's magnificent wildlife than would otherwise be possible.

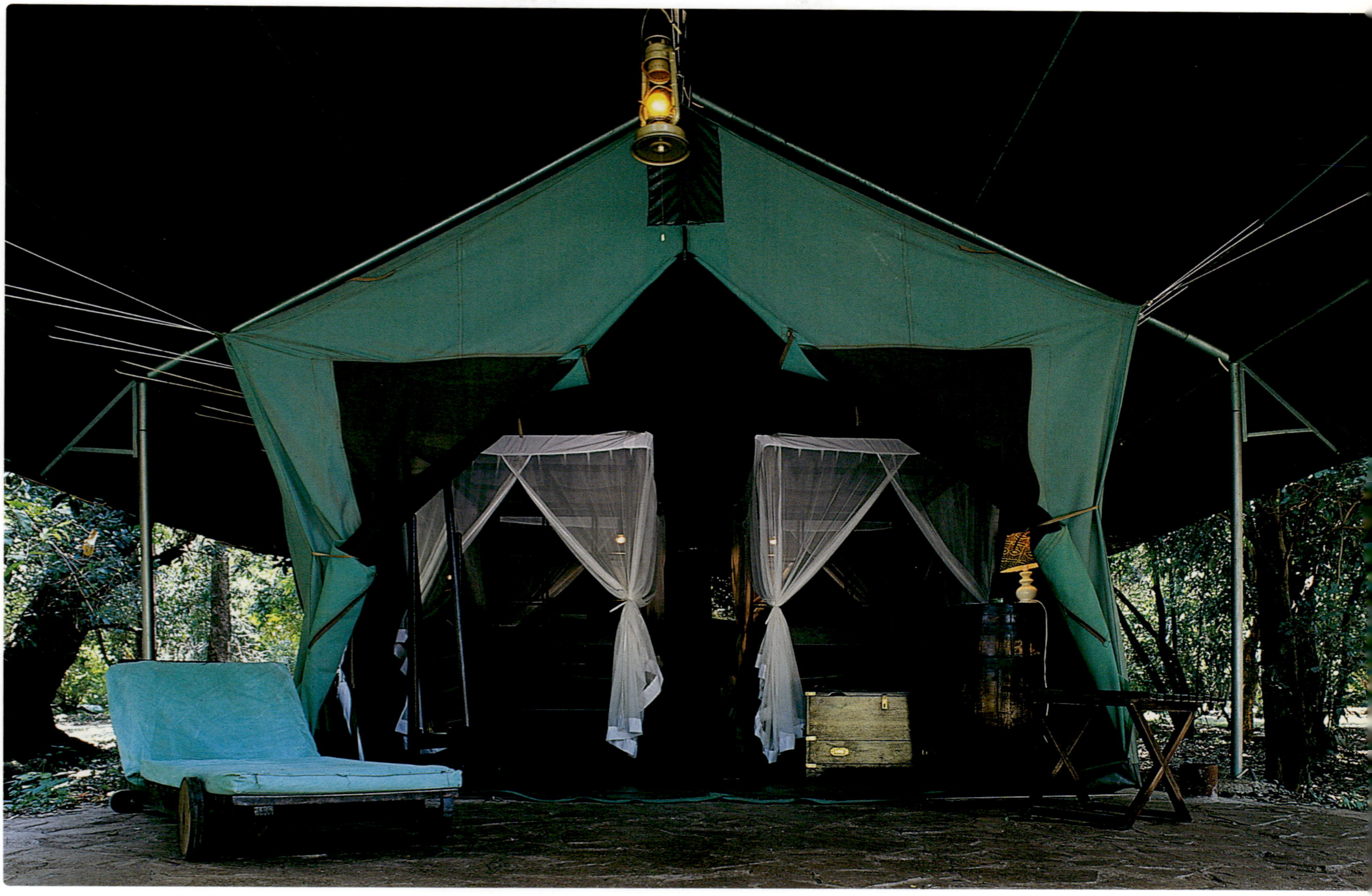

The Mara Intrepid's Lodge, in the heart of the Masai Mara game reserve, is a haven of luxurious charm. The harmonious way the buildings (apart from a few ill-judged extensions) blend into the scenery make this one of the best camps in the region.

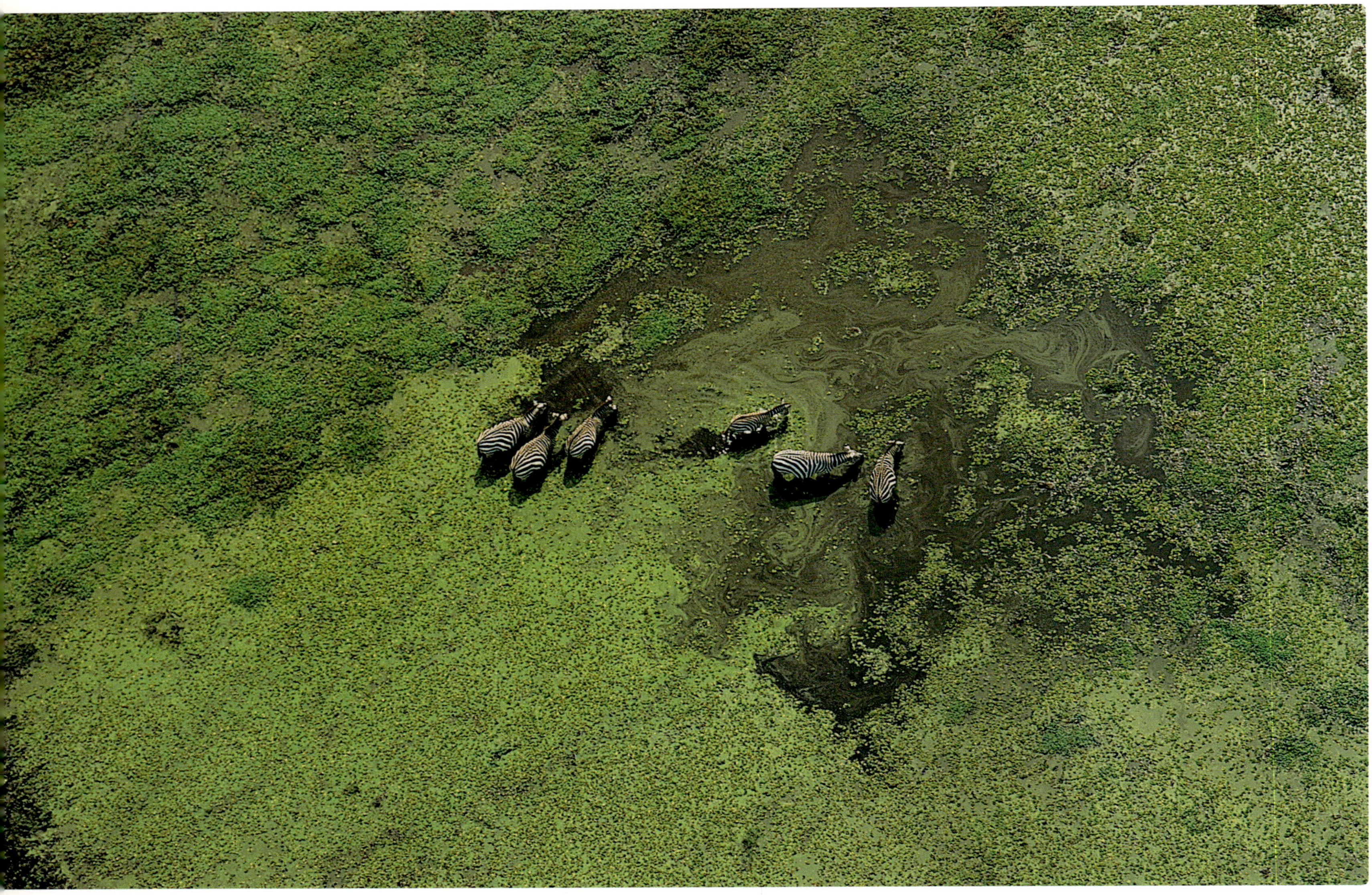

The subspecies called Grant's zebras live in structured harems led by a dominant female. In the Amboseli National Park, they spend most of the day in the marshlands.

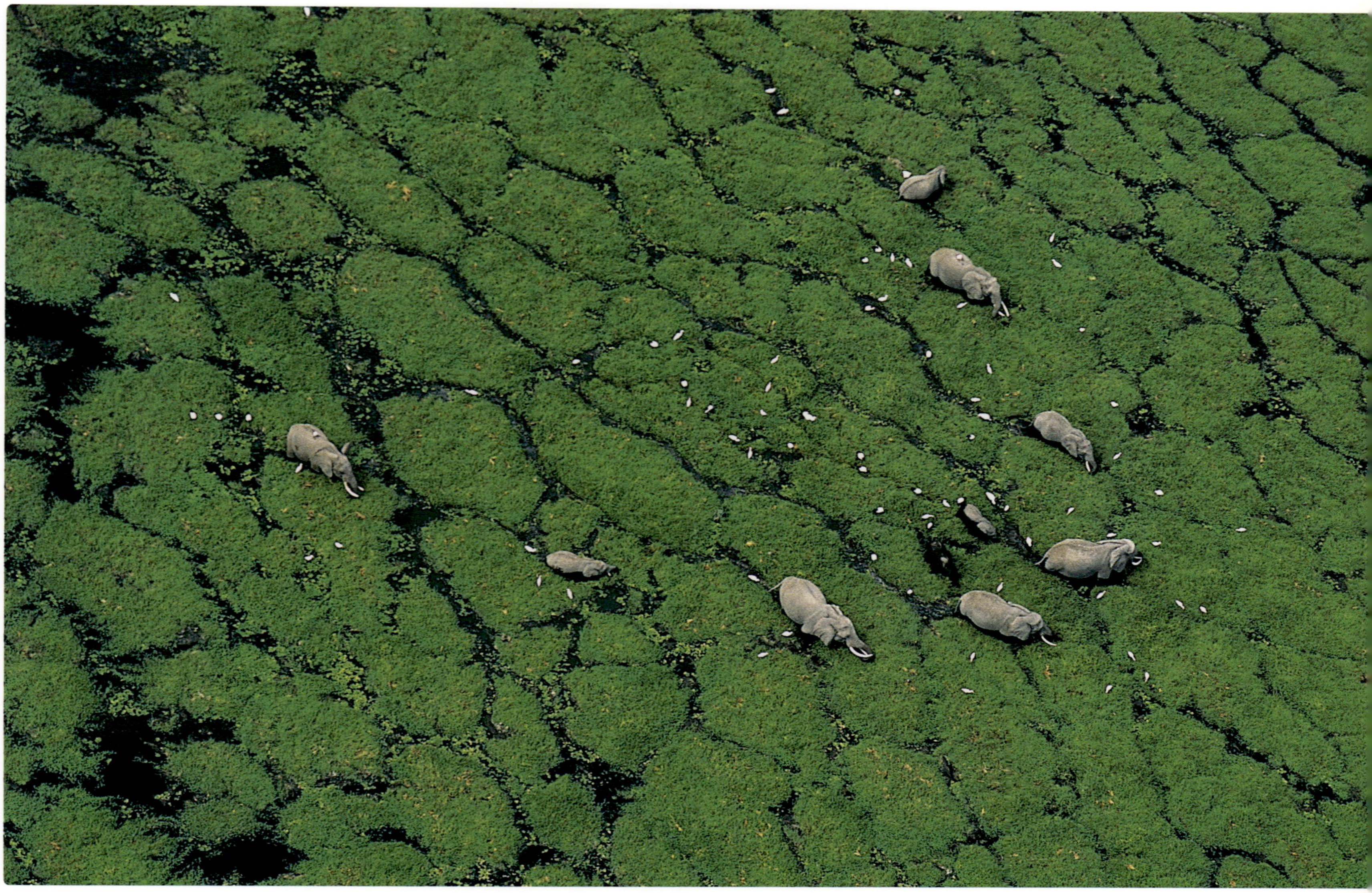

Cynthia Moss is a conservationist who has devoted much of her life to protecting the open spaces that are the natural habitat of Kenya's elephants. In Amboseli, she has focused her attention on keeping their migration routes open.

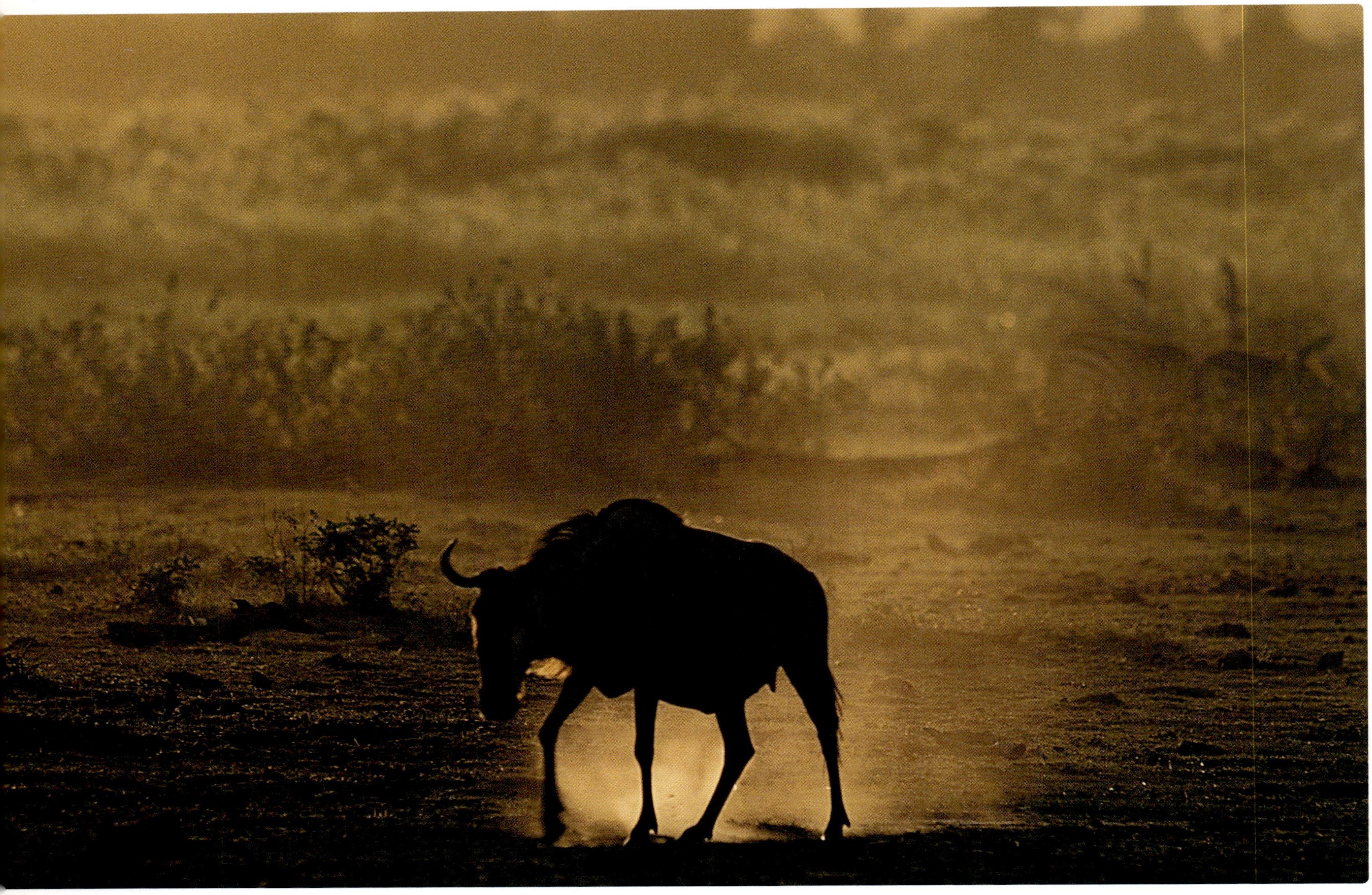

The migration period is extremely dangerous for many species. It is not uncommon to see a young wildebeest separated from the herd and calling piteously for its mother. Alone, it has little chance of survival.

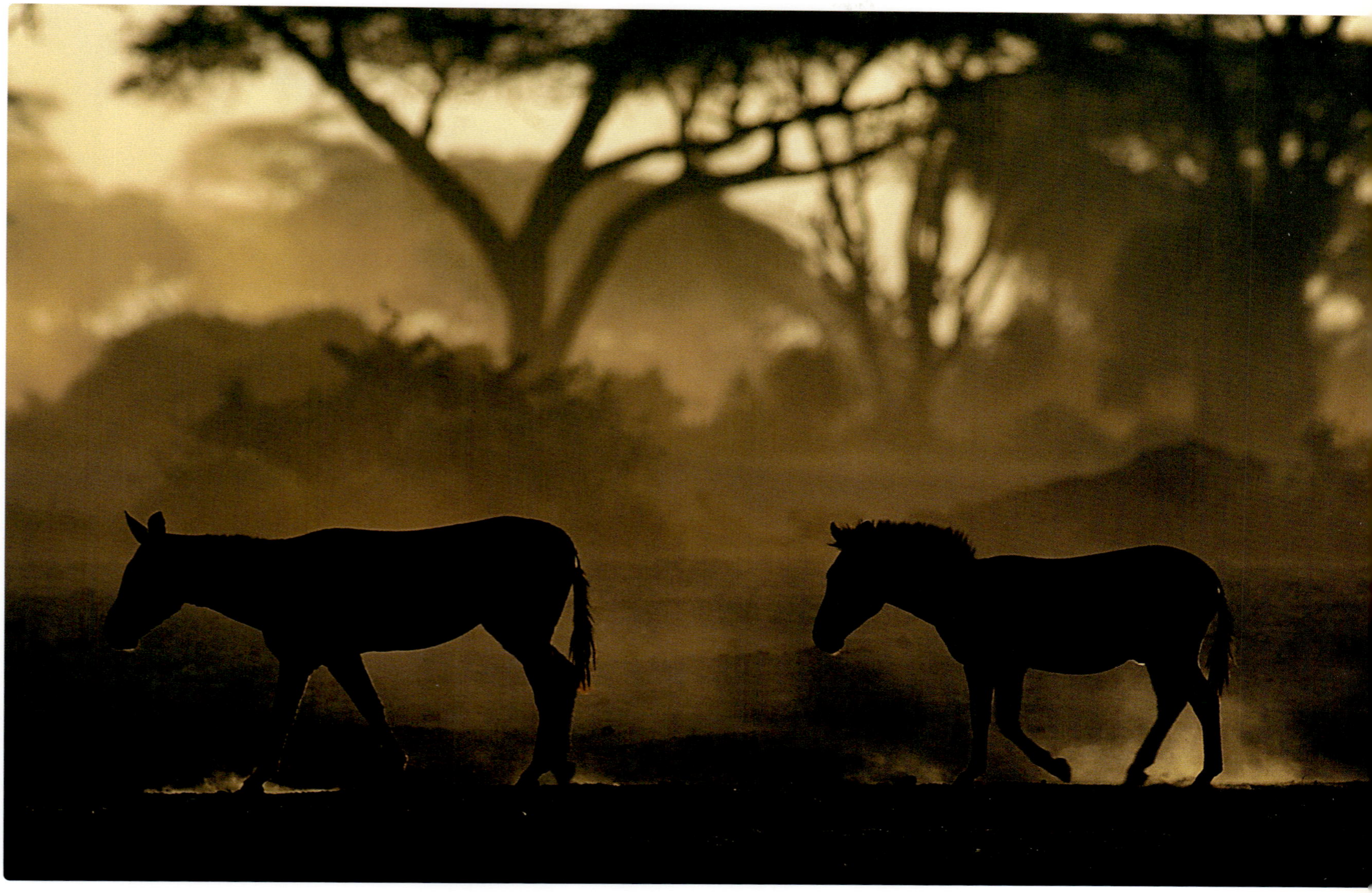

In the gathering dusk, the last rays of light seem to blend the black and white of the zebra's stripes. This makes the animals vulnerable to attack by big cats, which are confused in bright sunlight by the shimmering effect of the stripes.

Kenya boasts a range of hotels to suit every budget. However, the lack of a concerted program of tourism development has held the country back. Nowadays, the government is aiming to promote the country as a wildlife haven. Hotels like the Samburu Intrepid's play a major part in this image.

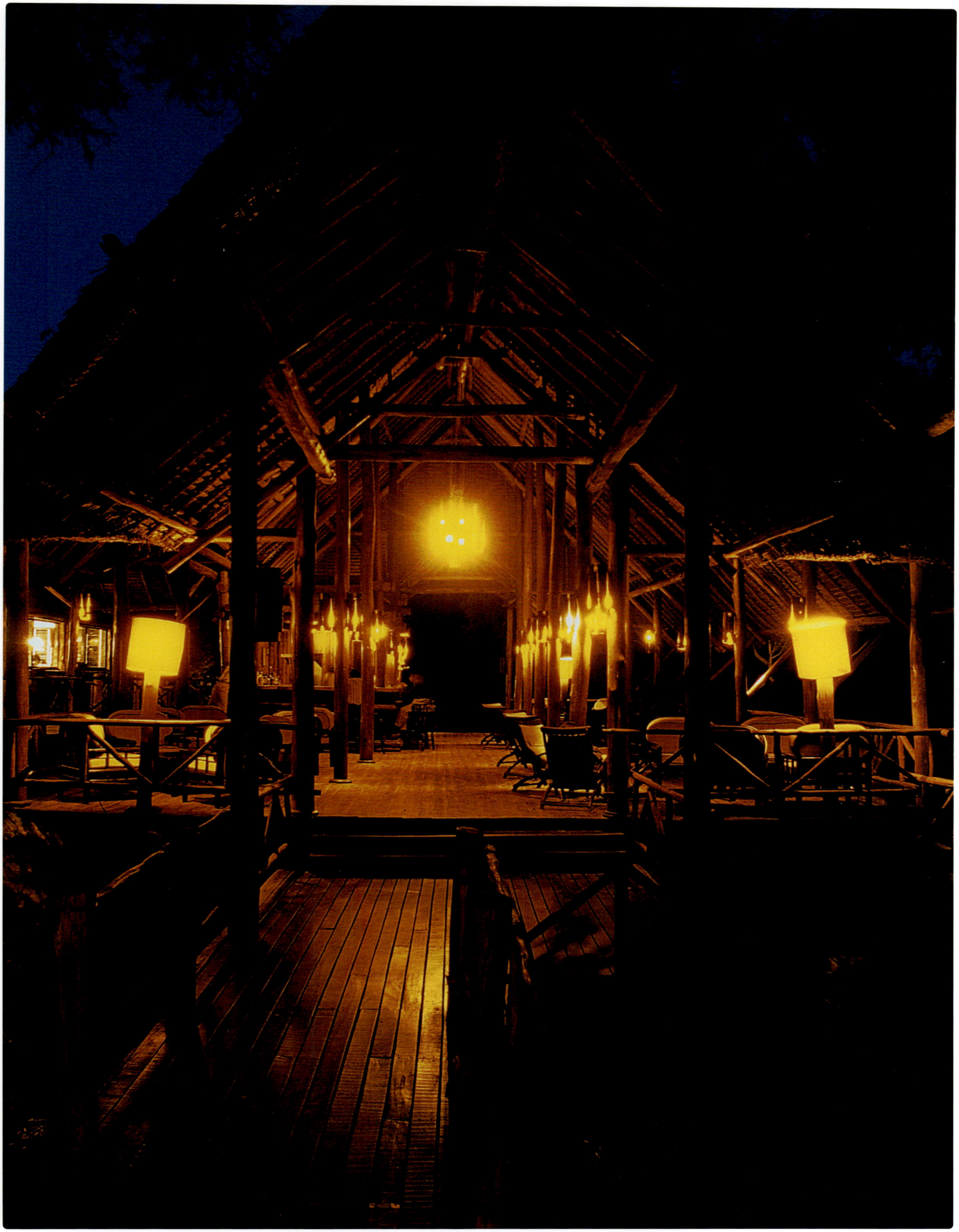

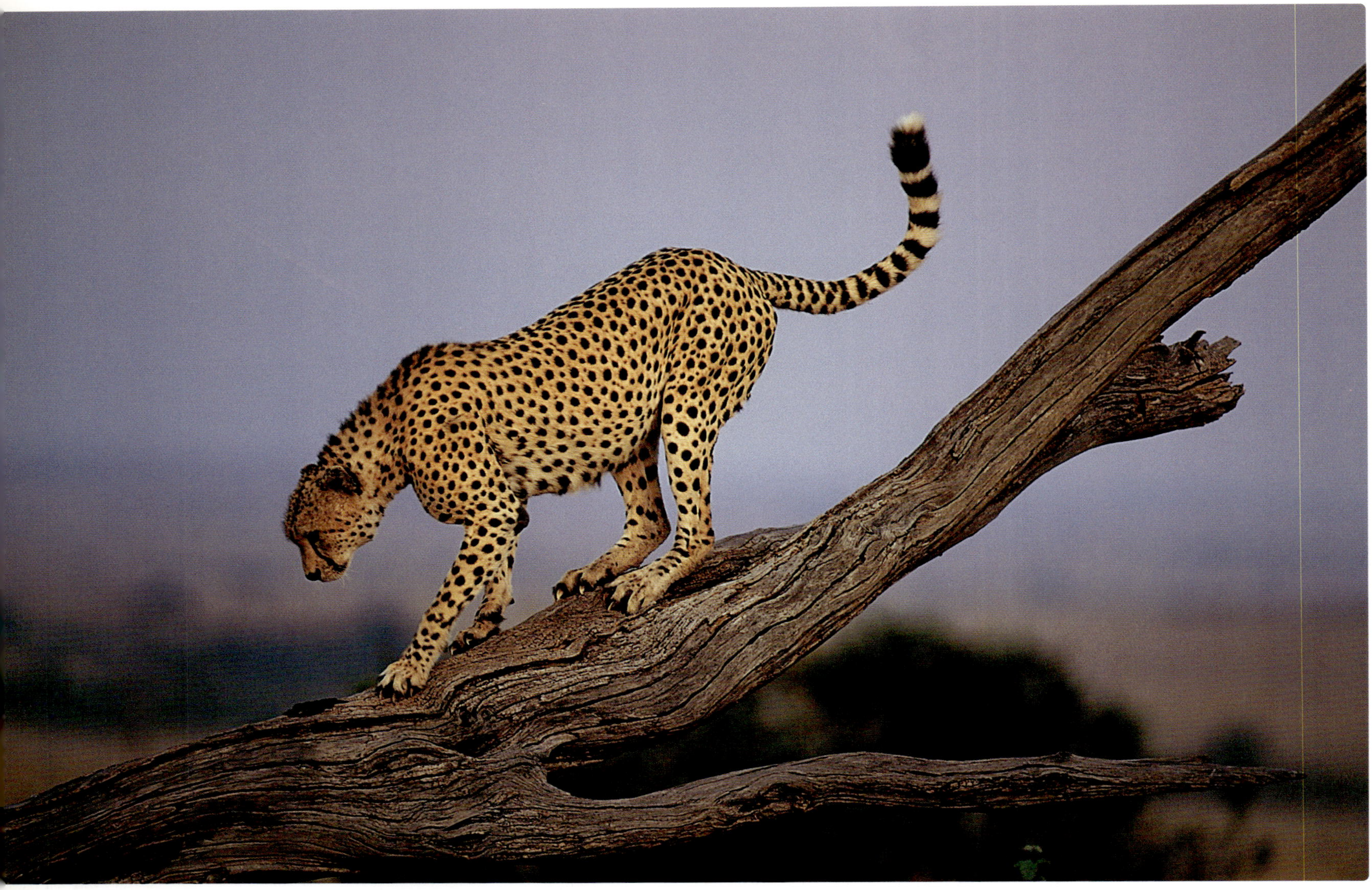

The cheetah is the fastest animal on land. Before sprinting for the kill, cheetahs seek out an elevated spot such as a tree stump or anthill to watch for their prey. The sprint demands a great deal of energy, so they only attack if they are reasonably sure of the kill.

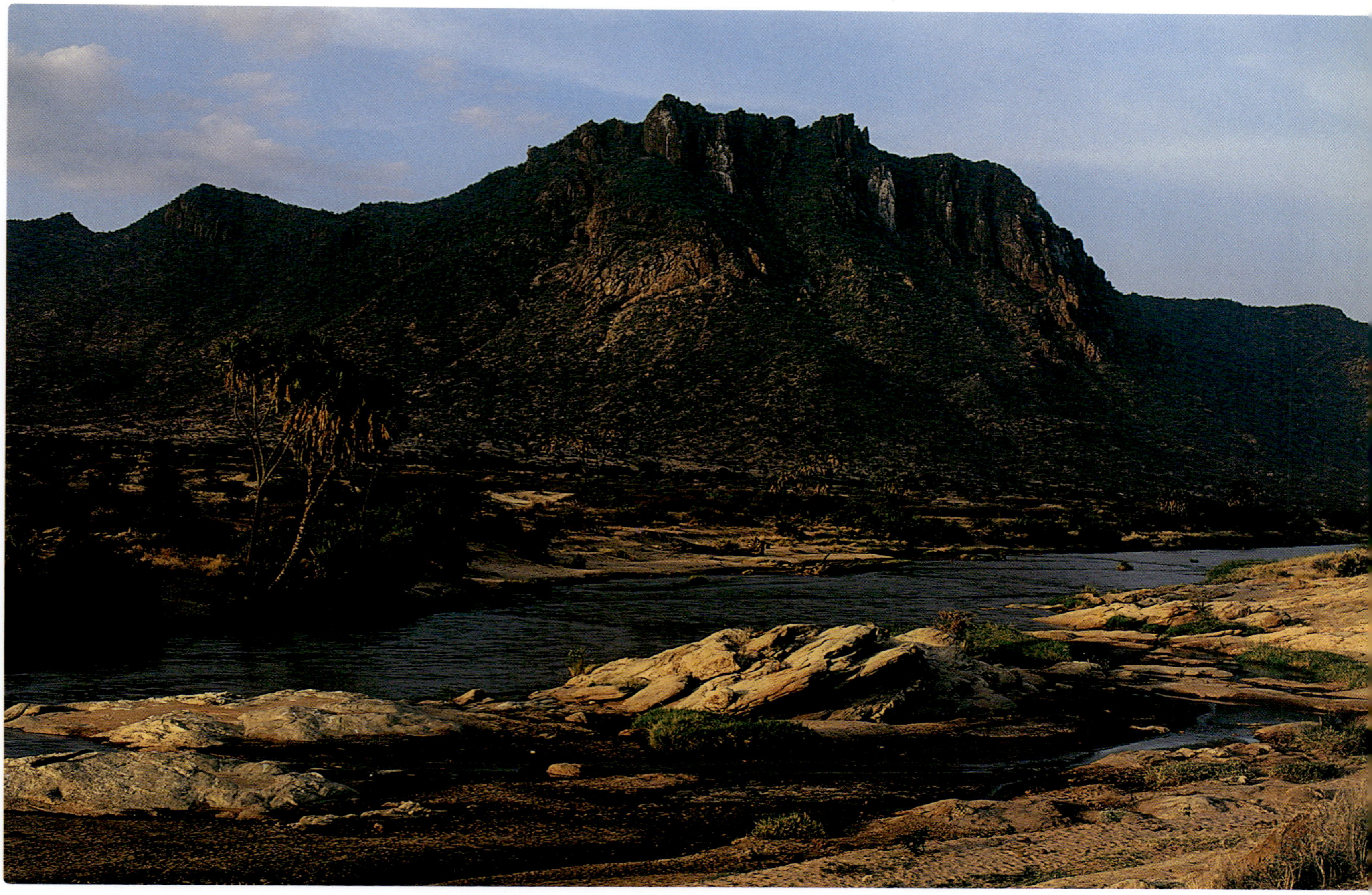

Shaba reserve still holds memories of Joy Adamson, the world-famous conservationist who was studying leopards here when she was killed by poachers. Her book *Born Free* tells of her lifelong love of big cats.

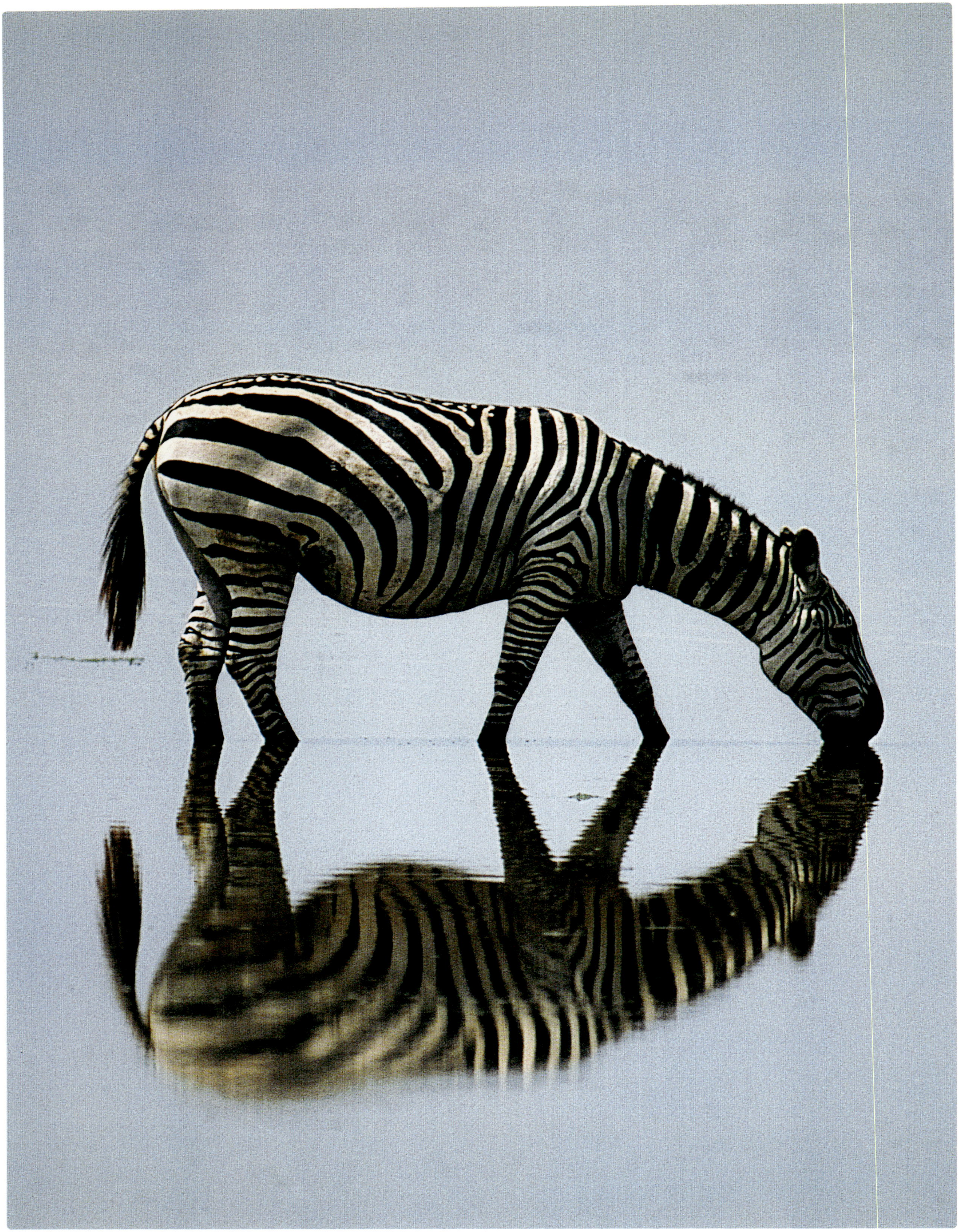

FACING PAGE:

The rainy season temporarily turns Amboseli into a vast lake where animals of all sorts come to drink. Special tracks have been opened to enable vehicles to visit all year round.

FOLLOWING PAGES:

The legendary Treetops Hotel in the Aberdares National Park. Visitors sit up at night to watch the animals attracted by the salt licks and the watering hole.

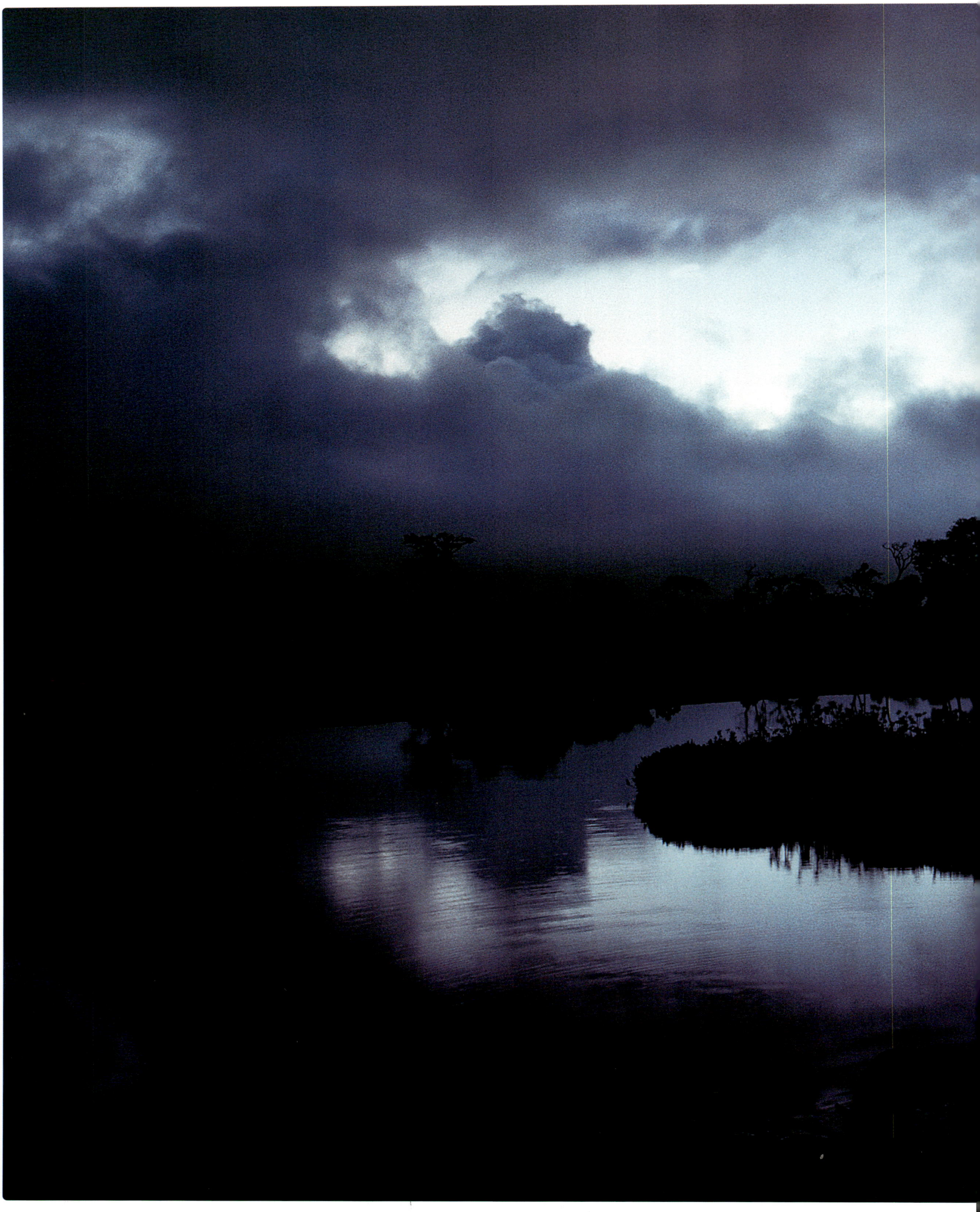

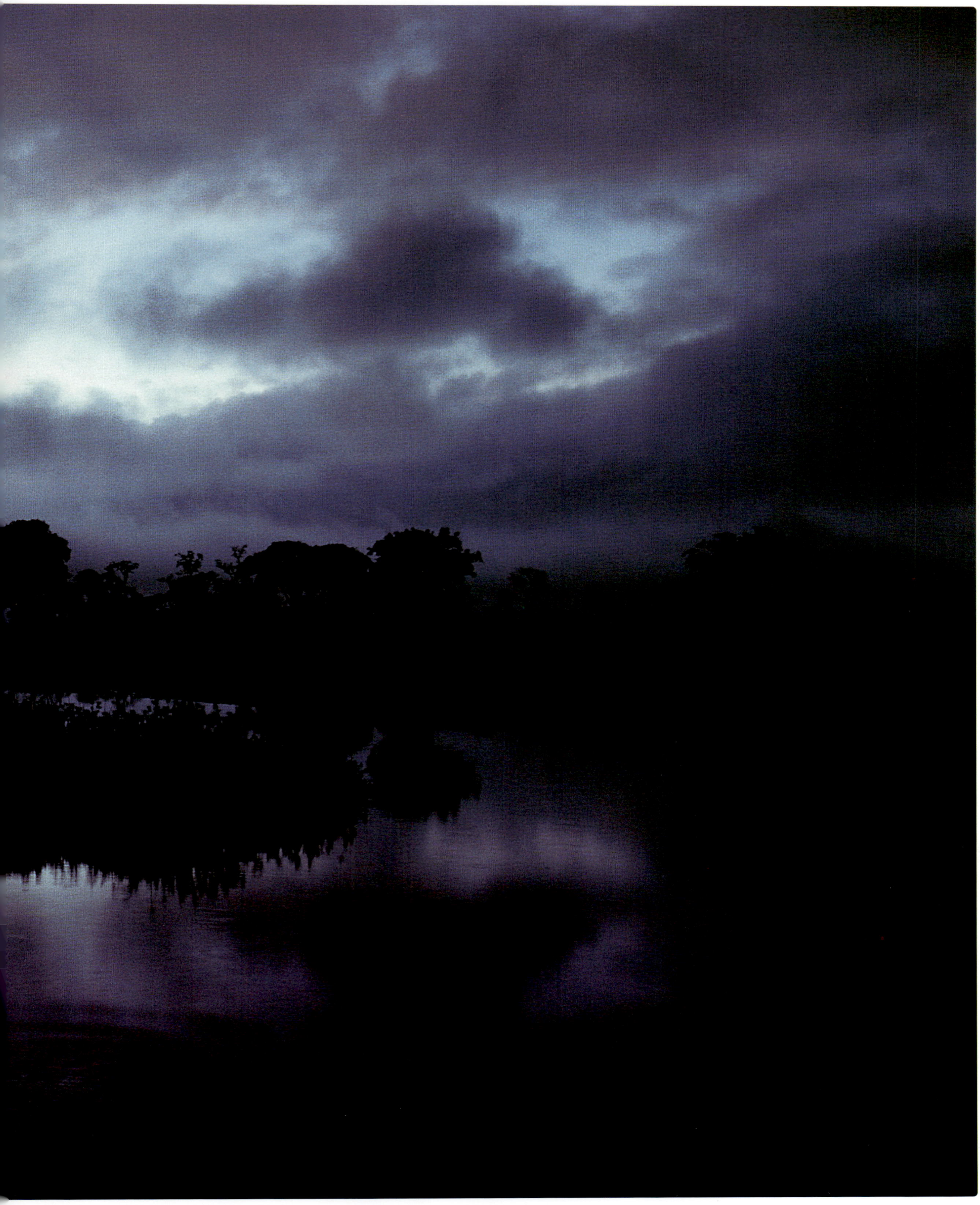

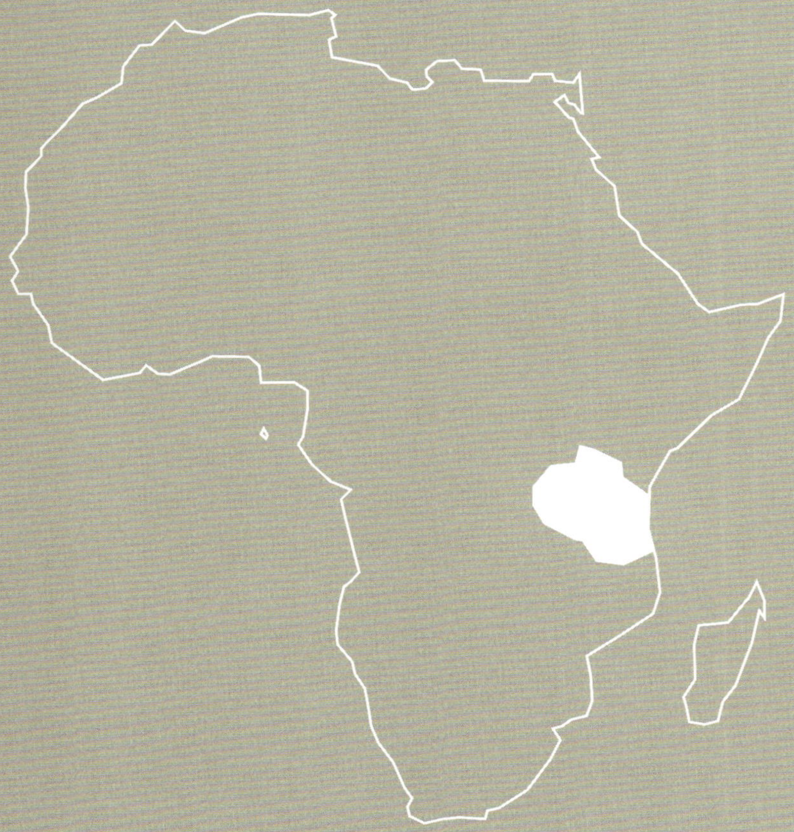

CHAPTER TWO

TANZANIA

THIS IS ONE OF THE CRADLES OF HUMANITY. TODAY, ONLY A FEW GAME LODGES IN CANVAS OR ROUGH-HEWN STONE, TUCKED DISCREETLY INTO THE LANDSCAPE, ALMOST INVISIBLE WHEN SET AGAINST THE MAJESTY OF THE SCENERY, BEAR WITNESS TO THE PRESENCE OF THE MODERN WORLD.

The horizon is a deep, magical, timeless blue on the cusp of the sky and the mountains. The N'Gorongoro crater is suffused with warm, honeyed light that caresses and softens the lines of this stark landscape like something out of an impossible dream. The crater reminds me of a great ark that has somehow escaped the passage of time, or a brand-new, unspoiled planet, wreathed in mist like a caul. It is a world of plants, animals, and minerals, where the black rhinoceros reigns supreme.

Tanzania was for many years held back from realizing its potential as a tourist destination by the hidebound socialist vision of the government that isolated the country from the modern world. However, this means that the country has been spared the worst excesses of the modern hotel industry and is still a land of wide open spaces and perfectly unspoiled landscapes. This is where the great annual migrations begin. This is one of the cradles of humanity. Today, only a few game lodges in canvas or rough-hewn stone, tucked discreetly into the landscape, almost invisible when set against the majesty of the scenery, bear witness to the presence of the modern world.

Tanzania only began opening up to the international marketplace in 1990 when Hassan Myinyi's government launched a liberal investment policy. This late start meant the country was well placed to learn from the mistakes of its neighbor, Kenya. Tanzania was able to avoid the problems caused by an overly rapid expansion of the tourism sector. Thanks to its three outstanding natural sites—Mount Kilimanjaro, the Serengeti National Park, and the N'Gorongoro Crater, Tanzania has developed an enviable reputation for the quality of the tourist experience it has to offer.

Tanzania and Kenya have been divided since the British and German governments decided to carve up East Africa between them in 1886. There is no natural feature to mark the border between the two countries, which is just a line on a map. The savanna stretches to the horizon, the animals and even the people are the same, but at some point we change country. Two-thirds of Tanzania's 364,9000 square miles (945,000 square kilometers) are savanna and scrubby grassland, while the remaining third is high-altitude forest.

Most visitors cross from Kenya into Tanzania at the border checkpoint of Namanga. From there, the road slopes down to Arusha, where most safari organizers are based. Thirteen miles (twenty-one kilometers) to the east of the little town, a ten-mile (sixteen-kilometer) track leads us to the Arusha Park, formerly known as the Meru Crater National Park. The park is a relatively small 53 square miles (137 square kilometers), but is a precious haven for zebra, giraffes, cobs, guib antelopes, buffaloes, hyenas, elephants, and black-and-white colobus monkeys. The altitude varies from 5,000 to 15,000 feet (1,524 to 4,572 meters) above sea level. It takes three days and the services of an experienced guide to reach the summit of Mount Meru, the third highest in Africa, which offers unparalleled views of its neighbor, Mount Kilimanjaro.

Although many people believe the best views of Kilimanjaro are from the Kenyan side of the border, the story goes that the mountain has been part of Tanzanian territory ever since Queen Victoria gave it to her grandson Kaiser Wilhelm as a birthday present. It has been set in a national park of 292 square miles (756 square kilometers) since 1973. It should be borne in mind that Kilimanjaro is sacred to the Masai people. It takes five or six days to climb the mountain and conquer the permanent snowcap of its highest peak, Kibo.

There are five possible routes up the mountain. The least known and to my mind the most interesting is Shira. Your only company is likely to be the elands, antelopes, buffaloes, and elephants that cross your path. Thousands of tourists attempt the arduous ascent of the 19,340 feet (5,895 meters) of Kilimanjaro every year. Many more, however, prefer to visit Lake Manyara, some 72 miles (115 kilometers) from Arusha, stopping in the village of Mto-wa-mbu, the "mosquito village," which today has a flourishing cottage industry making and selling handcrafted items for tourists. Most of Lake Manyara National Park's 125 square miles (325 square kilometers) consist of the lake itself. It is particularly interesting to visit after a very wet rainy season, like in 1998, when the waters rise, concentrating the animals in the ever-smaller patches of dry land, which are at best a few kilometers wide, caught between the waters of the lake and the Rift Valley. If you are very lucky, you might spot a lion taking refuge up a tree. You are bound to see some antelope species as well as countless pink flamingos and some of the 380 other bird species. From there, an appalling hairpin road, accessible only in all-terrain vehicles, winds thirty-eight miles (sixty kilometers) to the

PRECEDING PAGES:
The deep blue, almost purple depths of Lerai give the N'Gorongoro crater a mysterious, haunting presence. Many antelopes, including large numbers of wildebeest, live here because of the permanent watering holes.

FACING PAGE:
The fringes of the great migration sweep through the heart of the N'Gorongoro crater. In their neverending quest for food, the animals leave not a blade of grass. Hunger drives them north to the plains of Kenya. It is a harsh and often cruel life for wildebeest.

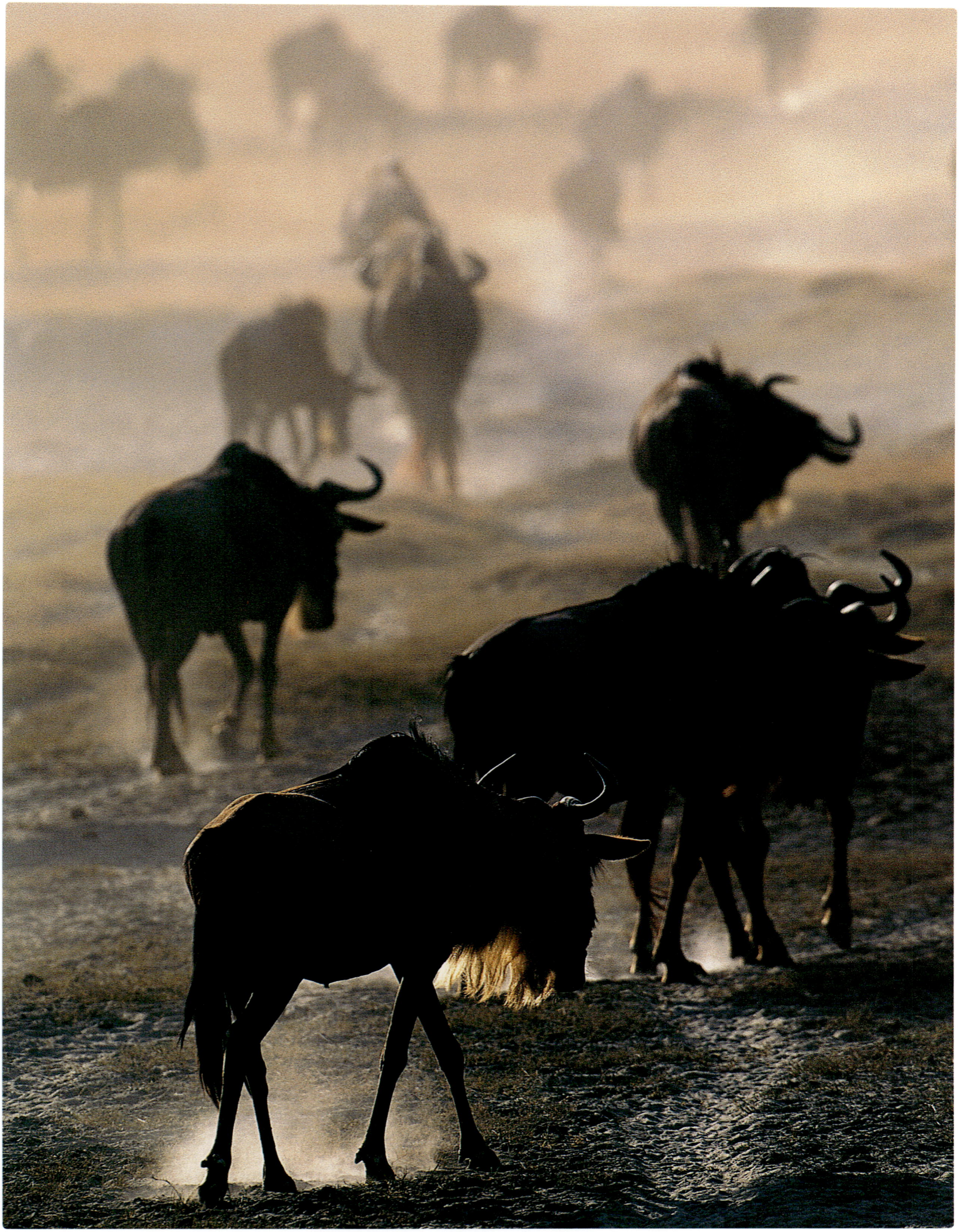

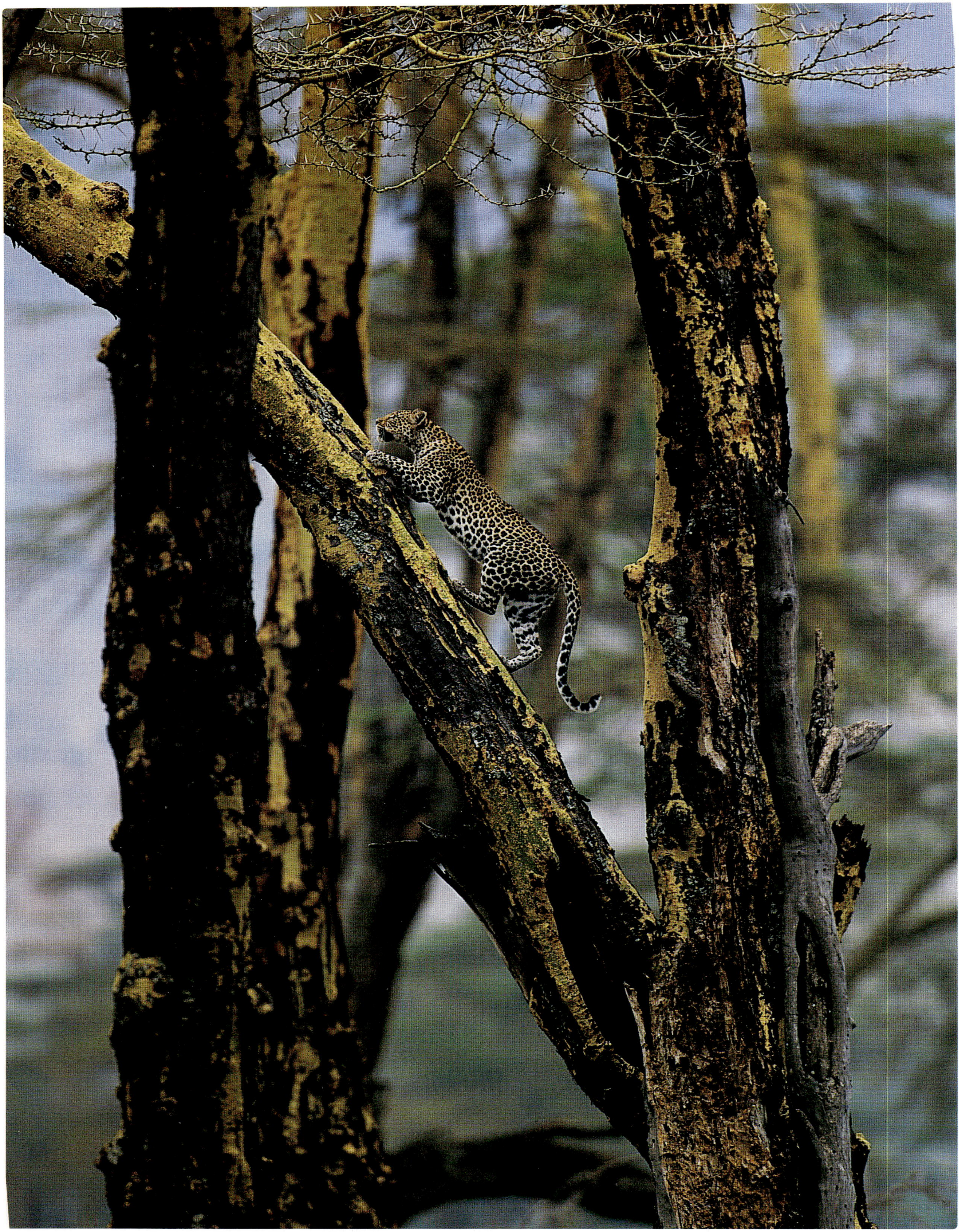

lip of the N'Gorongoro crater, passing through a rainforest of acacias, ficus, croton trees, and albizias. The Heroes Point observatory is marked by a rhinoceros statue in honor of all those who have given their lives in the cause of conservation. On the horizon, you can make out the misty, indistinct summits of Lolmalasin, Oldeani, Oldoinyo, Lemagrut, Olmoti, and Empakaai. This is pristine, untouched territory. However, the real attraction here is the first view of the N'Gorongoro crater.

The crater is Tanzania's foremost tourist attraction. Strictly speaking, it is not a crater, but a caldera—a large, circular volcanic depression formed by the inward collapse of the cone. It was formed two and a half million years ago by the collapse of a gigantic volcanic cone, and with a diameter of nearly thirteen miles (twenty kilometers), it is the largest—and the most beautiful—in the world. It is now part of the 3,205-square-mile (8,300-square-kilometer) N'Gorongoro Conservation Area, a territory created in 1959 to allow the Masai people to maintain their ancestral tradition of living alongside the wildlife. The conservation area is a mixture of forests, savanna, and bushland, mountains, and extinct volcanoes. The crater itself occupies a mere three percent of the zone, which was placed on UNESCO's World Heritage list in 1978. However, it offers a range of landscapes and animal species that is truly exceptional. Standing on the crater's lip above the plain, you can make out the dark masses of the herds as they wander among the lakes, marshlands, streams, and forests. There are three narrow roads winding between the aloes and the candelabra trees. They are barely more than dirt tracks with deep ruts gouged by the torrential rain during the wet season. The roads wind down the flanks of the crater, descending six hundred meters (650 yards) to the plains below. The views are spectacular. Each bend opens up a new vista of buffaloes, zebras, elephants, wildebeest, and gazelles. At first light or in the last rays of the dying sun, you might even see one of the few remaining black rhinoceroses with a pair of egrets or a red-billed oxpecker hitching a ride on its back. The best place to see these magnificent beasts is between Gorigor and the Mandusi swamps. Just a few individuals remained in the late 1980s. The numbers have now risen to nineteen thanks to the recent release of a mother and calf brought over from Addo Park in South Africa. In the early 1960s, the crater was home to over a hundred individuals. Contrary to what you might expect from their names, the black rhinoceros (*diceros bicornis*) and his white cousin (*ceratotherium simum*) are the same color, blending in with the colors of the savanna. In fact, the white rhinoceros got its name from a faulty translation of the Dutch *weit*, meaning broad or wide. The two species do differ in terms of size. The black rhinoceros is smaller, weighing up to 590 pounds (1,300 kilograms), while the white rhino can weigh anything up to three tons. The white rhino is also reputed to be a more placid beast than its black relative. Black rhinos are legendary for their aggressiveness, often charging tourists, primarily as a form of intimidation when they feel threatened. Even the most experienced guides steer well clear of black rhinos. The behavior of animals in the wild depends a great deal on their surroundings and the time of day. Animals' brains are wired in similar ways to our own, and each individual interprets the signs it detects as its own nervous system dictates. In the animal kingdom, nothing is ever entirely predictable.

THE ROADS WIND DOWN THE FLANKS OF THE CRATER, DESCENDING SIX HUNDRED METERS (650 YARDS) TO THE PLAINS BELOW. THE VIEWS ARE SPECTACULAR. EACH BEND OPENS UP A NEW VISTA OF BUFFALOES, ZEBRAS, ELEPHANTS, WILDEBEEST, AND GAZELLES.

The presence of permanent watering holes in the hollow of the crater means that large numbers of animals have chosen this as their home. Regularly, in the first few months of the year, part of the great antelope migration passes through. Long lines of wildebeest wander endlessly along the salt-encrusted shores of Lake Makat. Herds numbering fifteen thousand wildebeest or five thousand zebras and buffaloes have been counted. The presence of water also brings in tribesmen with their livestock, which generally leads to a decline in the wild animal population. At dawn, you can sometimes see Masai tribesmen leading vast herds of cattle to pasture in the Munge and Mandusi swamps. The rapid growth in livestock numbers thanks to the recent influx of tourist money into parts of the region has had a considerable impact on the wildlife. Today, there is a real danger of wild animals and livestock competing for the all too slender natural resources. The park authorities are aware of the problem and are trying to deal with it before the situation becomes too critical, but there are no easy answers.

The road that curves round the western flank of the crater leads to the Serengeti. This is the birthplace of humanity. Here, between the vast plains and the great rent in the earth's surface

FACING PAGE:
To the east of Lake Makat, the forest of Lerai offers a magnificent display of gigantic yellow acacias, also known as the fever tree because a decoction of its bark is a powerful painkiller. Occasionally, you might spot a pair of leopards slouching on a branch. To take this kind of picture, you need plenty of patience. It can take a full day's wait in your vehicle—it is far too dangerous to wander into the forest on foot.

THE DEFINING IMAGE OF THE REGION—EVEN IF IT IS PERHAPS A LITTLE MISLEADING—IS THAT OF AN ENDLESS EXPANSE OF GOLDEN GRASS REACHING AS FAR AS THE EYE CAN SEE UNDER A CLOUDLESS BLUE SKY, WITH HERE AND THERE AN OUTCROP OF POLISHED ROCK CALLED A KOPJE. THESE GRANITE OUTCROPS ARE OVERGROWN WITH ACACIAS, ALOES, AND HIBISCUS, AND PROVIDE COVER FOR MONGOOSE, DIK-DIKS, LEOPARDS, COBRAS, AND CHEETAHS.

called the Rift Valley, one of our ancestors 3.6 million years ago decided that standing up straight on his two hind feet would give him a certain advantage over other species. A series of footprints set in volcanic ash on the flanks of the N'Gorongoro crater prove that this is where humanity began. Paleontologists are still arguing about whether our earliest ancestor was *orrorin tugenensis*, discovered in Kenya in 2000, or *sahelanthropus tchadensis*, found in Chad in 2002. In a field where concrete evidence is everything, there can be no disputing that our early ancestors walked here in Laetolil. The site is not far from the famous Olduvai gorges where so many fossil species have been patiently unearthed since the beginning of the twentieth century. Perched above the strata of rock laid bare by successive generations of digs, a modest yet fascinating museum exhibits a collection of dusty fossils. They tell the story of the amazing species that our ancestors might have hunted, including horned giraffes, giant boar, and three-toed horses—all long since extinct.

The name Serengeti is taken from the Masai term *siringet*, meaning a vast plain. While two-thirds of the Serengeti is in fact covered with copses and forests, the first impression on leaving the Olduvai gorges behind is one of the immensity of the open space. The defining image of the region—even if it is perhaps a little misleading—is that of an endless expanse of golden grass reaching as far as the eye can see under a cloudless blue sky, with here and there an outcrop of polished rock called a kopje. These granite outcrops are overgrown with acacias, aloes, and hibiscus, and provide cover for mongoose, dik-diks, leopards, cobras, and cheetahs. One very common animal in these parts is the rock hyrax, an odd-looking creature that resembles a rabbit, but which is in biological terms the elephant's closest relative. Just before you arrive at Naabi Hill, a track leading off to the right takes you to Gol Kopjes, where several families of cheetahs have taken up residence. To visit this site, you must have requested special permission and paid an entrance fee. But the Serengeti's best-known spectacle takes place on the plains, when the great annual migration gets underway from the Naabi Hills and the shores of Lake Ndutu. Some 1.8 million animals, including 1.3 million wildebeest and 280,000 zebra, as well as large numbers of gazelles, elands, topis, and giraffes, leave the arid plains in search of fresh sources of water. The migration begins at the start of the dry season, in May or June, after the calves are born in February and March. Some animals migrate as far as Lake Victoria, but the majority crosses over into Kenya. The Tanzanians get rid of the dry grass by setting enormous fires that pollute the atmosphere over vast tracts of eastern Africa, so that the grass will grow fresh and green straight after the first rains. The Serengeti is also renowned for the numbers of big cats in the region—around a thousand lions, five hundred cheetahs, four thousand hyenas, and a few dozen leopards. Many live in the heart of the park around Seronera.

The Tanzanian government is keen to retain some control over the tourism industry and is trying to limit the number of hotels in the north of the country, preferring to attract tourists to the great nature reserves in the south of the country. Selous Game Reserve in particular is noted for its buffaloes, elephants, antelopes, and lions. Selous is thought to be the largest nature reserve in the world, at 21,080 square miles (54,600 square kilometers), a large part of which is hunting territory. However, it is much less frequented by tourists than N'Gorongoro or the Serengeti. Camps in Selous are few and far between. Two of the better-known ones are Sand River and Selous Camp, both of which are in sites of outstanding beauty. While Tanzanian game lodges do not quite have the cachet of the upscale Kenyan camps, the decision to focus on the top end of the safari market has proved a shrewd one. Tanzania is no longer the poor relation. While Tanzania has followed its own path, Kenyan safaris—far cheaper, far less effort required from the tourist—have seen bookings fall dramatically. Paradoxically, Tanzania has benefited from its late start and the difficult economic conditions of ten or fifteen years ago, which have meant that it has not fallen into the trap of exploiting its wealth of attractions. Tourism is indeed a double-edged sword: it brings wealth, but in so doing, it irrevocably changes the place tourists come to experience.

FACING PAGE:
Both male and female elephants have tusks, but those of the male are larger. They are simply huge incisors that have been known to weigh up to two hundred and twenty pounds (a hundred kilograms) apiece for the largest animals. Ivory poaching has been a major cause of the fall in elephant numbers.

FOLLOWING PAGES:
The hollow of the N'Gorongoro crater regularly fills with a layer of mist that seems to rest on the luxuriant vegetation typical of the humid climate. Here, we are 7,544 feet (2,286 meters) above sea level. The Lerai road is only open to vehicles driving down the slope. It descends 1,980 feet (six hundred meters) into the valley, offering magnificent views at every turn.

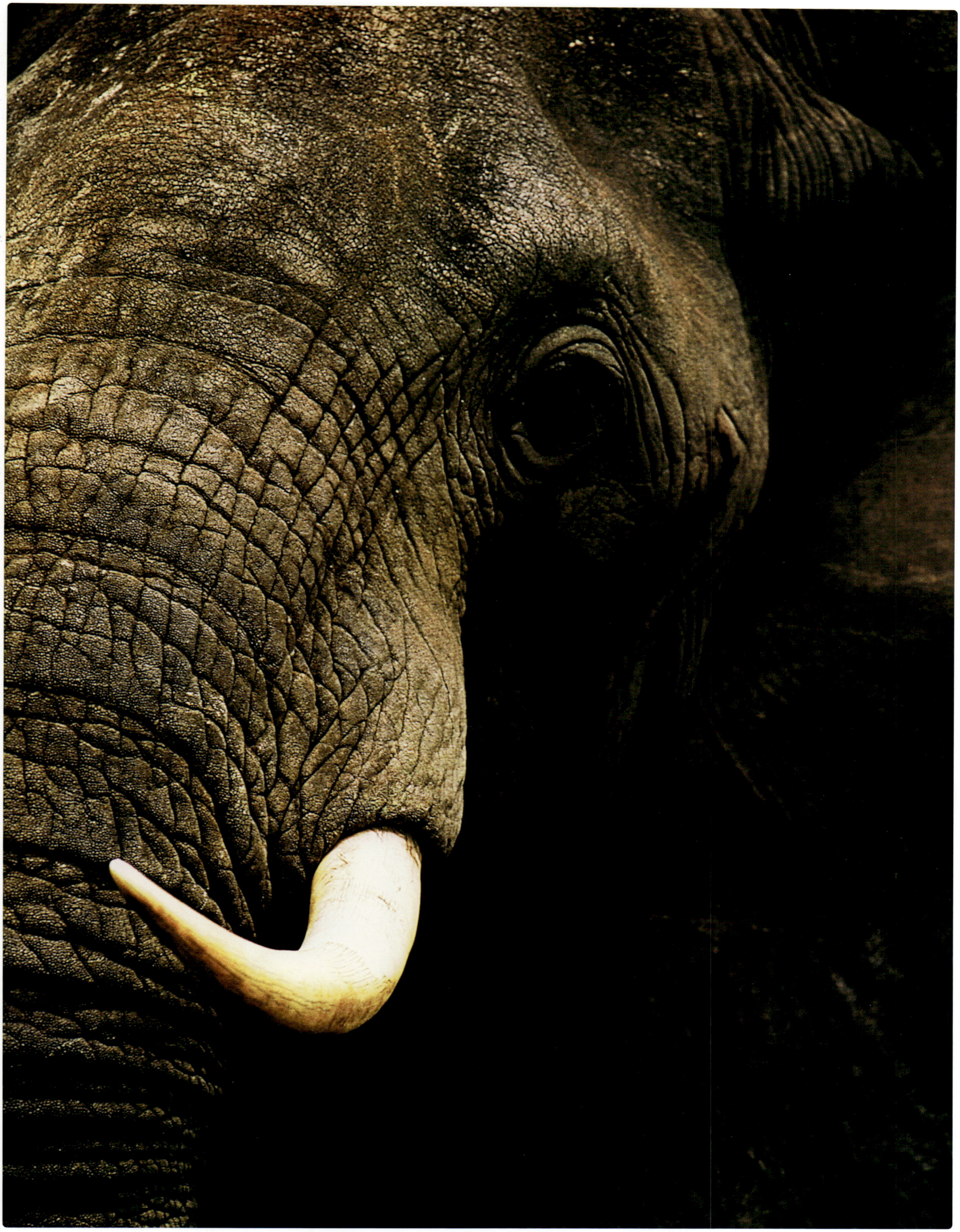

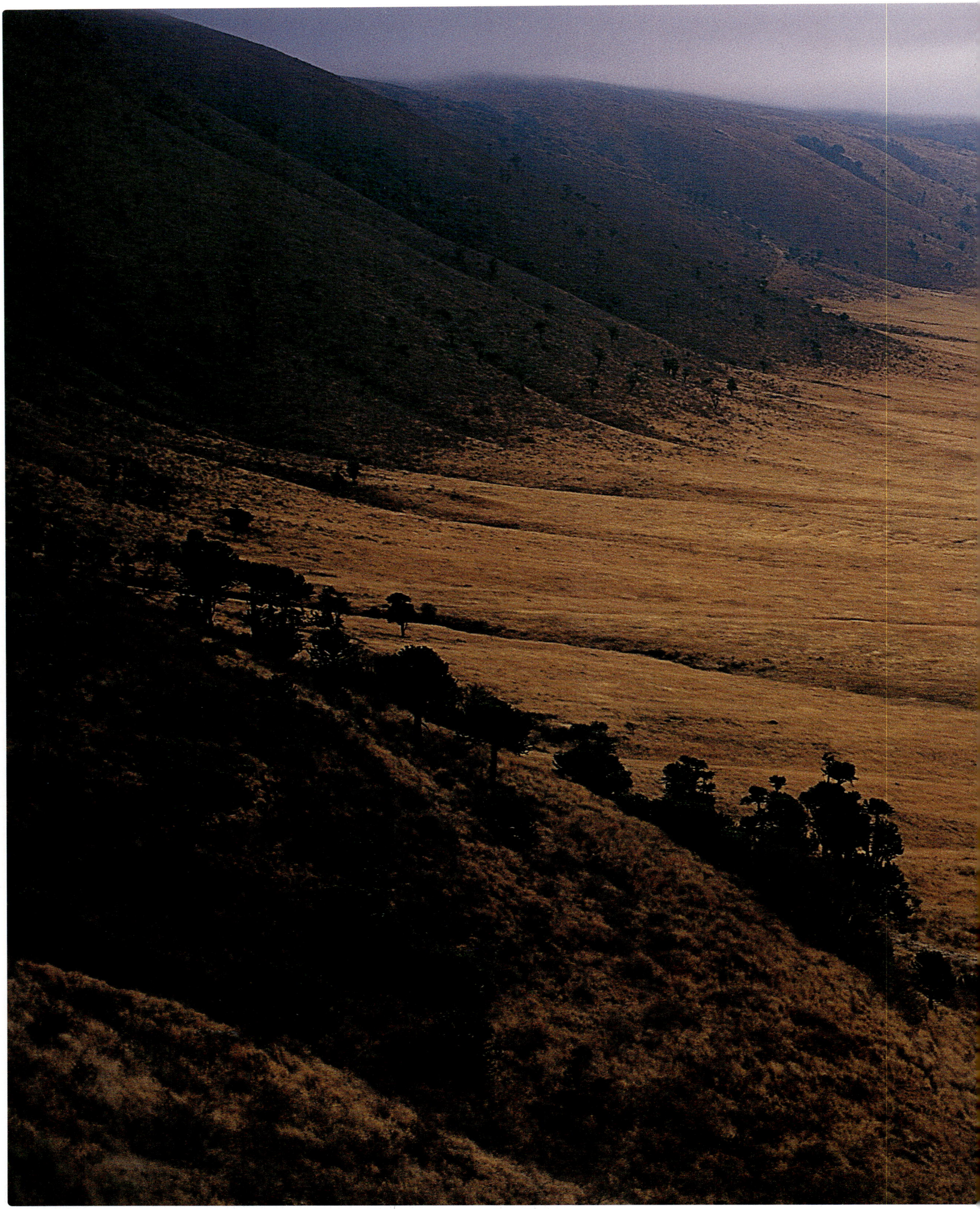

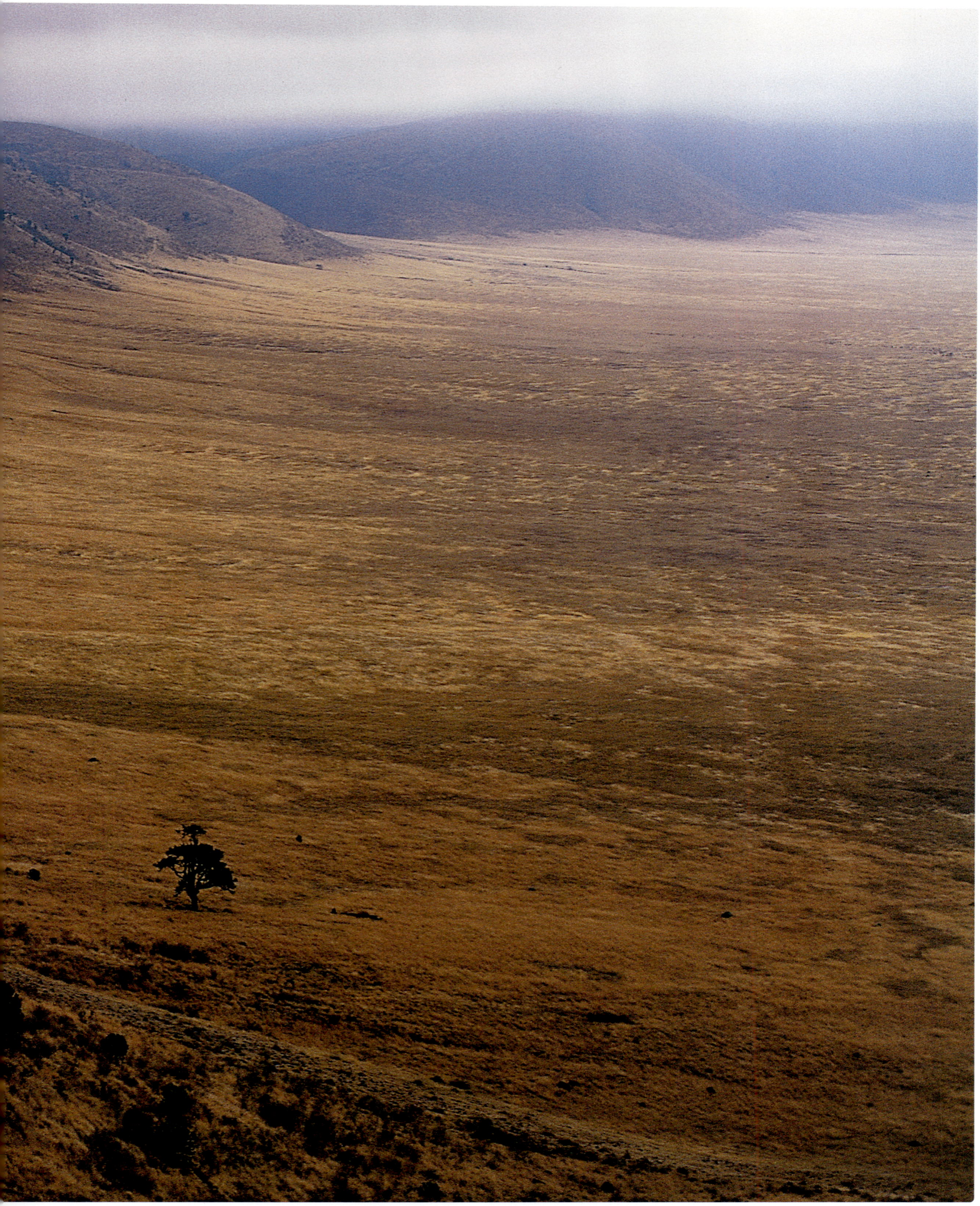

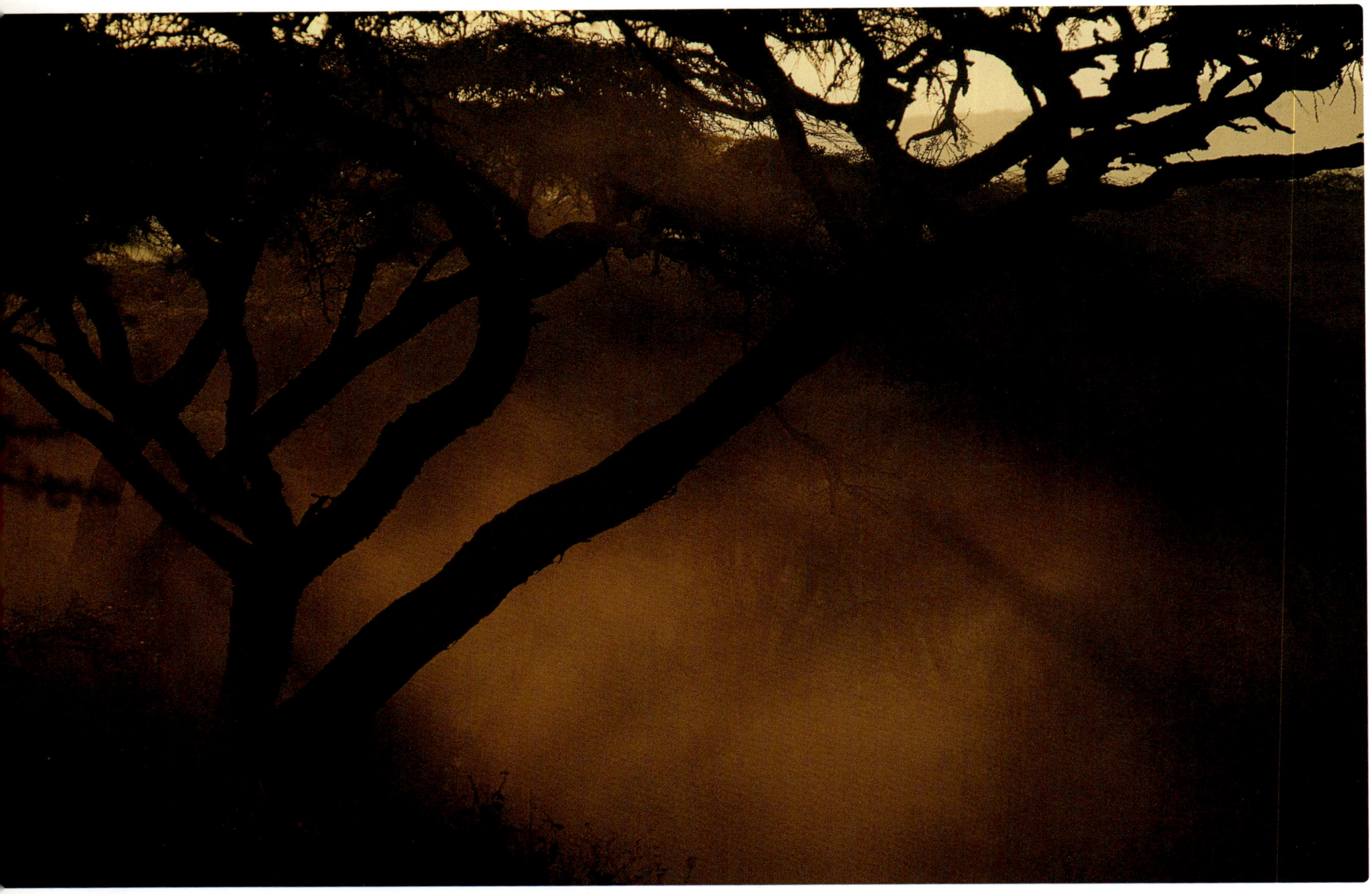

Night falls quickly at the equator, and the sunsets seem all the shorter since it is forbidden to drive in the national parks after dark. It is immensely frustrating to have to leave just as nature is putting on one of her finest spectacles.

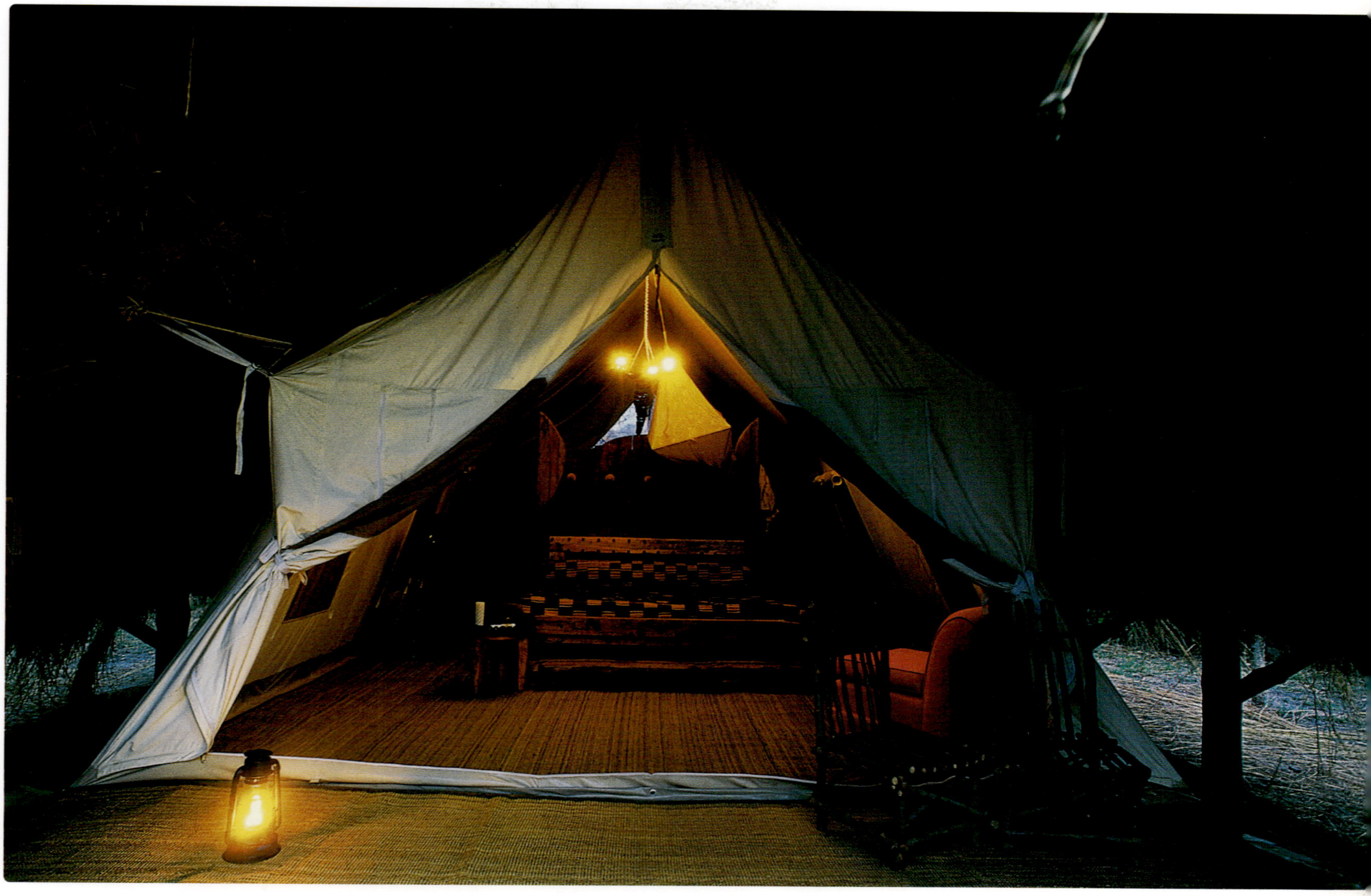

The bush camp architecture style was designed by the Italian Silvio Rech. The Maji Moto camp on Lake Mangana has proved highly influential in terms of game lodge design, both in neighboring countries and in South Africa. Part of the Serena hotel chain, the Maji Moto lodge was backed by the Conservation Corporation investment group. The group has built high-quality safari lodges such as this one in the Serengeti, on Lake Manyara, and in N'Gorongoro, making an important contribution to the Tanzanian tourist industry.

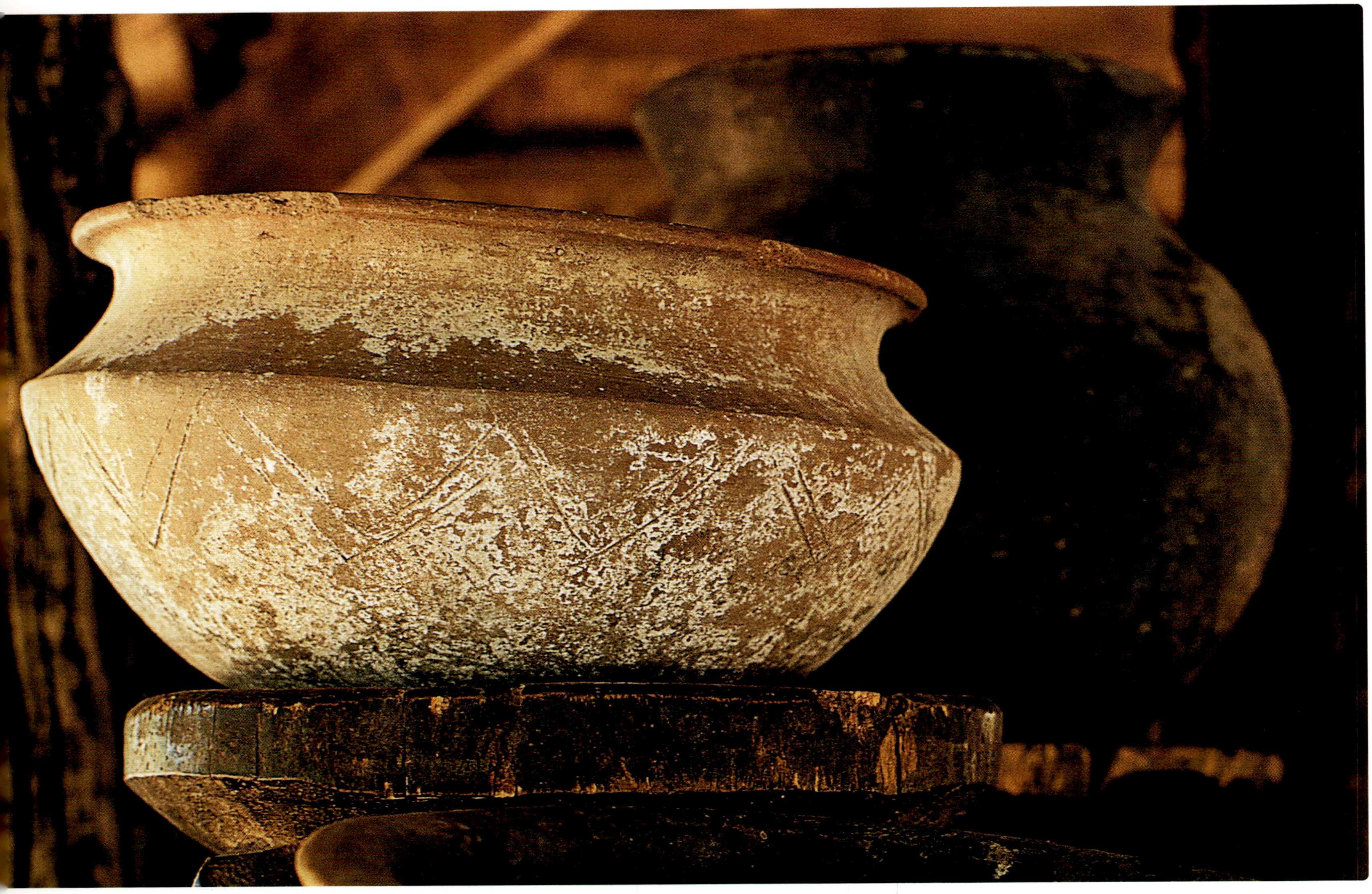

ABOVE:
The tools and utensils that lie in the corner of Masai huts are used for decoration in the safari lodges. These pots, jugs, and gourds are prized for their beauty and bring a touch of local color to the Grumeti game lodge in the Serengeti. The development of tourism in the region has led to changes in the lifestyles of the local tribes. In particular, they now produce many more such decorative objects for sale as a means of saving up some money to buy a few head of cattle.

FACING PAGE:
Looking from a distance like a trail of ants, the migrating wildebeest follow each other for dozens of miles across the arid savanna where every drop of water has been scorched from the earth. It is heartrending to hear the groans of the beasts as they search for relief from their raging thirst. One in ten of these animals will die in the trek across the savanna. Yet this annual migration is vital to the survival of the species.

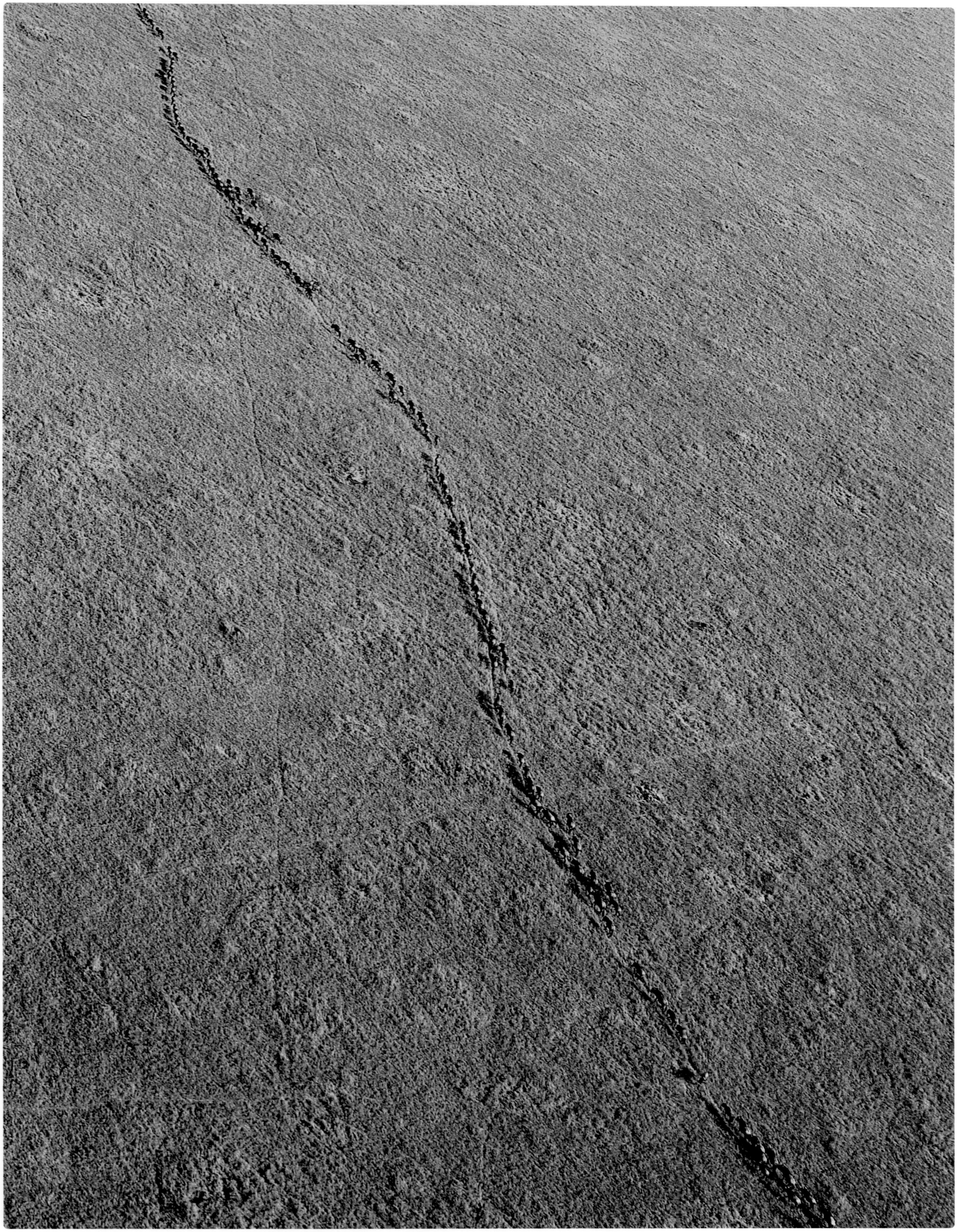

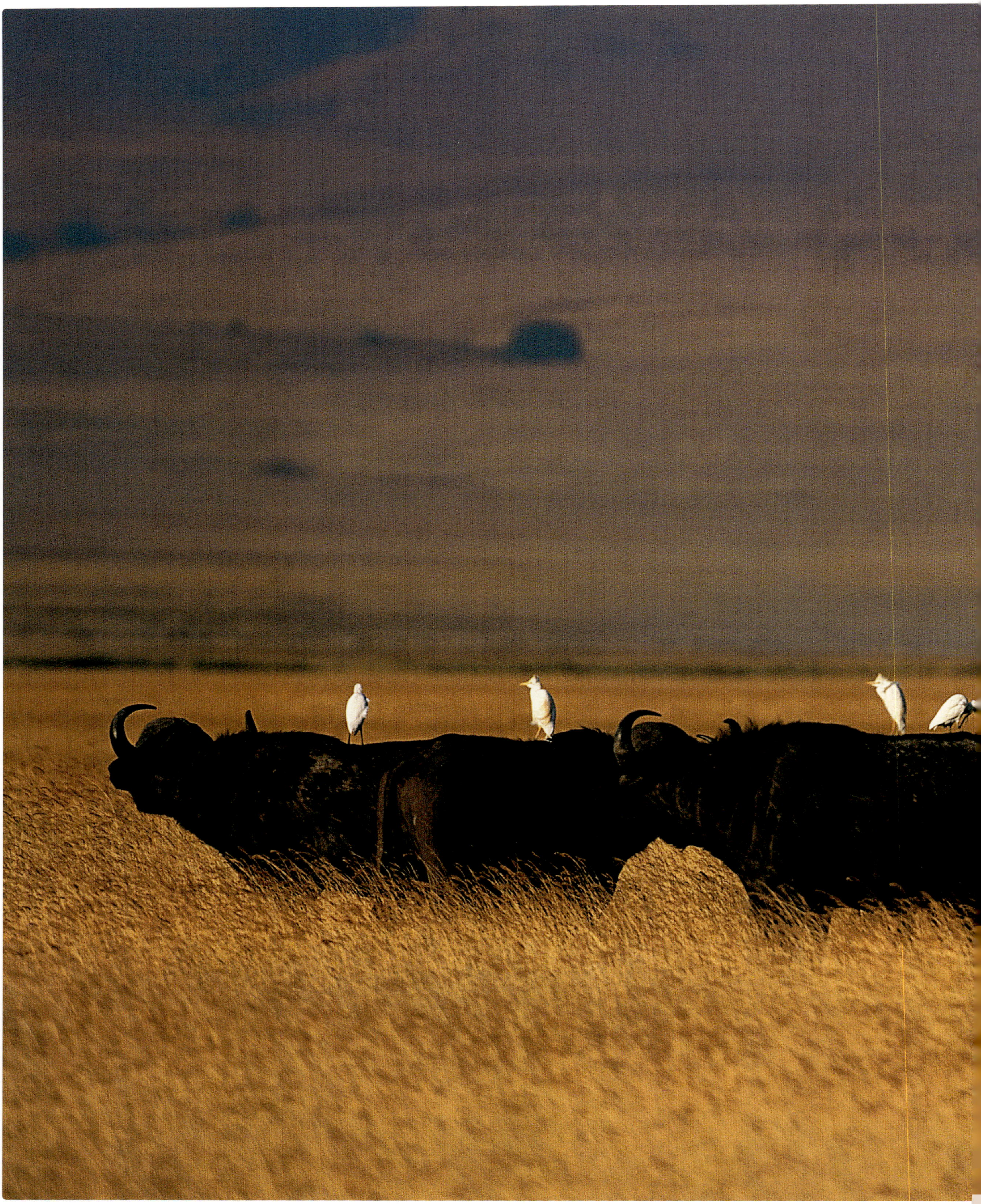

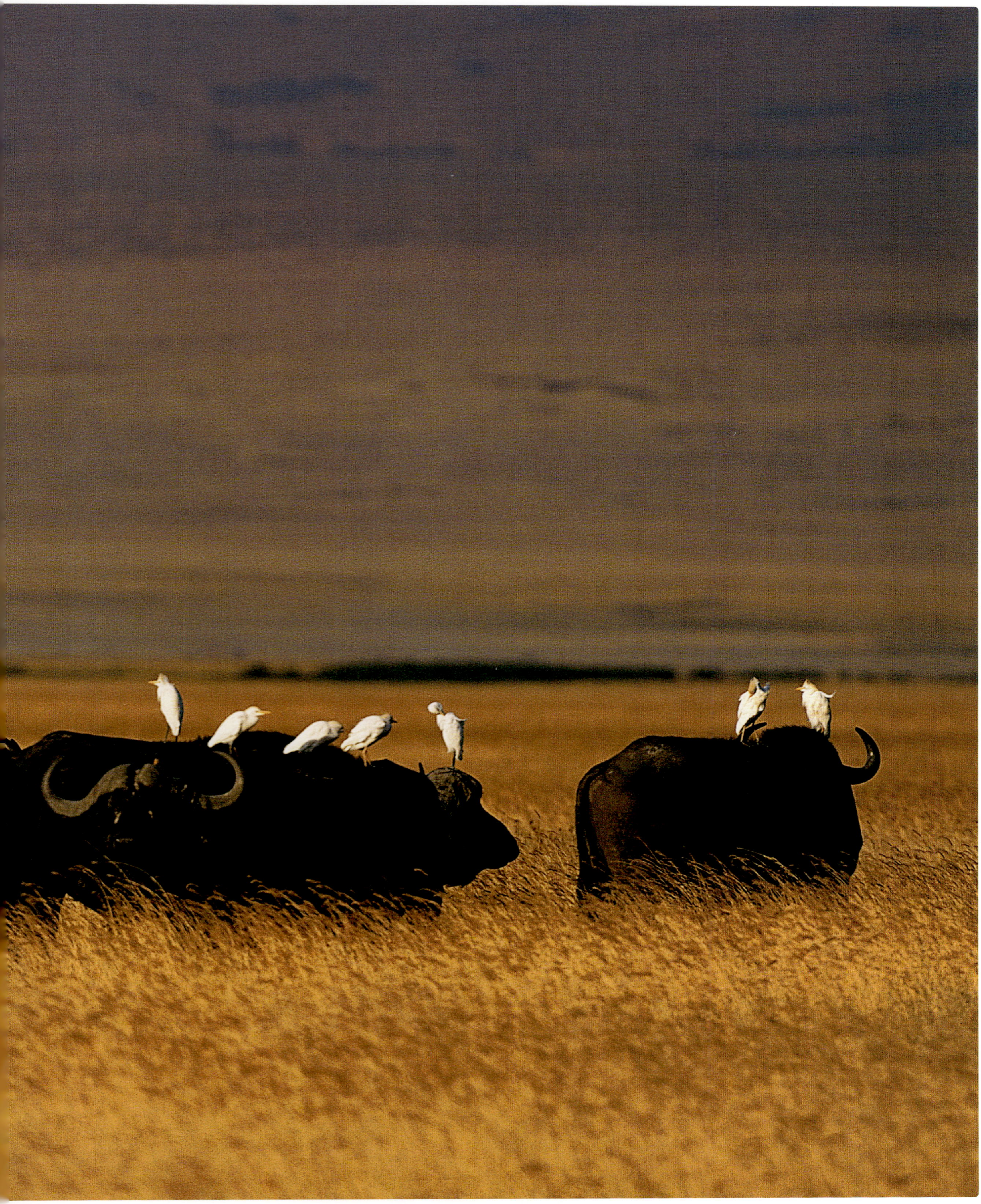

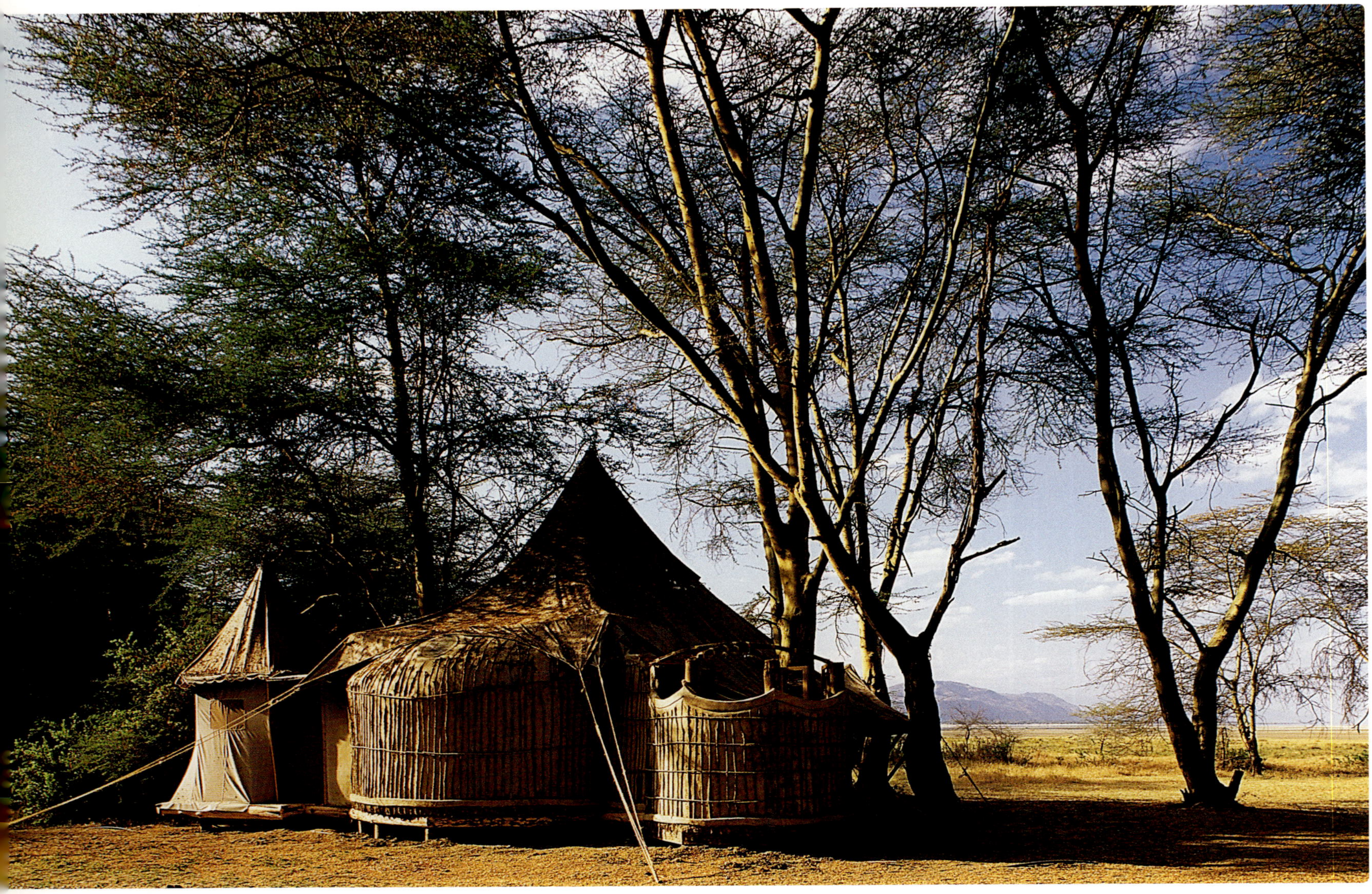

PRECEDING PAGES:

Buffaloes usually live in groups numbering several hundred individuals, but when the dry season begins, they separate into much smaller clusters. The young males leave the herd, returning only for the breeding season. They prefer open territory so they can see lions approaching. If threatened, they huddle together in a compact group, presenting a formidable challenge to any predator. White egrets perch on the backs of the buffaloes, providing a valuable service as they feed on the ticks and other parasites that make the creature's life a misery.

ABOVE:

Tanzania's hotel industry was for a long time hugely underdeveloped, but in recent years it has caught up with its neighbors in Kenya. A number of international leisure chains have invested in the country, building excellent hotels such as the Maji Moto on Lake Manyara. These new establishments far outclass the hotels run by the Tanzanian government. The Tanzanian authorities have now put in place a policy of privatization, handing the management of the TAHI chain over to private investors in 2002.

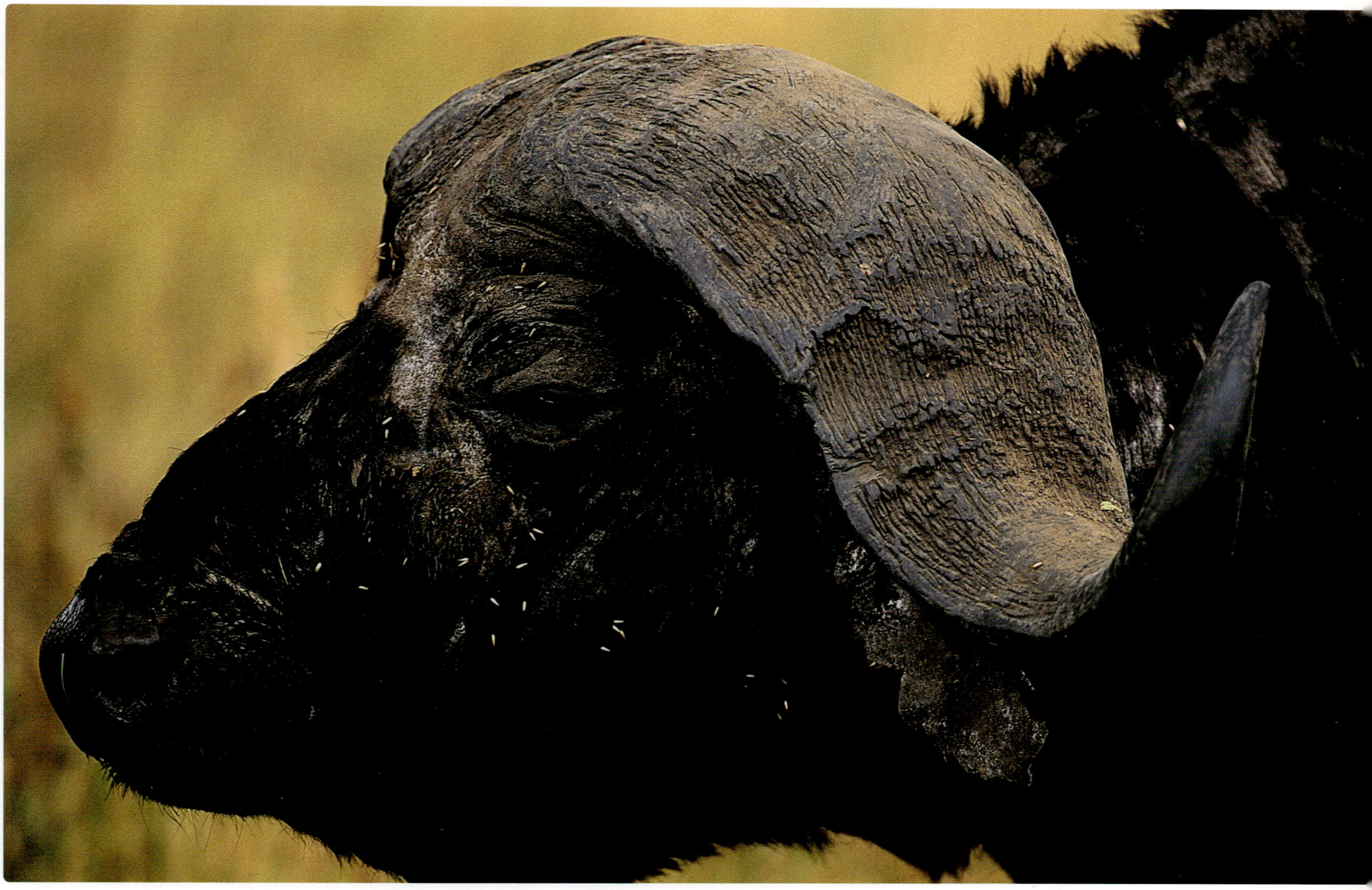

ABOVE:
Buffaloes are incapable of regulating their internal body temperature. To keep cool in the searing heat, they must drink between thirty and forty liters of water per day. This is also the reason why, in the heat of the day, they will remain motionless for hours on end, or seek out a mud bath or watering hole to wallow in.

FOLLOWING PAGES:
Lions are unpredictable creatures. They are at home everywhere, from the open savanna to the steaming heat of the mopane forests and the semi-arid fringes of the desert. They are not shy and will approach game lodges. As they have on occasion been known to attack tourists, it is advisable to be escorted to your tent. Some Masai have even chosen to exchange their traditional red robes for a ranger's green jacket. From the Engitati observatory, they keep an eye on the tourists to make sure none are foolish enough to forget that here they have to follow the rules of nature.

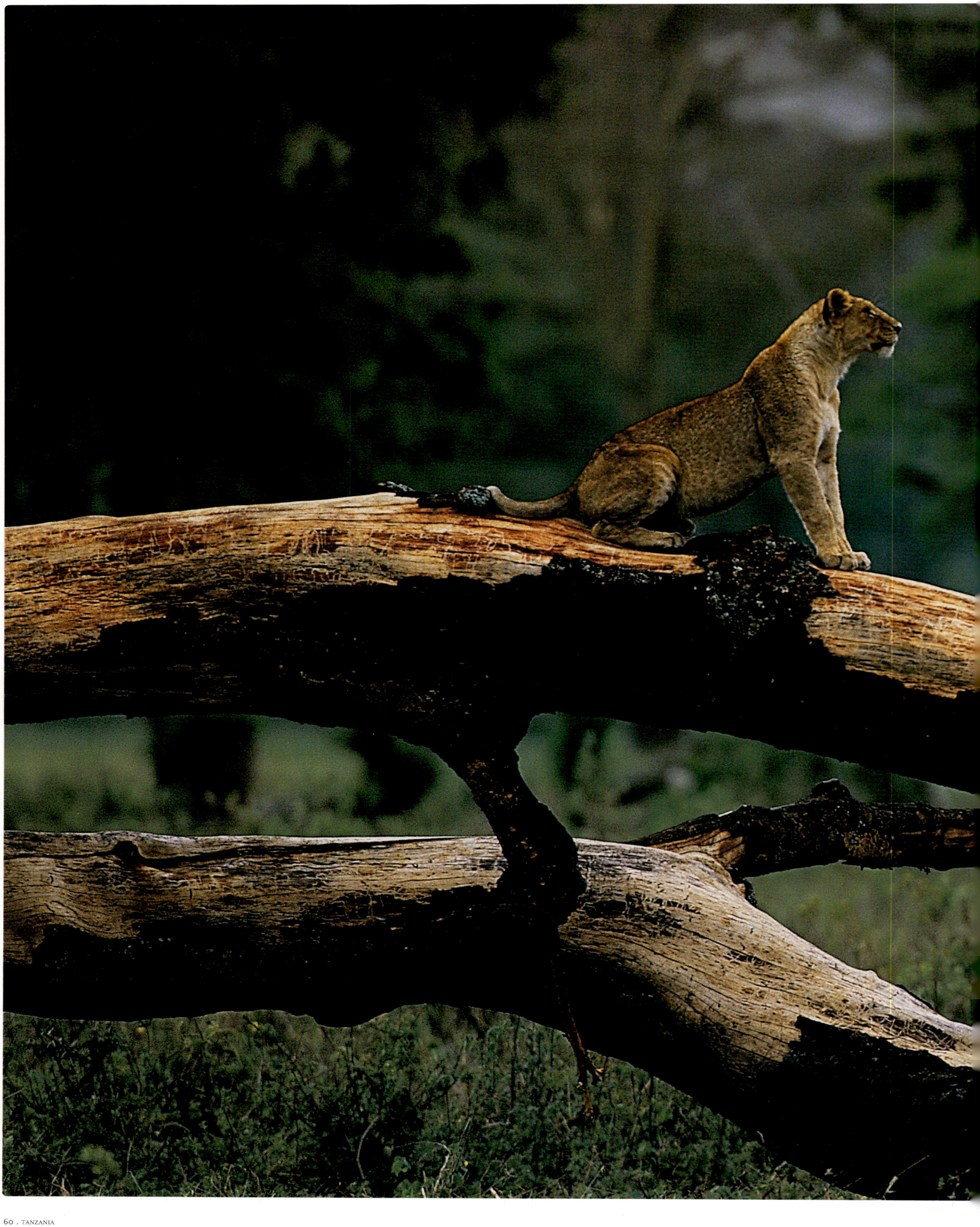

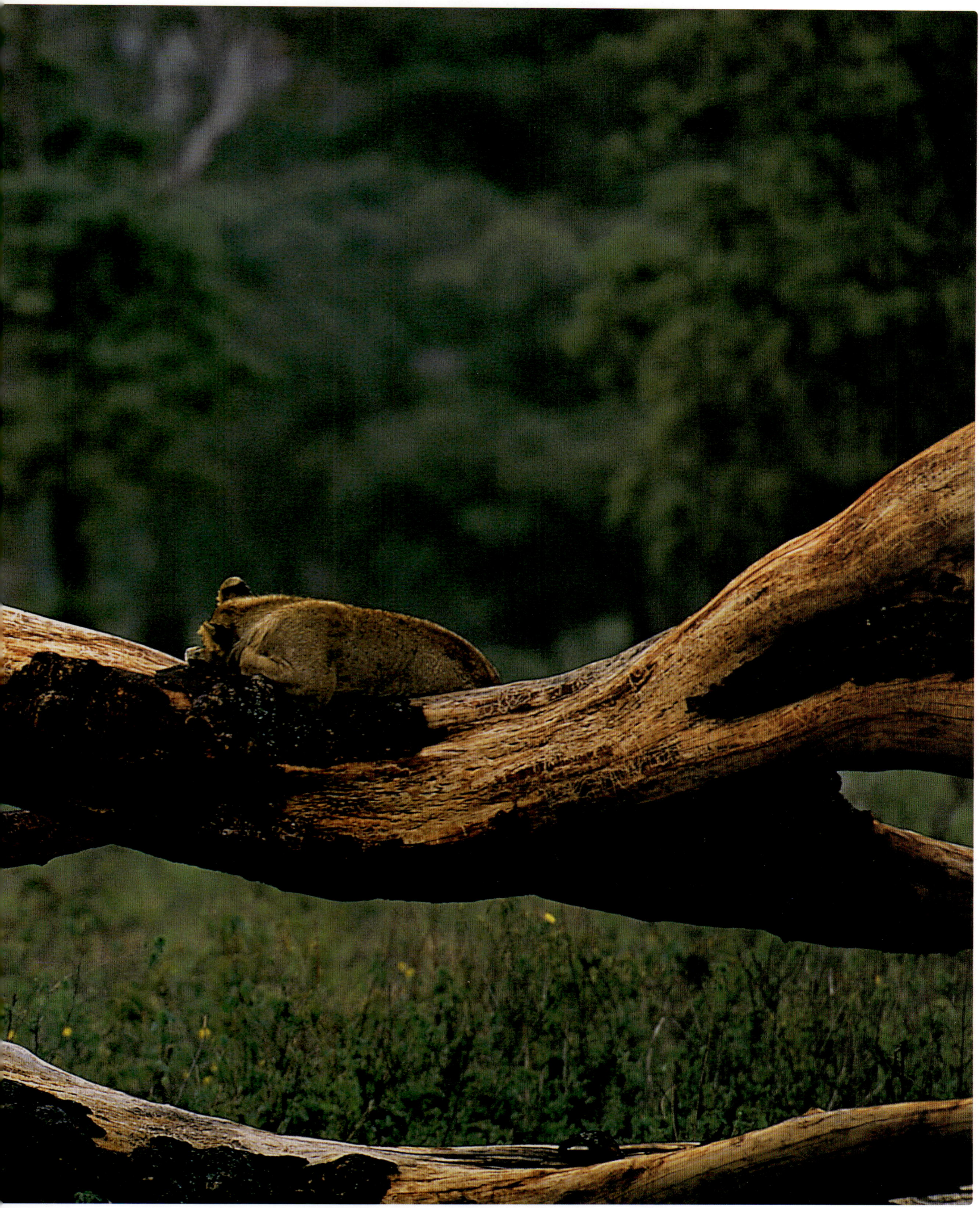

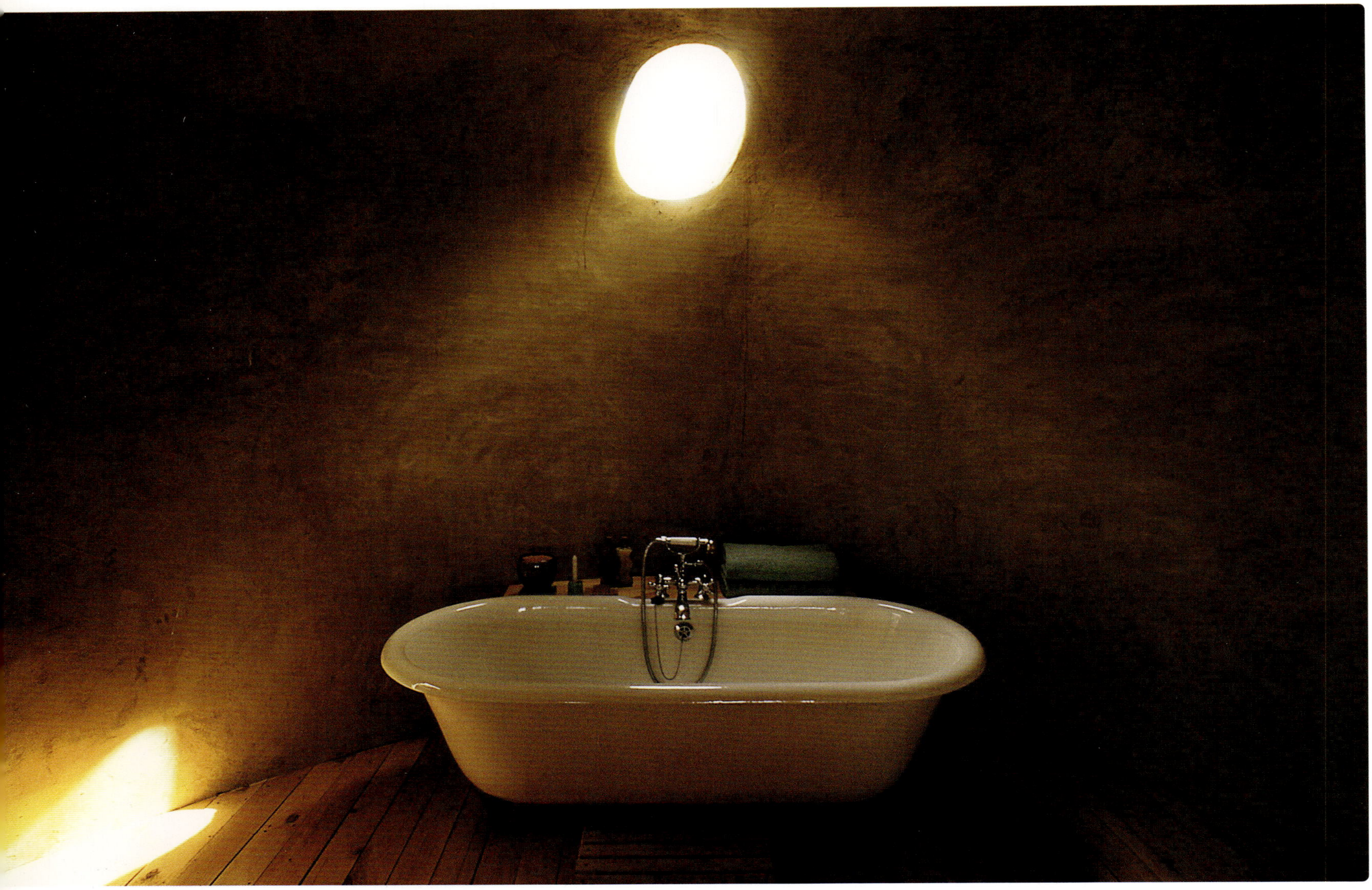

The simple elegance of the Maji Moto Lodge was inspired by the clean lines of the natural world. The lodge was built using all local materials and traditional architectural design and techniques. The result is breathtaking. The luxurious comfort of the lodge, all in brown canvas and polished wood, is magically reminiscent of the African roots of humanity. The light falling through the canvas walls of the tents onto the dull sheen of the wooden floor reminded me of a forest clearing where, thousands of years ago, our ancestors might have set up camp for a few nights.

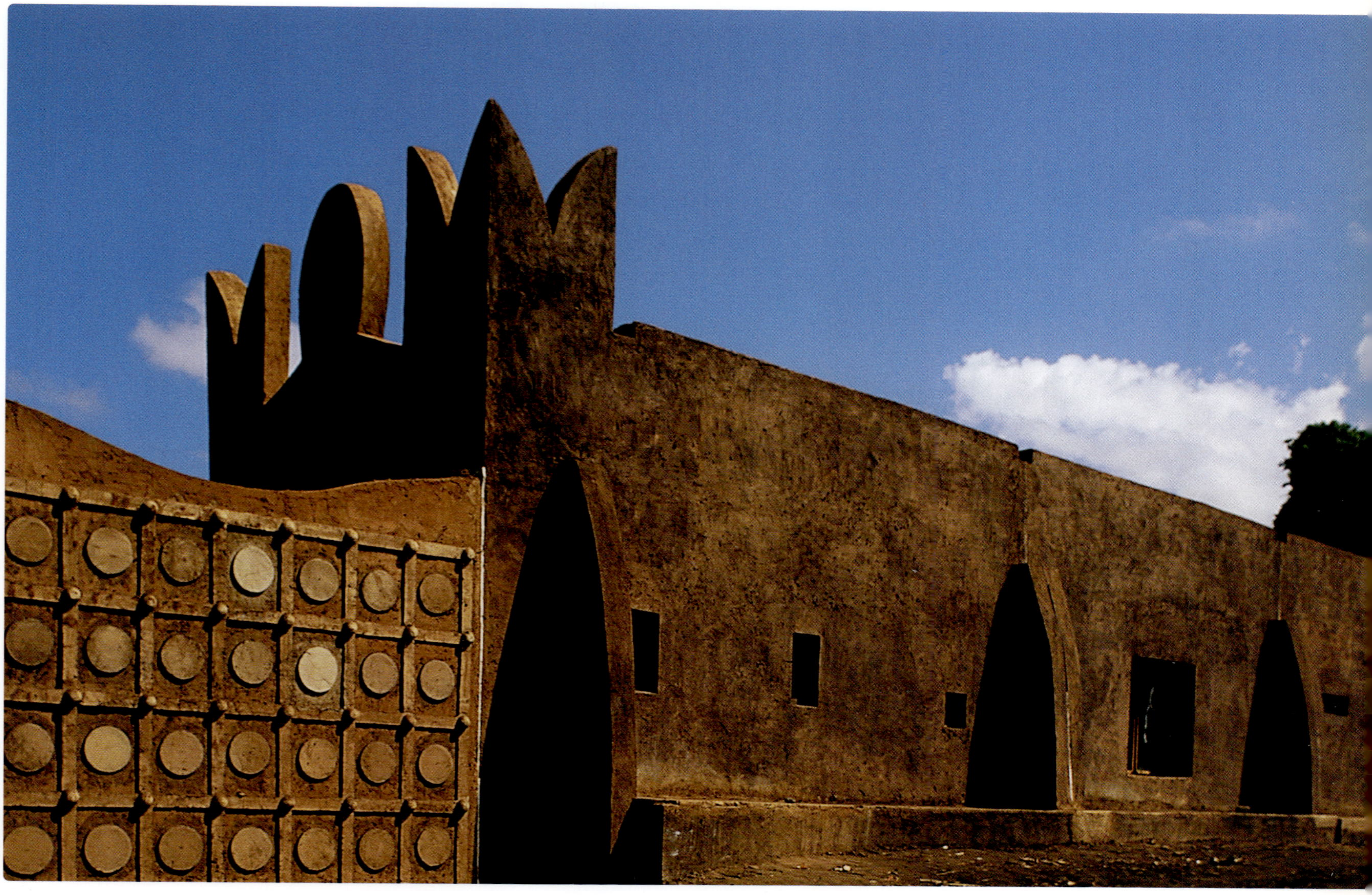

As its name suggests, Crater Lodge stands on the lip of the N'Gorongoro crater. The stunning buildings were designed by the award-winning Italian architect Silvio Rech. Their construction cost 5.5 million dollars. The design is a masterful blend of elements drawn from traditional African architecture and the elegant Colonial style. The lodge, inaugurated in 1997 by the Tanzanian president Benjamin Mkapa, is the undisputed flagship of the Tanzanian tourist industry. Its success, in large part due to the remarkable, almost Surrealist design of the site, has unfortunately inspired a number of entrepreneurs to work on pale imitations of the lodge. The increasing number of hotels in the area is of course bringing in more and more tourists, diminishing the magnificent tranquility of the plains.

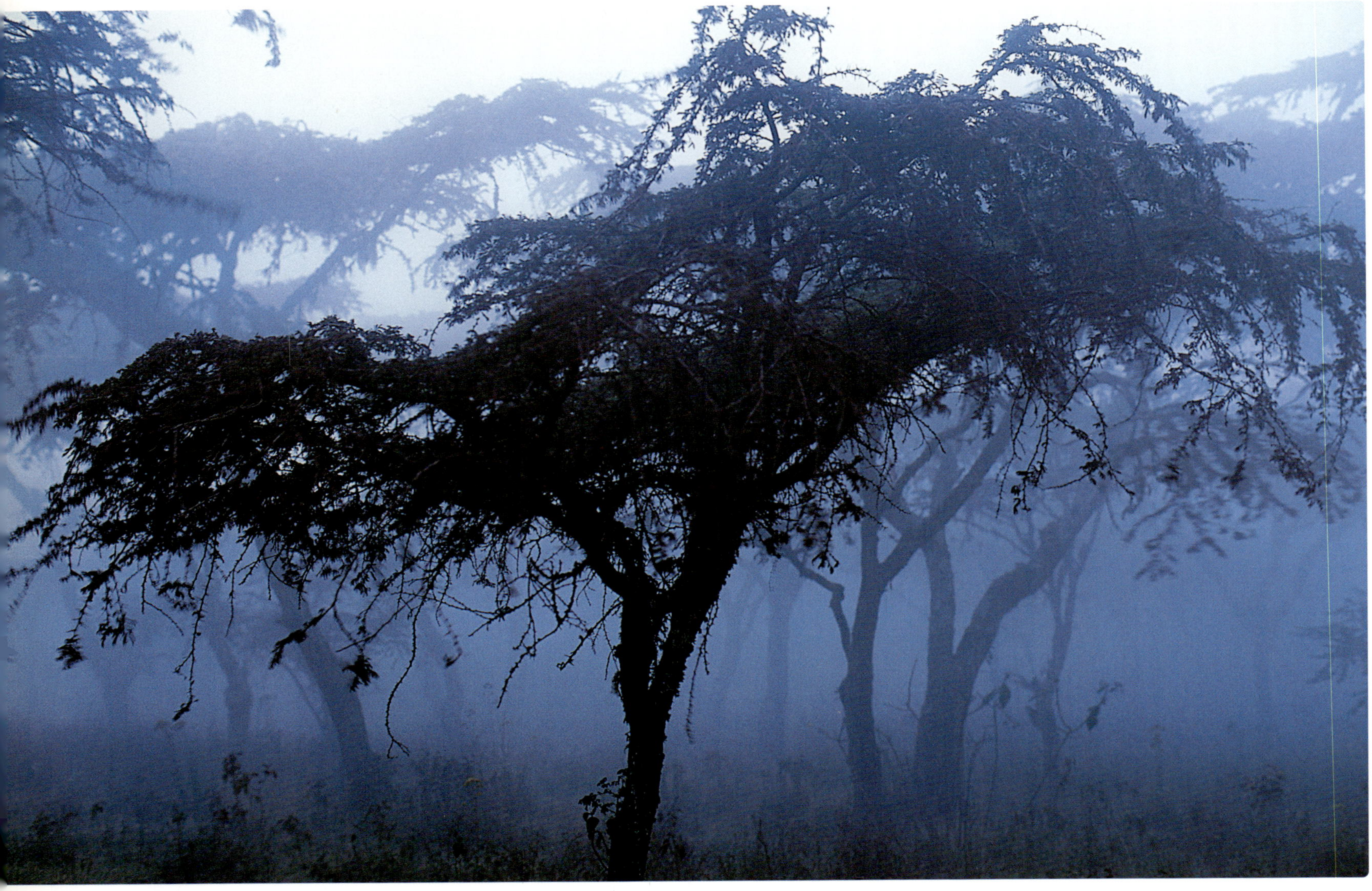

The rainy season lasts from March to June. The rainforest on the lip of the N'Gorongoro crater takes on an eerie, ghostly character as veils of mist shroud the trees. The mysterious silhouettes hint at the presence of acacias, ficus, croton trees, and albizia or silk trees whose branches are overgrown with long strands of lichen like old men's beards.

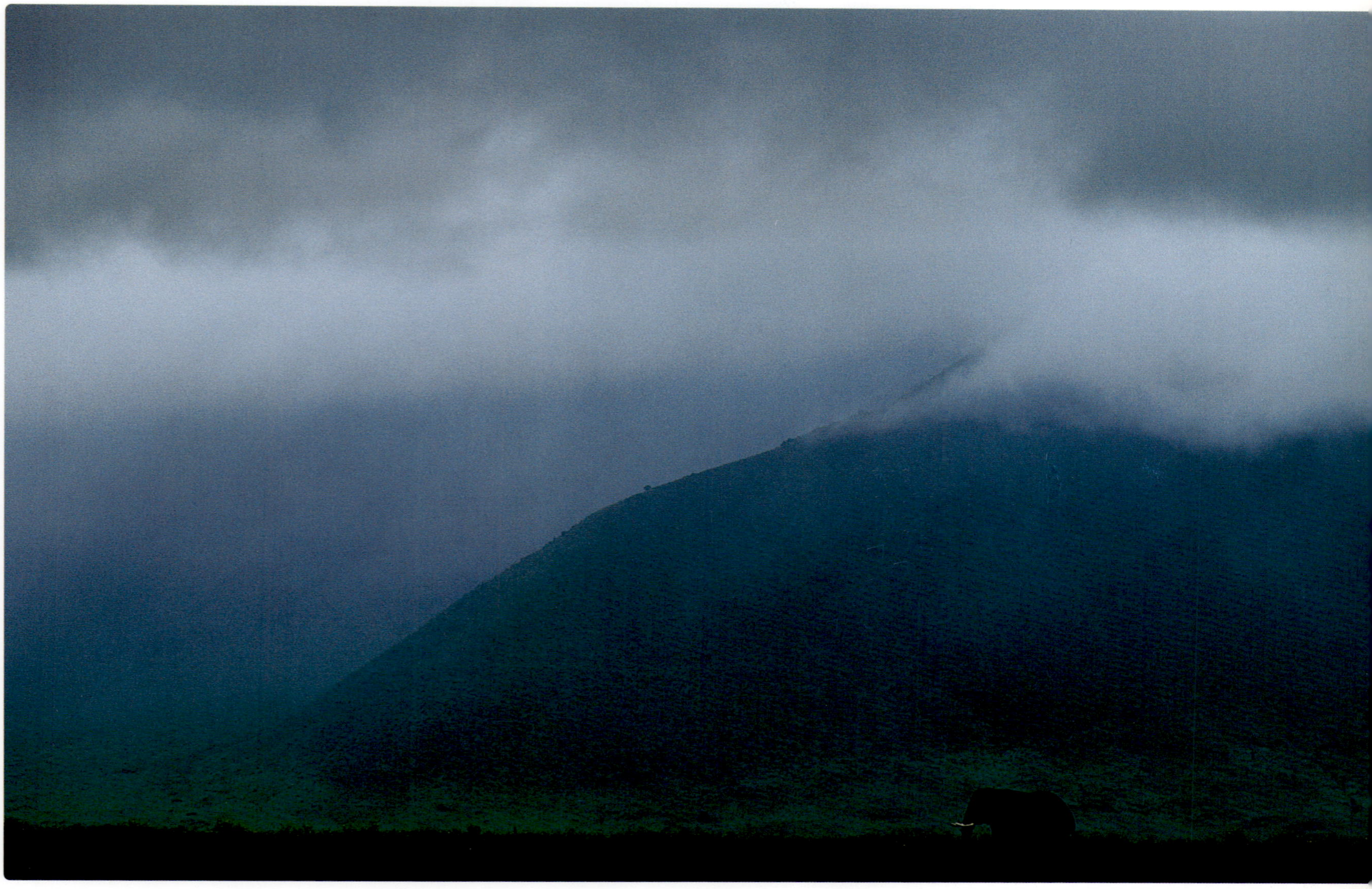

ABOVE:

Many of the dirt tracks that crisscross the Serengeti are simply washed away by the pounding rains during the wet season. While the occasional ray of sun sets the earth gently steaming, the general atmosphere is gloomy and damp. The rainy season has a vital role to play in the life of the savanna, replenishing the water tables and ensuring that the animals and plants will live another year.

FOLLOWING PAGES:

While it is hard work reaching the bottom of the crater during the rainy season, the spectacle that awaits those who persevere is breathtaking. The dry scrub of the savanna bursts into flower. This magnificent bull elephant was standing quite alone in a flowering meadow. He must have been surprised and displeased by our intrusion, for he charged our vehicle several times. We backed up hurriedly and returned to our own world.

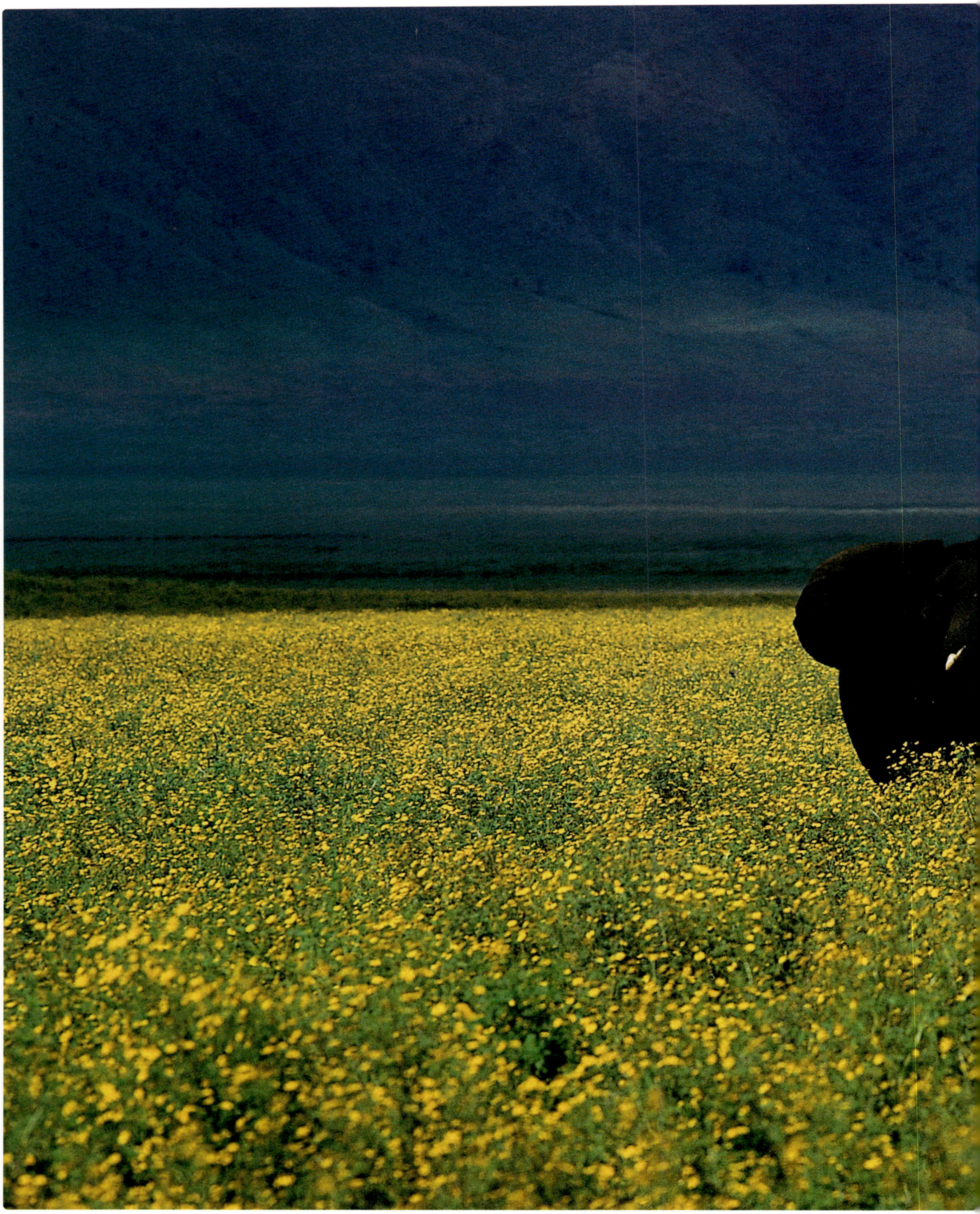

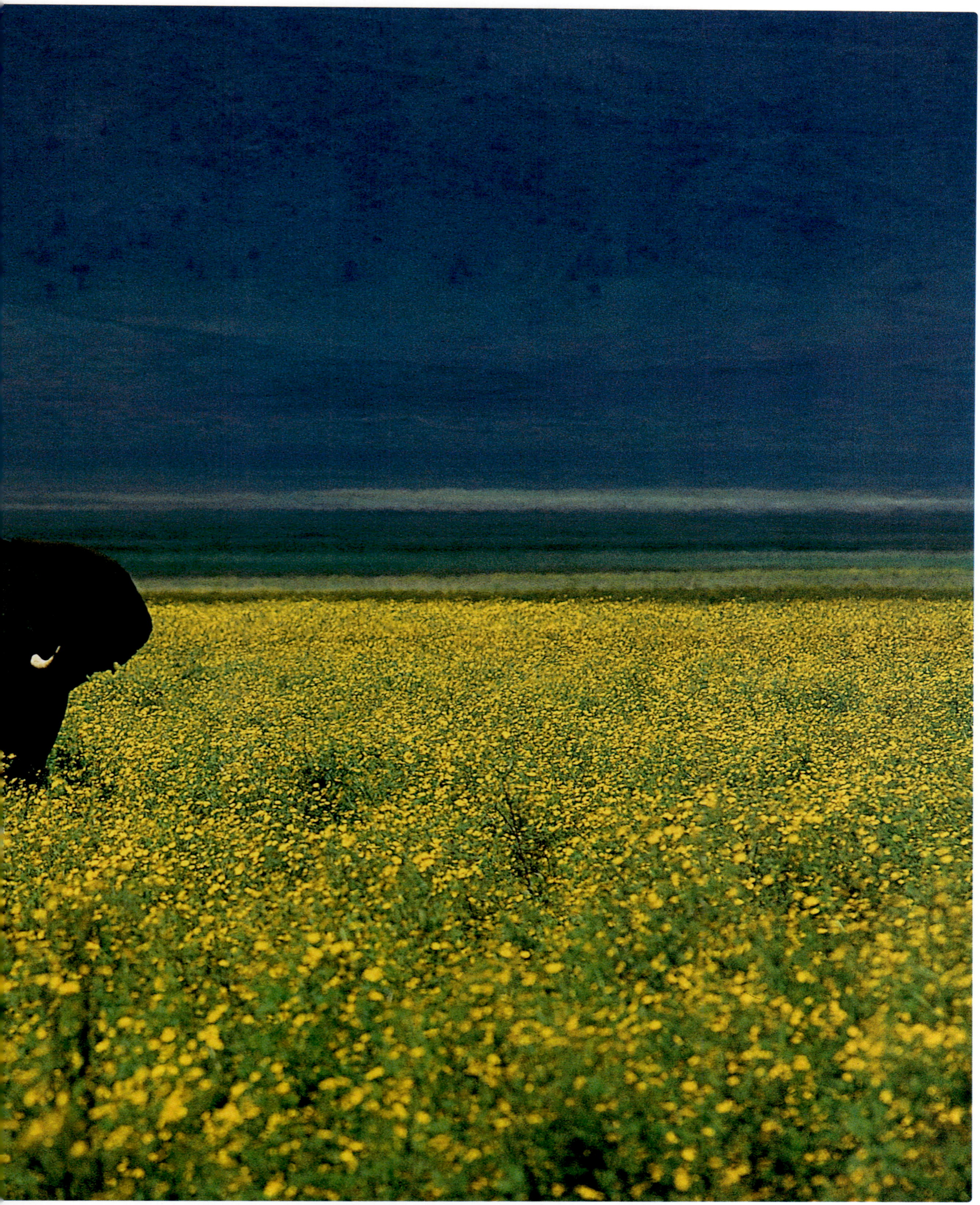

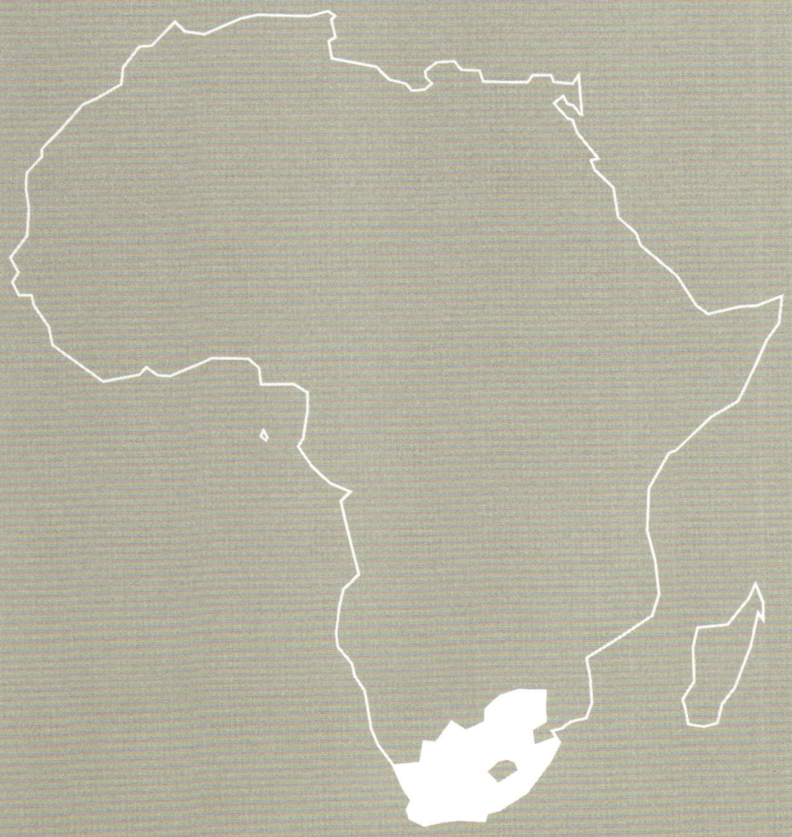

CHAPTER THREE

SOUTH AFRICA

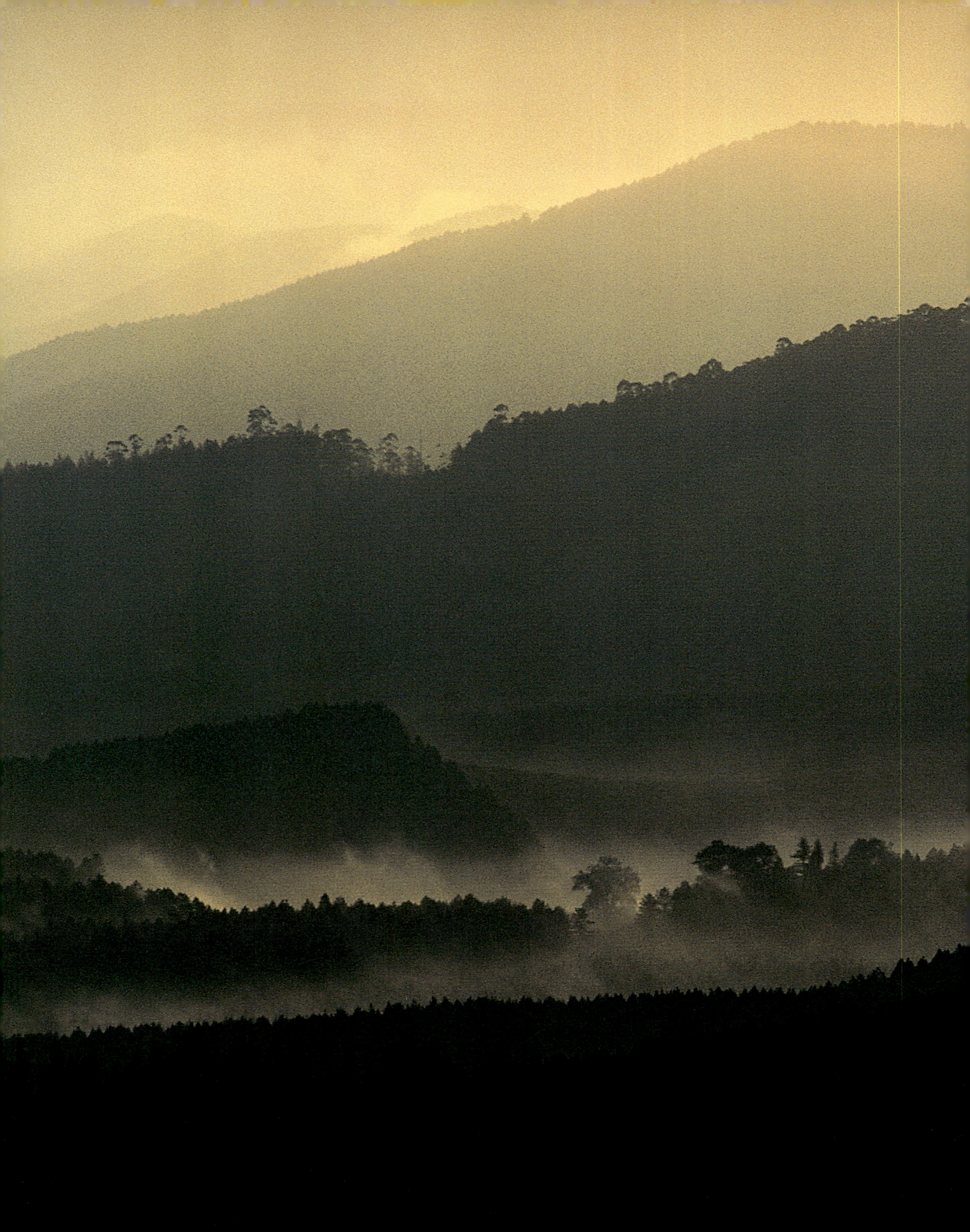

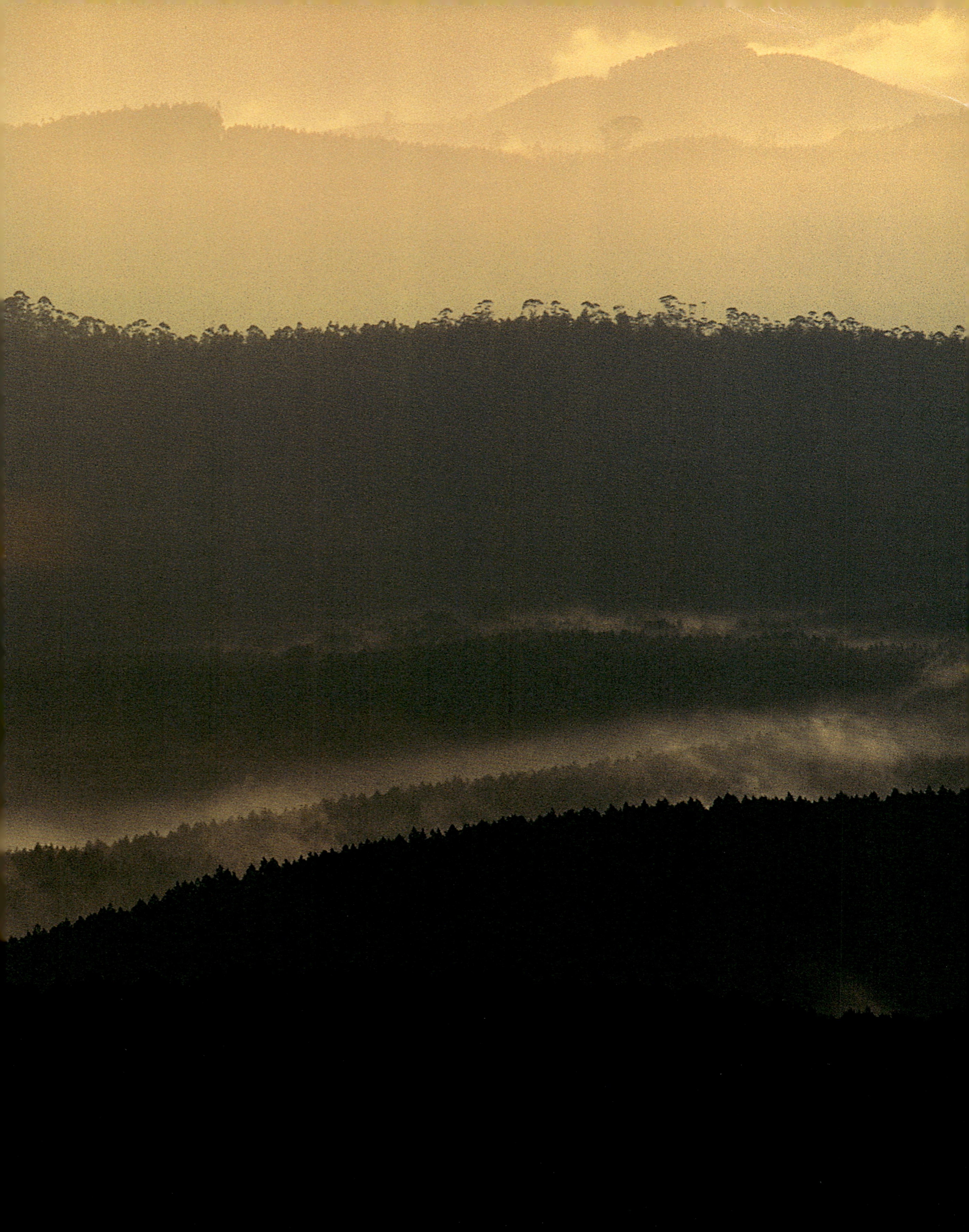

BOTH THE PRIVATE GAME RESERVES AND THE GREAT NATIONAL PARKS PROMISE THE VISITOR THE CHANCE TO SEE A HUGE VARIETY OF FLORA AND FAUNA. THE KRUGER PARK, SOUTH AFRICA'S ANSWER TO THE TAJ MAHAL OR THE EIFFEL TOWER, IS ARGUABLY THE MOST IMPRESSIVE OF ALL. ITS REPUTATION WAS ORIGINALLY BUILT ON THE FACT THAT IT COULD BOAST THE "BIG FIVE," A BOAST NOW SHARED BY MANY OTHER PRIVATE PARKS, THANKS TO REINTRODUCTION PROGRAMS.

The sun is still low on the horizon. The moss and lichen on the branches of the monkey orange tree glow in the incandescence of its rays. It is a picture of utter peace. Then on the other side of the clearing, I hear some strange cracking sounds, as if someone were snapping branches. A pride of lions is devouring the wildebeest they killed during the night. Two females and six half-grown cubs are fighting over the carcass, swiping with their claws and trying to bite each other. I have never felt so isolated from civilization—but then I see an electric fence, just a few feet behind the bushes.

In South Africa, there are clear limits to the wilderness. The creatures that once wandered the whole land are now kept in strictly defined areas, behind fences. Many species have had to be reintroduced into the wild, having seen their natural habitat destroyed to make way for farmland and housing. The country now has a wildlife development program, having recognized the potential importance of this sector of the economy. The great wildlife parks in South Africa are vast, but whichever direction you travel in, you will eventually come to a fence. There is no chance of seeing the great animal migrations like the ones Tanzania can offer. The country's safaris are more like those of Kenya, offering magnificent scenery, but within a relatively limited area. The big attraction, as elsewhere in Africa, is the chance of seeing the "Big Five," the five species that most people associate with Africa—lions, leopards, buffaloes, rhinoceroses, and elephants. South Africa has a number of game parks, some national, some private. There are twenty-four national parks and three hundred or so smaller national game reserves. Alongside the national parks are an increasing number of privately owned game reserves, whose owners by and large take their responsibilities as guardians of the natural environment extremely seriously. Among the private lodges to have sprung up in the last few years, generally on lands that were formerly used for growing crops or grazing, are such exclusive tourist complexes as Makalali, Welgevonden, Marakele, Lapalala, Shamwari, Amakala, Kariega, Kapama, Thornybush, Timbavati, and Tswalu. Some of the best game lodges, such as Phinda, are absolute references in the world of safaris. They have taken great care to design a hotel that fits in with the wild majesty of the landscape. This is more than can be said for many hotels, unfortunately. Many of them remain rather charmless.

Both the private game reserves and the great national parks promise the visitor the chance to see a huge variety of flora and fauna. The Kruger Park, South Africa's answer to the Taj Mahal or the Eiffel Tower, is arguably the most impressive of all. Its reputation was originally built on the fact that it could boast the "Big Five," a boast now shared by many other private parks, thanks to reintroduction programs. The Kruger's legendary reputation still brings in the visitors, though. The main entrance to the park is dominated by a monumental bust carved in white stone, representing the park's founder, Paul Kruger, the first president of South Africa, who decided to create the park in 1898. In those days, South Africa was far smaller than it is today, covering the territory that is now Transvaal province. The park has borne the name of its founder since 1926. The park was originally limited to the zone lying between the Crocodile and Sabi rivers, a tract of land measuring 1,114,000 acres (460,000 hectares) that was overrun by ivory smugglers and slave traders. The idea behind the park was to protect the wildlife from the indiscriminate massacres committed by hunters for the biltong market. Biltong is dried game meat, found everywhere in South Africa. Unfortunately, the Boer War meant that Paul Kruger was unable to bring the project to fruition. The lands of the Lowveld became a battlefield and most of the animals were killed and eaten. After the war, the famous naturalist Abel Chapman wrote a highly enthusiastic report recommending the park be extended as far as the Limpopo River. The project was taken up by the English government at the very end of Victoria's reign. It was entrusted to a thirty-five-year-old Scot, Major James Stevenson-Hamilton. He devoted every moment of the next forty-four years to his mission. In 1903, the park grew considerably when a vast tract of land known locally as Shingwedre, lying between the Letaba and Luvuvhu rivers, was brought within its boundaries. At the same time, the park authorities negotiated the acquisition of a number of patches of land along the border with Mozambique, between the Sabie and Shingwedre reserves, founded by the Boers and the English respectively. The people living on the expropriated land that was to become national park territory were offered compensation in the form of what is now the Sabi Sand private reserve. Kruger Park was further enlarged in 1968 by the inclusion of the land between Quant and Crook's Corner, a triangle of land between South Africa, Mozambique, and Zimbabwe from the Limpopo to the Luvuvhu. This stretch of land was previously a refuge for smugglers, traffickers, thugs, and undesirables of all sorts. The park's current boundaries were approved in 2000, based on a project masterminded in 1997 by John Hanks, director of the Peace Parks Foundation. President Thabo Mbeki's government was determined to make wildlife conservation a top priority. The result of John Hanks' plan was the creation of an immense wildlife park measuring 8.7 million acres (3.5 million hectares).

PRECEDING PAGES:
The Drakensberg Mountains, enshrouded in mist, are the stuff of legend. Their name means "dragon mountain" in Afrikaans. It is said that J.R.R. Tolkien was inspired by this majestic landscape to write *The Lord of the Rings*.

FACING PAGE:
Walking through the long grass at dusk, it is all too easy to imagine that every shadow, every tree root, is an animal waiting to pounce. Most animals will have heard you coming and slunk away silently.

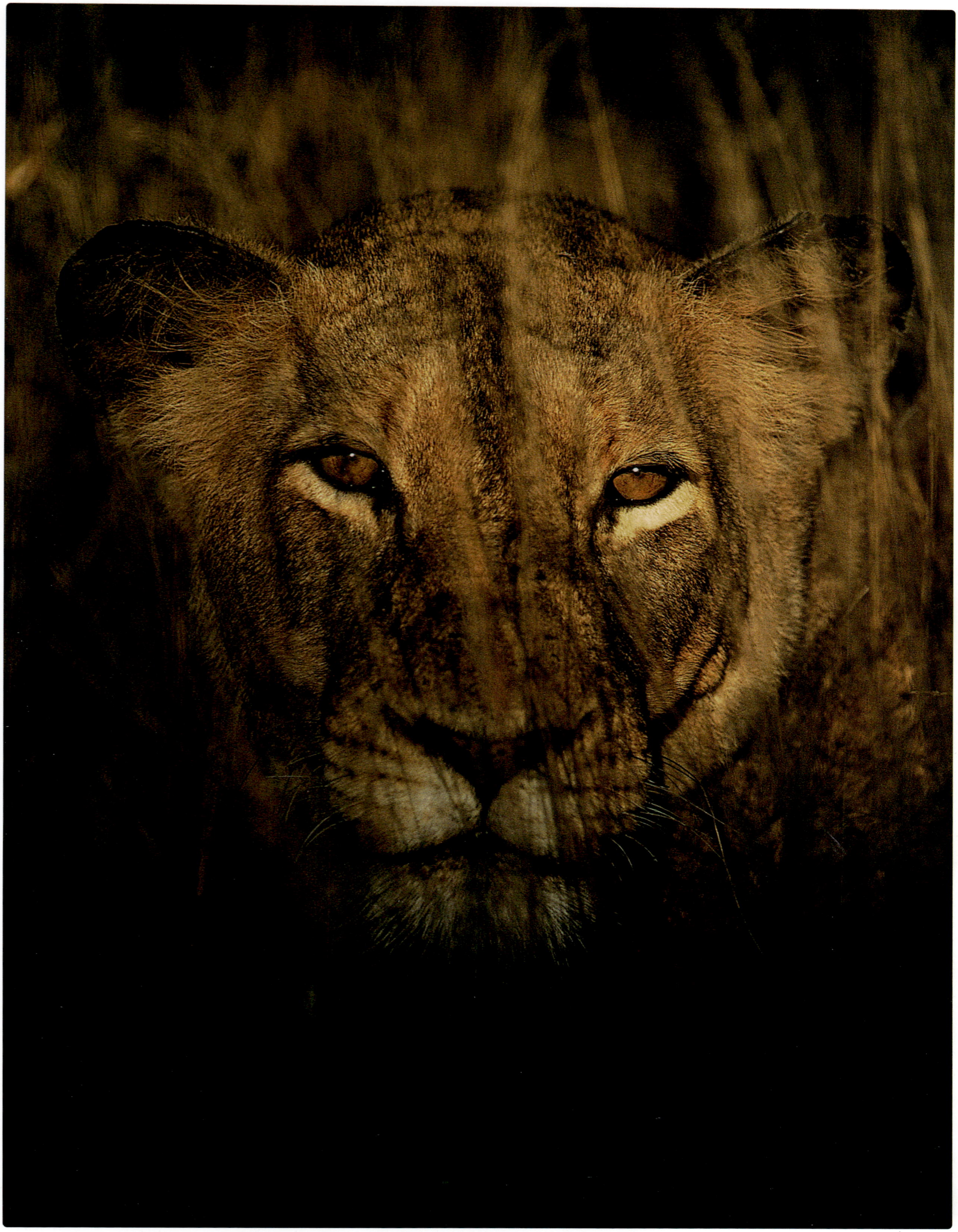

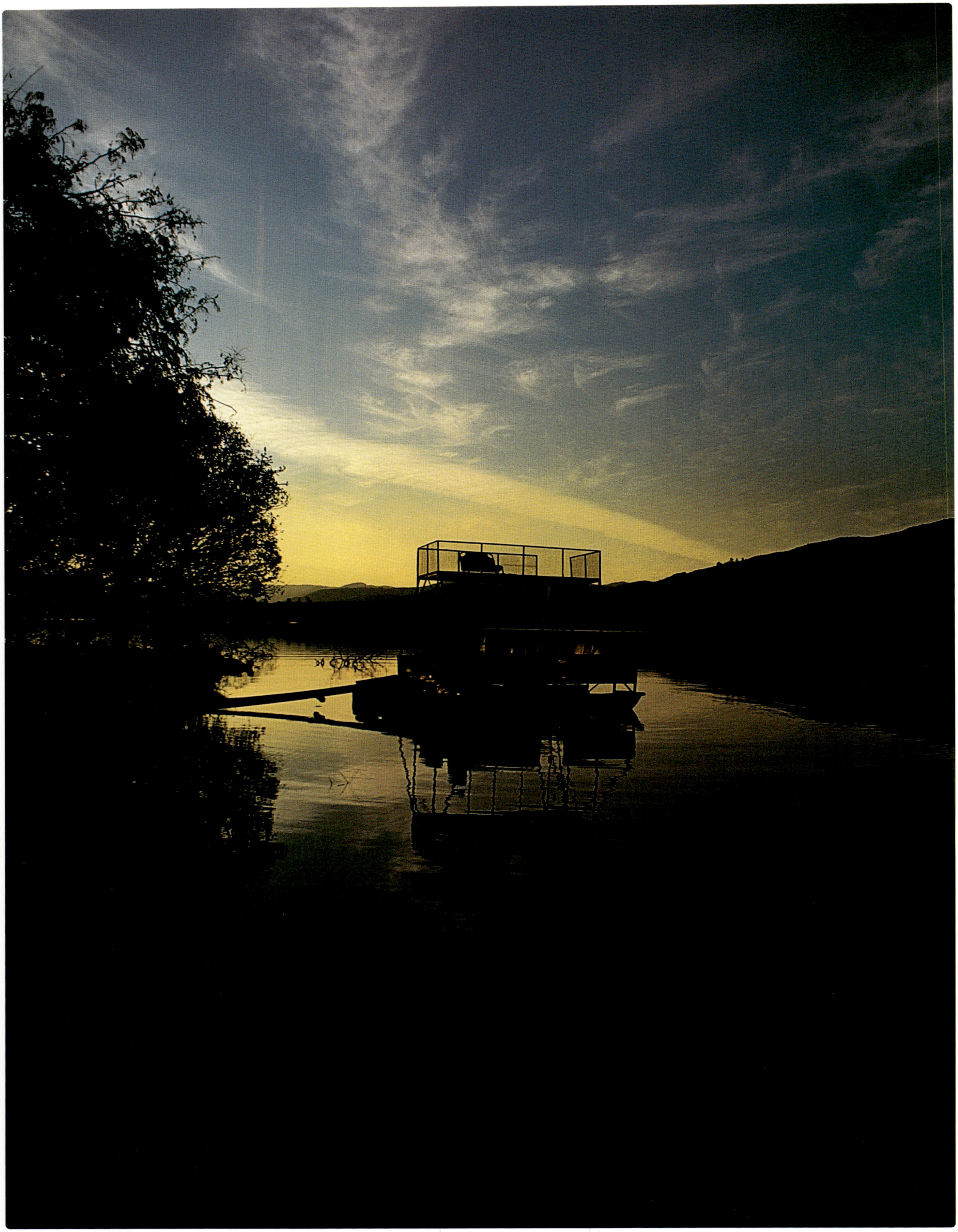

SINGITA AND OTHER RESERVES SUCH AS LONDOLOZI AND MALA MALA OFFER SOME OF THE MOST STUNNING SCENERY IN THE REGION, THE NORTHERNMOST PROVINCE IN SOUTH AFRICA. THEY ALSO GIVE VISITORS A BETTER THAN AVERAGE CHANCE OF SEEING A LEOPARD, SOMETHING WHICH IS RARE ENOUGH TO BE THE REAL HIGHLIGHT OF ANY SAFARI.

It was initially called the GKG Transfrontier Park before being rebaptized the Greater Limpopo Transfrontier Park (GLTP). The GLTP includes Kruger Park in South Africa, Gonarezhou Park in Zimbabwe, and the Coutada 16 zone in Mozambique, currently reserved for hunting expeditions. The vast park was inaugurated in December 2002 by the presidents of the three countries. In the future, it is planned to expand the park to 23.5 million acres (9.5 million hectares)—about the size of Hungary—by incorporating Zinave and Banhine parks in Mozambique. It will then be the largest game reserve in the world, far larger than Selous in Tanzania. It is a gargantuan undertaking. The cost of electric fencing on the Mozambique side of the park alone is estimated at 6.2 million euros, to be financed by the European Community and the World Bank. The project has been warmly welcomed by ecologists and politicians alike. Conservationists see the park as a means of solving the recurring problem of the elephant population in Kruger Park. The park can support a total of some eight thousand individuals. On several occasions in the years prior to 1996, several hundred elephants had to be culled to stabilize the population. Politicians see the project as a source of foreign revenue and of job creation—it is estimated that one full-time job in the tourism sector is created for every eight tourists—and of building up a positive image for their country, particularly important in South Africa after the shame of apartheid.

The earliest visitors to Kruger Park in 1927 would drive along the only road in the region, from Lower Sabie to Olifants River. In those days, before the creation of the first permanent camp in 1931, visitors to the park had to bring their own tents and equipment and camp in rudimentary enclosures protected by piles of thorny branches. There were so few visitors that the animals took no notice of their presence, having no reason to fear them. This is still largely the case today. It is possible to get up close to lions, leopards, cheetahs, rhinos, and elephants in open-topped vehicles. James Stevenson-Hamilton quickly recognized the need for some form of control of the animal populations. He came up with a plan in 1946, which involved culling vast numbers of elephants and big cats. This practice continued throughout the 1950s. Despite the mass slaughter of countless thousands of animals, the South African part of the park still boasts a wildlife population of over 120,000, including some 23,000 zebras, 20,000 buffaloes, 14,000 wildebeest, 9,500 kudus, 9,000 elephants, 3,800 giraffes, 3,000 hippos, 1,700 rhinos, 1,500 lions, 900 leopards, 250 black rhinos, 200 cheetahs, and 150 African hunting dogs.

The new government in South Africa is doing all it can to speed up the process of privatizing the lodges and other facilities at the Kruger National Park. The difference between the private sectors of the park and the areas that remain under government control is striking. The nationalized areas are much cheaper and far more crowded. Most of the tourists here are South Africans. The privately owned areas are far more exclusive and expensive and attract a well-heeled international clientele. While much of the pleasure of a safari lies in seeing the animals in their natural habitat, the quality of the accommodation is also an important factor. It also makes an enormous difference to be able to see the animals without a horde of minibuses in the background. Many of the private camps offer the services of experienced rangers who accompany visitors through the bush, teaching them to look for signs such as animal tracks and helping them get up close to any creatures they come across. There is no denying that the rangers employed by the private camps are generally far more skilled than are those working in the nationally owned areas.

Kruger National Park now has a large number of private reserves very close to the public areas. From the extravagant luxury of Sabi Sabi to the sparse yet comfortable surroundings of Gomo Gomo, the park offers safari experiences for all budgets.

The most famous private game reserve in South Africa is probably Sabi Sand Wildtuin, which takes its name from the two rivers that water the land. The land originally belonged to nineteen different farmsteads and hunting reserves with evocative names such as Nantes, Toulon, Alicecot, Sparta, Exeter, Mala Mala, and Charleston. For the last twelve years or so, animals have been free to cross over from its 154,000 acres (62,300 hectares) into the national park. The banks of the Sand River are like heaven on earth. In the heart of a 44,480-acre (18,000-hectare) private reserve known as Singita, a local word meaning "miracle," the Ebony Lodge, opened in 1993, and the famous Boulder Lodge are excellent places to stay to discover the wealth of local flora and fauna. Singita and other reserves such as Londolozi and Mala Mala offer some of the most stunning scenery in the region, the northernmost province in South Africa. They also give visitors a better than average chance of seeing a leopard, something which is rare enough to be the real highlight of any safari.

As various species prefer different types of habitat, one excellent way of spotting animals is to wait somewhere where their favorite food is found in abundance. If you wish to see large herds of antelopes and other herbivores, such as zebras, wildebeest, buffaloes, and white rhinos, it is obviously best to head for the open grasslands. This is also where you will find their principal predators: cheetahs and lions. To see species that feed on leaves, including elands, giraffes, gerenuks, and black rhinos, as well as the more solitary species of predators, you should find a stretch of

FACING PAGE:
The Venda region is a land of sacred forests with enchanted lakes lying deep in their shadowy heart. Here, it is hard to tell truth from legend. Shiluvari is the ideal place for an introduction to this culture and for bird-watching on Lake Albasini.

EVERYTHING YOU EVER LEARNED IS BLOWN AWAY BY THE KEENING WIND. YOU ARE ALONE AND VULNERABLE IN A LANDSCAPE THAT IS HARSH AND BARE. NATURE IS TOTALLY INDIFFERENT TO YOUR PRESENCE. IT IS A LAND OF OBSTINACY AND SACRIFICE, WHERE PLANTS STRUGGLE TO SET DOWN ROOTS IN A LANDSCAPE OF RED OR TAWNY DUNES CONSTANTLY SHIFTING UNDER THE ACTION OF THE WIND.

tree-dotted savanna. Although most tourists want to see the big cats above all, other species such as elephants and rhinos are just as interesting. There are large numbers of rhinos—1,600 white and 400 black—in the Hluhluwe Umfolozi game reserve. This is the oldest reserve in the country, founded in 1897. The Hlathikhulu Lodge in the heart of the reserve gives impressive views over the range of hills with the Hluhluwe River winding its way through the valleys. It is a particularly magnificent spot to admire the sunrise.

Some distance away, at the far end of a vast alluvial plain reaching all the way to the Indian Ocean, are the thirty square miles (eighty square kilometers) of the Santa Lucia Park, lying between the cape of Santa Lucia and Sodwana Bay. The park has an unusual diversity of ecosystems, ranging from coral reefs, ponds, and lakes to marshes, dunes, savanna, and bushland. These precious biotopes are home to around 500 species of birds, 120 species of fish, and a number of buffaloes, hippos, and crocodiles. It richly deserves to have been named South Africa's first World Heritage Site. In December and January, thanks to an ingenious system of underwater cameras, visitors can watch the coelacanths and leatherback turtles gracefully gliding through the water. There are plans to launch a program to reintroduce forty or so elephants from the Kruger and Tembe parks into the Santa Lucia reserve, but as the estimated cost is 96 million euros, it may be some time before it comes to fruition.

About sixty-five miles (a hundred kilometers) west of Santa Lucia, you arrive at the verdant paradise of the Tembe and Ndumu reserves. This densely forested country hides many secret treasures. While Tembe is best known for its elephants, Ndumu is especially proud of its rhinos. In the heart of Ndumu reserve is a delightful old-fashioned little camp on the shores of Lake Banzi. Two hours' drive away, near the border with Swaziland, the Pongola reserve is the ideal destination for honeymooning couples. It has a large lake perfect for romantic boating trips. Romantic as it is, Pongola was founded in 1894 by President Paul Kruger for entirely prosaic reasons. The idea behind the reserve was partly to protect the wildlife from the indiscriminate slaughter it had suffered during the great hunting expeditions from the 1840s to the 1870s, but mainly to cut the English colony in Natal off from the sea.

Given its geographical situation and its difficult colonial heritage, the history of South Africa is rather untypical of Africa. Like its people, its landscapes vary tremendously, sometimes discordant but more often uniting to form a whole of a rare richness and complexity. From the Tsitsikamma rainforests to the dunes of the Kalahari, the rich ecosystems of South Africa each have their own game reserve dedicated to preserving the rare flora and fauna of the region. There are so many game parks in South Africa that it takes a very large book to list them all, as Alan Duggan's *Game Parks and Nature Reserves of South Africa* proves. Some of these parks have acquired legendary status, such as the Karoo Park, the Mountain Zebra Park, whose severe beauty unveils itself only to the most determined visitors, Addo Park with its three hundred elephants and its colonies of meerkats, Pilanesberg, which backs onto the famous holiday complex of Sun City, and finally Kalahari Gemsbok Park, now known as Kgalagadi Transfrontier Park. The park's original territory, measuring 2,400,000 acres (970,000 hectares), was expanded in 1938 to include 2,900,000 acres (1,087,000 hectares) in Bechuanaland. Its total area is now 7,040,000 acres (2,850,000 hectares). Lying across the South Africa-Botswana border near the frontier with Namibia, the park is an otherworldly, almost surreal place. Everything you ever learned is blown away by the keening wind. You are alone and vulnerable in a landscape that is harsh and bare. Nature is totally indifferent to your presence. It is a land of obstinacy and sacrifice, where plants struggle to set down roots in a landscape of red or tawny dunes constantly shifting under the action of the wind. The tallest trees are scrubby acacias and thorn-bushes. Until modern times, only the San people managed to master this most inhospitable of climates, where drought is the norm and where the searing heat of the day gives way to near freezing temperatures at night. Ever since the park was opened in 1931, with the intention of protecting the animals from the depredations of the big game hunters, San tribesmen have played a vital role as park rangers. From the very earliest days of the park, Johannes Le Riche hired the tribesmen to track poachers. Johannes was the first head ranger. He was succeeded by his brother Joseph and later by his sons Christoffel and Elias, who still play a key part in conserving the unique flora and fauna of the Kalahari. Thanks to the limitless devotion of the Le Riche family and the San tribespeople, the park is extremely rich in wildlife, particularly in the dry riverbeds of the Auob and Nossob, which form the natural frontiers of the park. Although the roads through the park are very few in number, visitors may come across springboks, blue wildebeest, oryx, hartebeest, kudus, cheetahs, lions, brown hyenas, jackals, ground squirrels, and meerkats—the cheeky, charming little creatures that have become the symbol of the Kalahari.

However rich the national parks and private reserves of South Africa, however glorious its flora and fauna, what draws people back to South Africa time and time again is the sense that this is a country that is seizing its chances with two hands to fulfil its destiny as the Rainbow Nation.

FACING PAGE:
As its name suggests, the blue crane has elegant slate-blue plumage. South Africa's national bird is found throughout the country and is featured on the five-cent coin.

FOLLOWING PAGES:
The undulating terrain of the Drakensberg region comprises a vast assembly of private reserves (Klaserie, Timbavati, Umbabat). Out of the dozen different lodges situated in this area, the little Ngala Game Lodge designed by Chris Browe is undoubtedly the most remarkable.

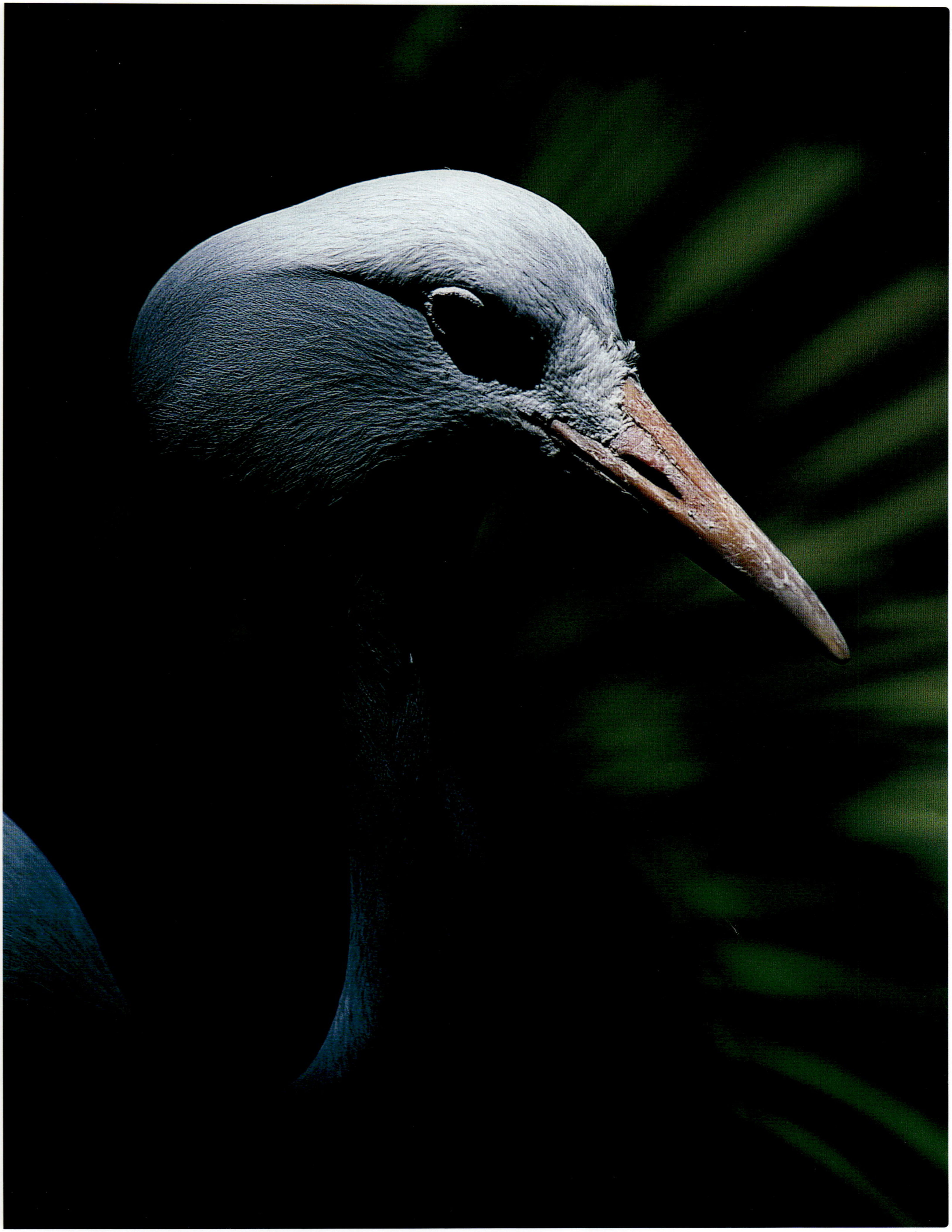

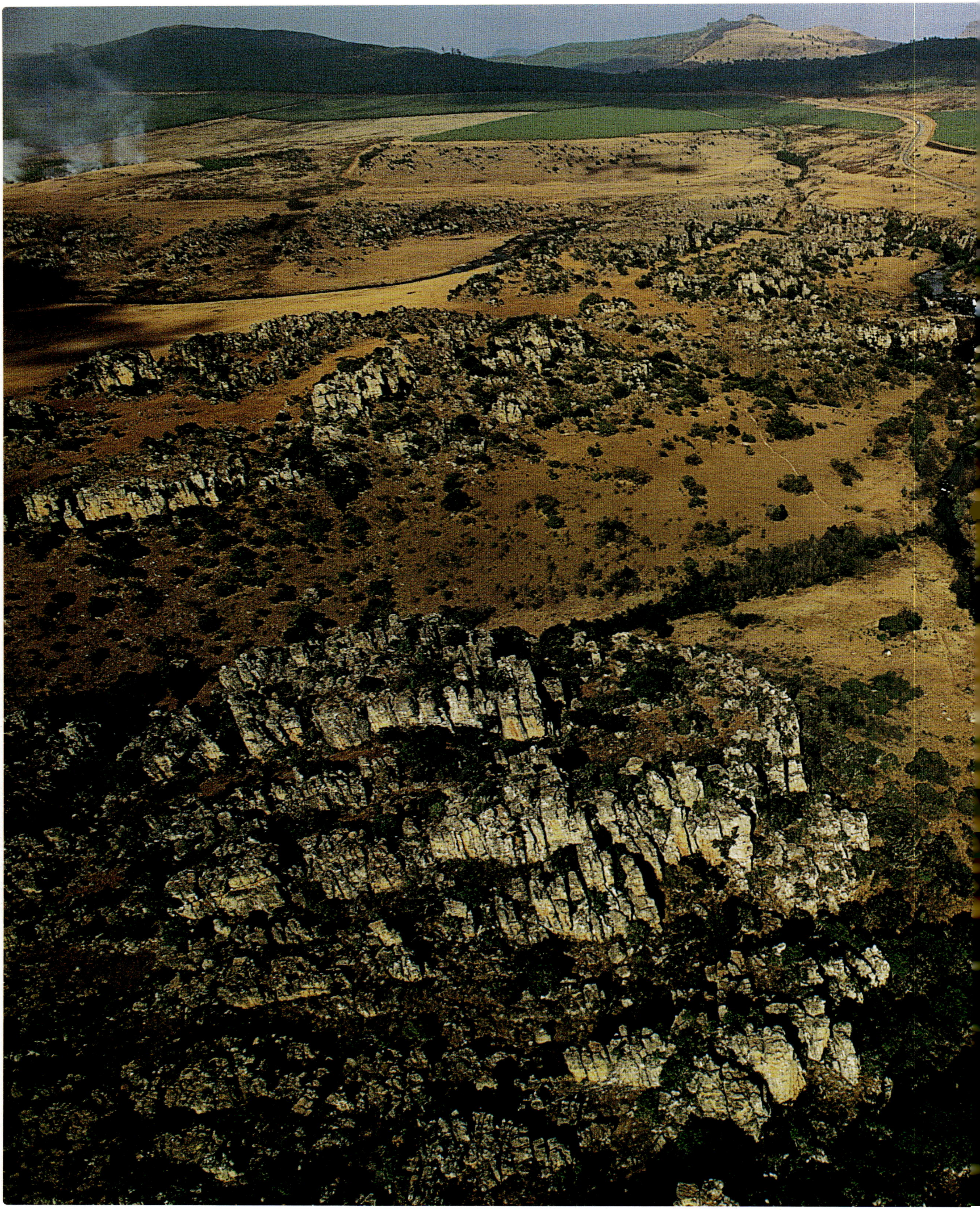

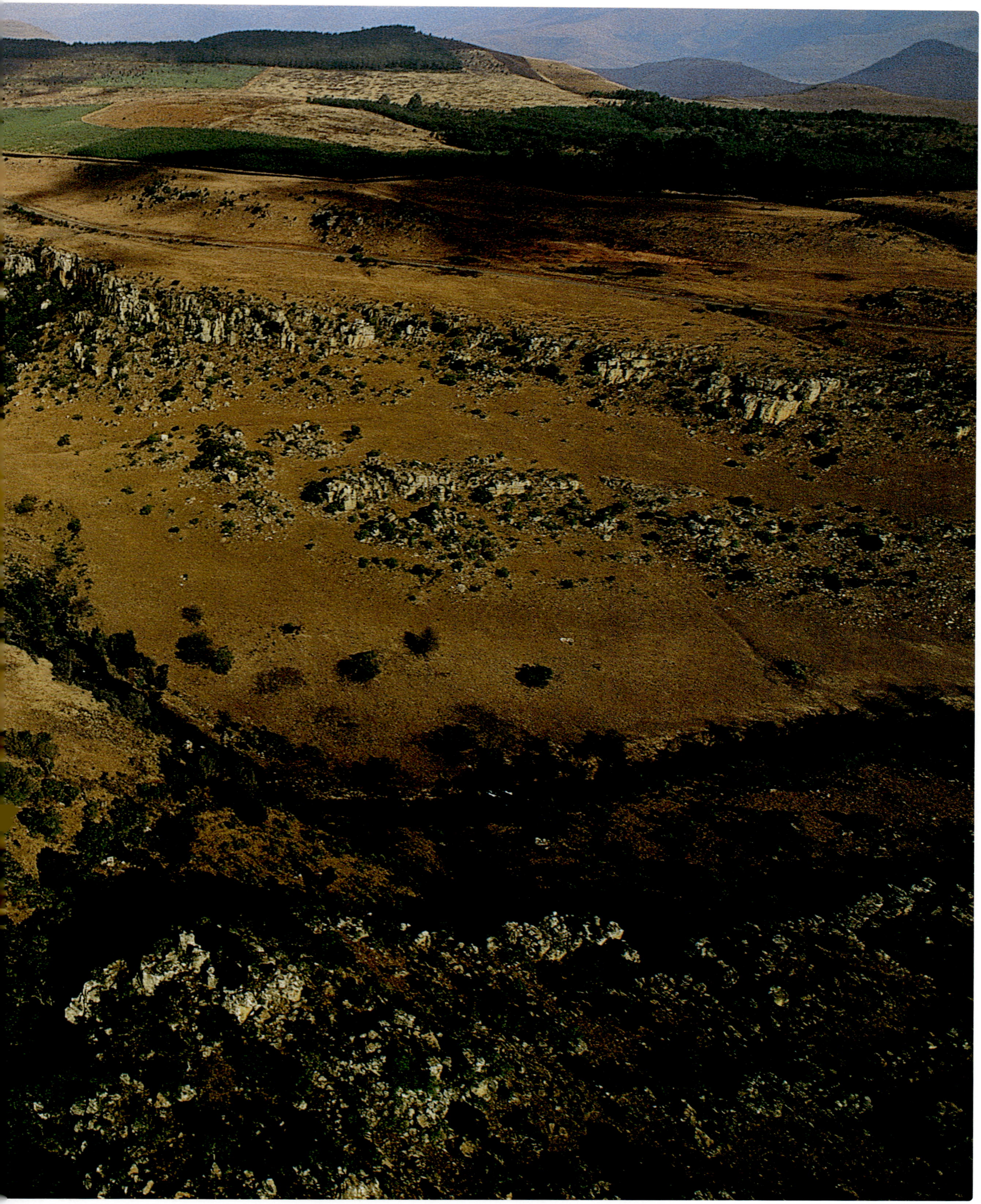

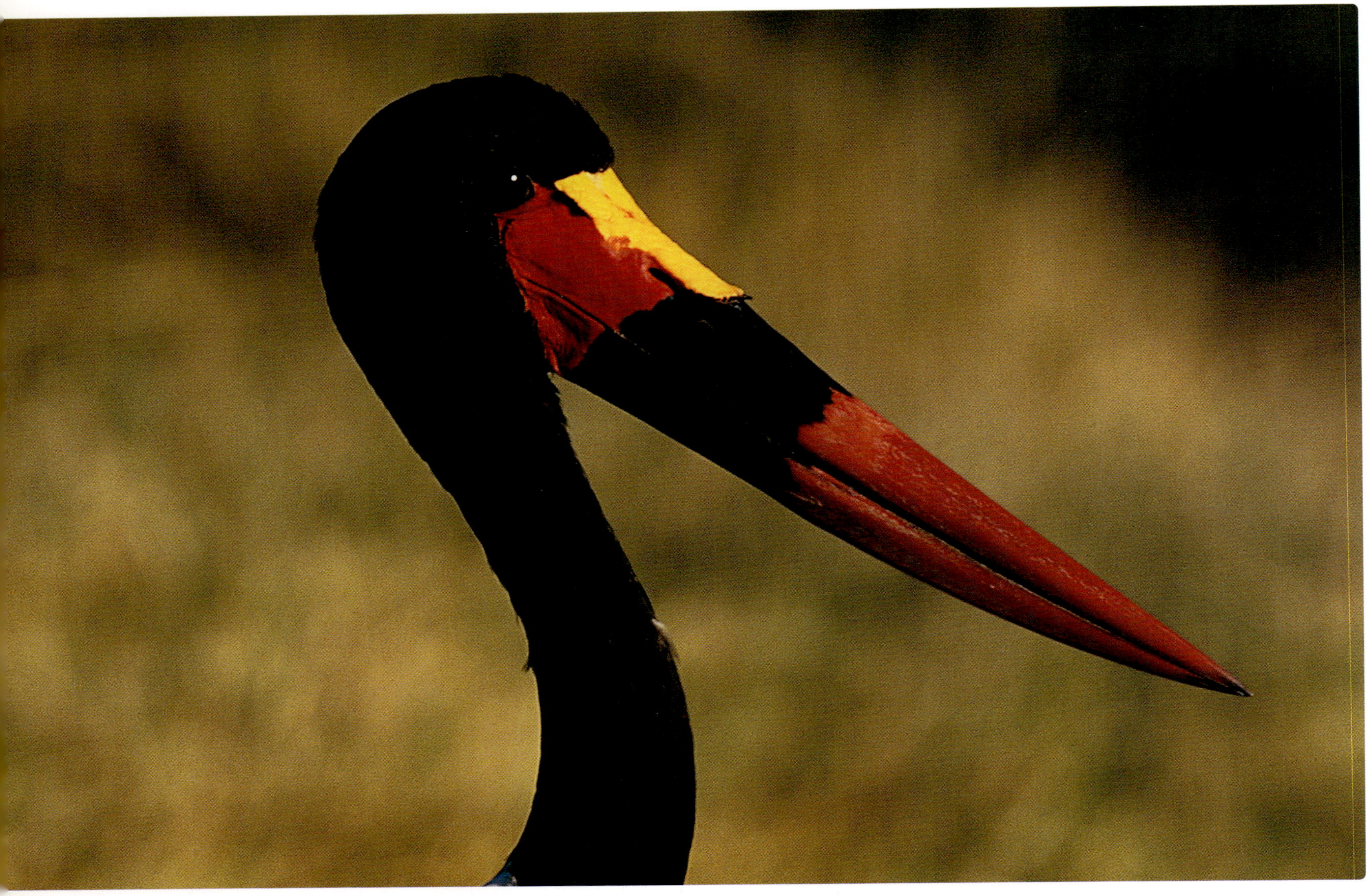

The jaribu is a magnificent stork easily recognizable thanks to its unusual beak. It mainly eats fish and can be found in the Santa Lucia wetlands in Zululand. It is a timid bird that is very difficult to approach.

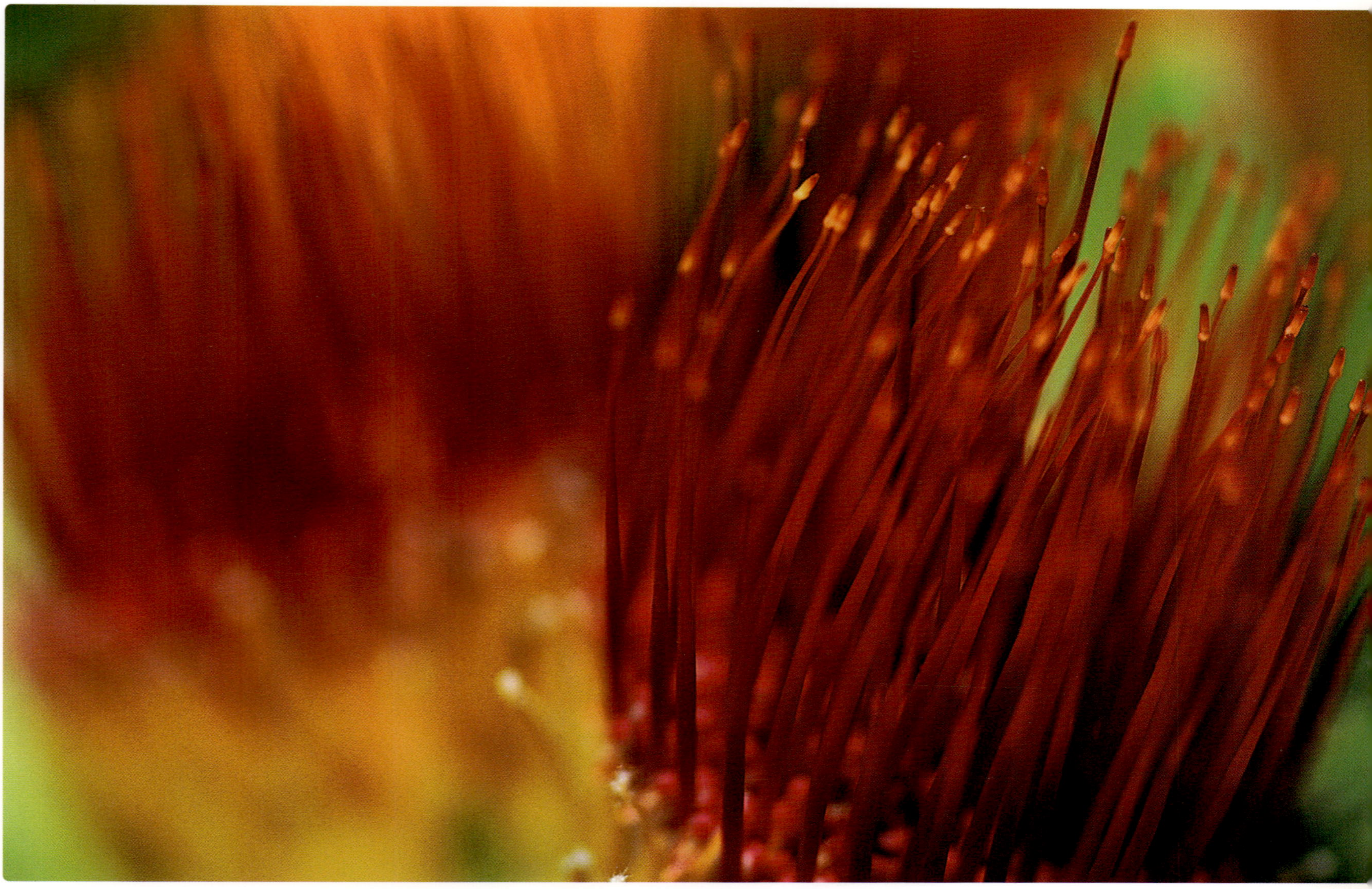

South Africa boasts an extraordinary range of magnificent plant species. The protea family, familiarly known as pincushions, is perhaps the most spectacular and varied. *Leucospermum oleifolium*, the Overberg pincushion, is a firework display in itself.

Just a few feet from the Goliath herons, Squacco herons, and white egrets, enormous crocodiles float motionlessly in the shallows, biding their time, taking no notice of the churning waters full of fish, easily within jaw's reach. To allow visitors to watch crocodiles hunting from a safe distance, Wilderness Safaris set up a camp on the shores of Lake Banzi in the Ndumu reserve at the end of the rainy season. The crocodiles in this region are truly enormous. They spend most of their time floating in the water like logs, with just their eyes and nostrils above the surface giving away their ominous presence.

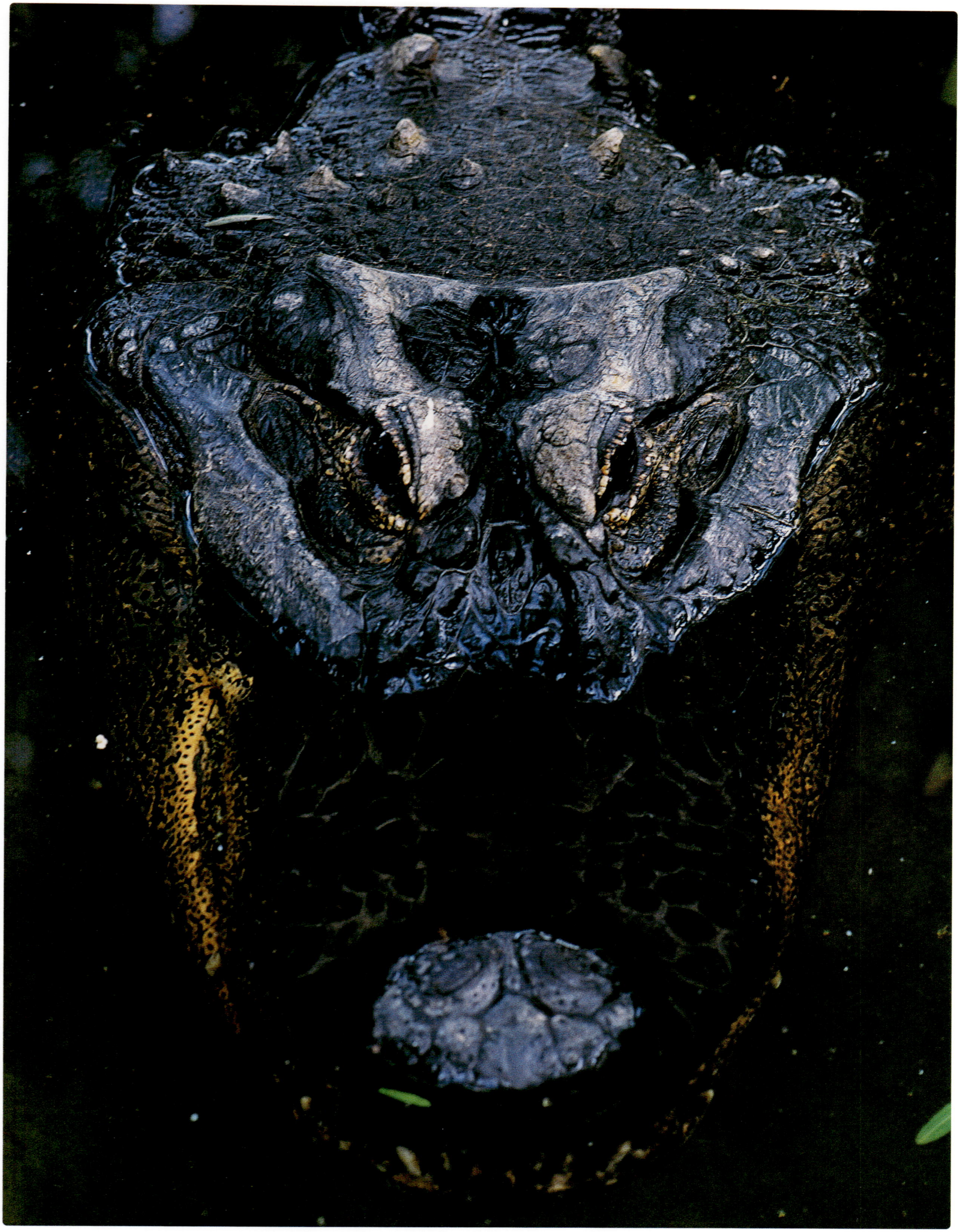

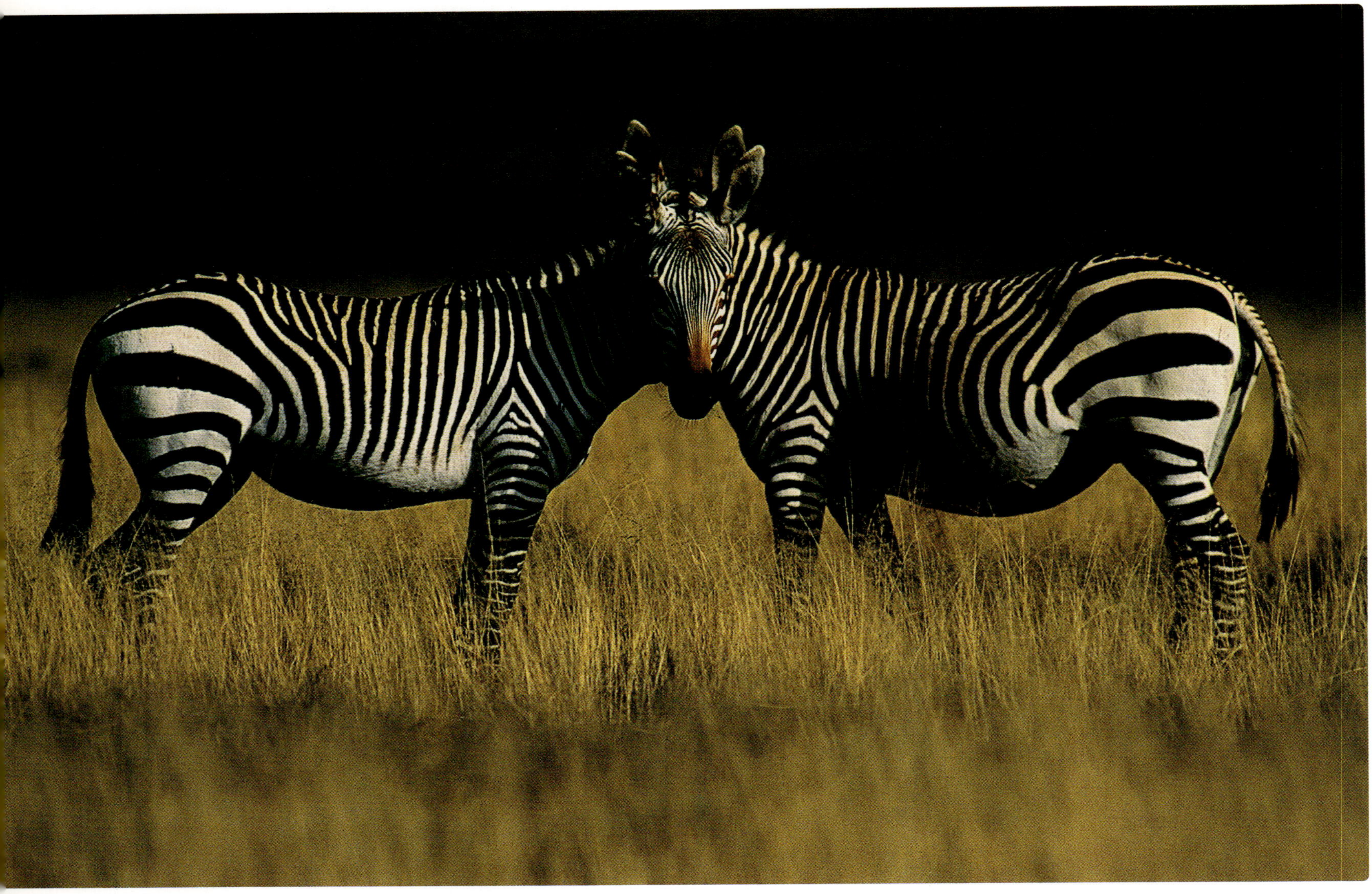

Mountain zebras have broad, closely spaced stripes with white underbellies. They live on the high, arid plateaus of the Mountain Zebra National Park near Cradock. The park is home to some three hundred individuals.

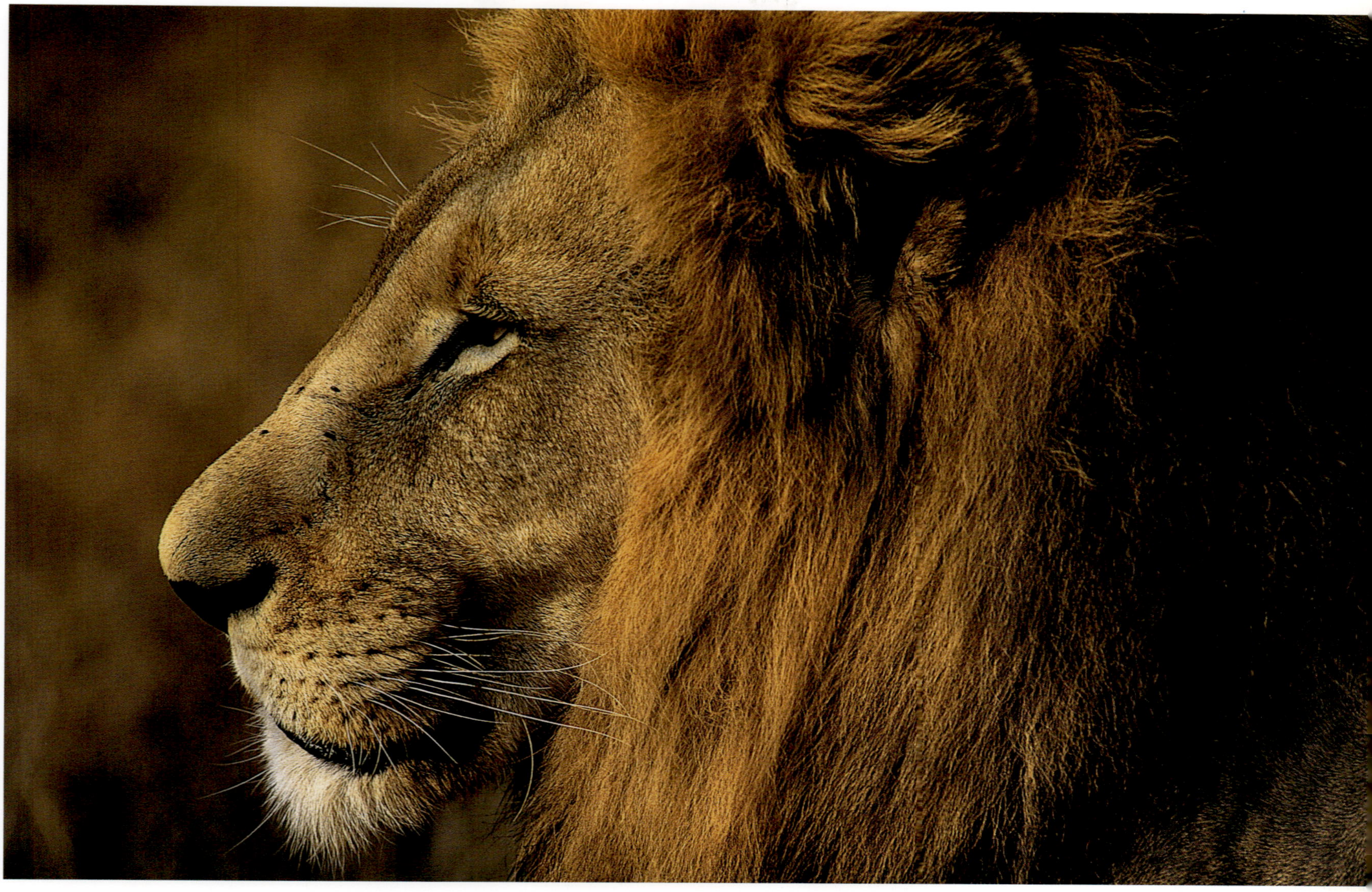

Coming face to face with a lion is always impressive. Africa's biggest carnivore can stand almost four feet (1.10 meters) at the shoulder and weigh up to 440 pounds (200 kilograms). Seeing such powerful beasts just a stone's throw from your vehicle, you cannot help but be gripped by a deep, primeval fear.

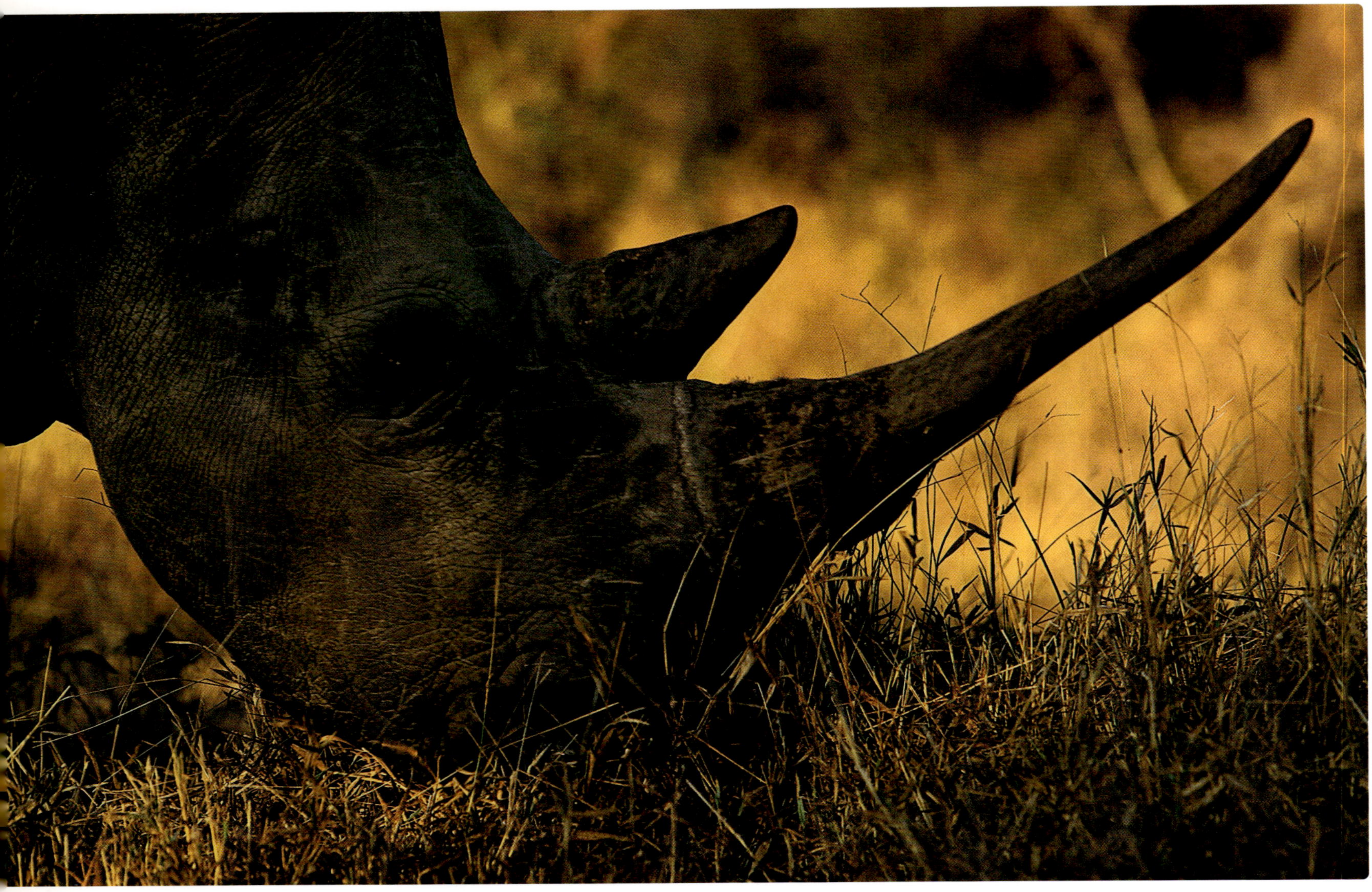

Kwazulu Natal has a number of vast natural reserves that are home to many rhinos. The Hluhluwe Umfolozi reserve has 1,600 white rhinos and 400 black rhinos. They are placid creatures and will let you approach them on foot if they do not feel threatened.

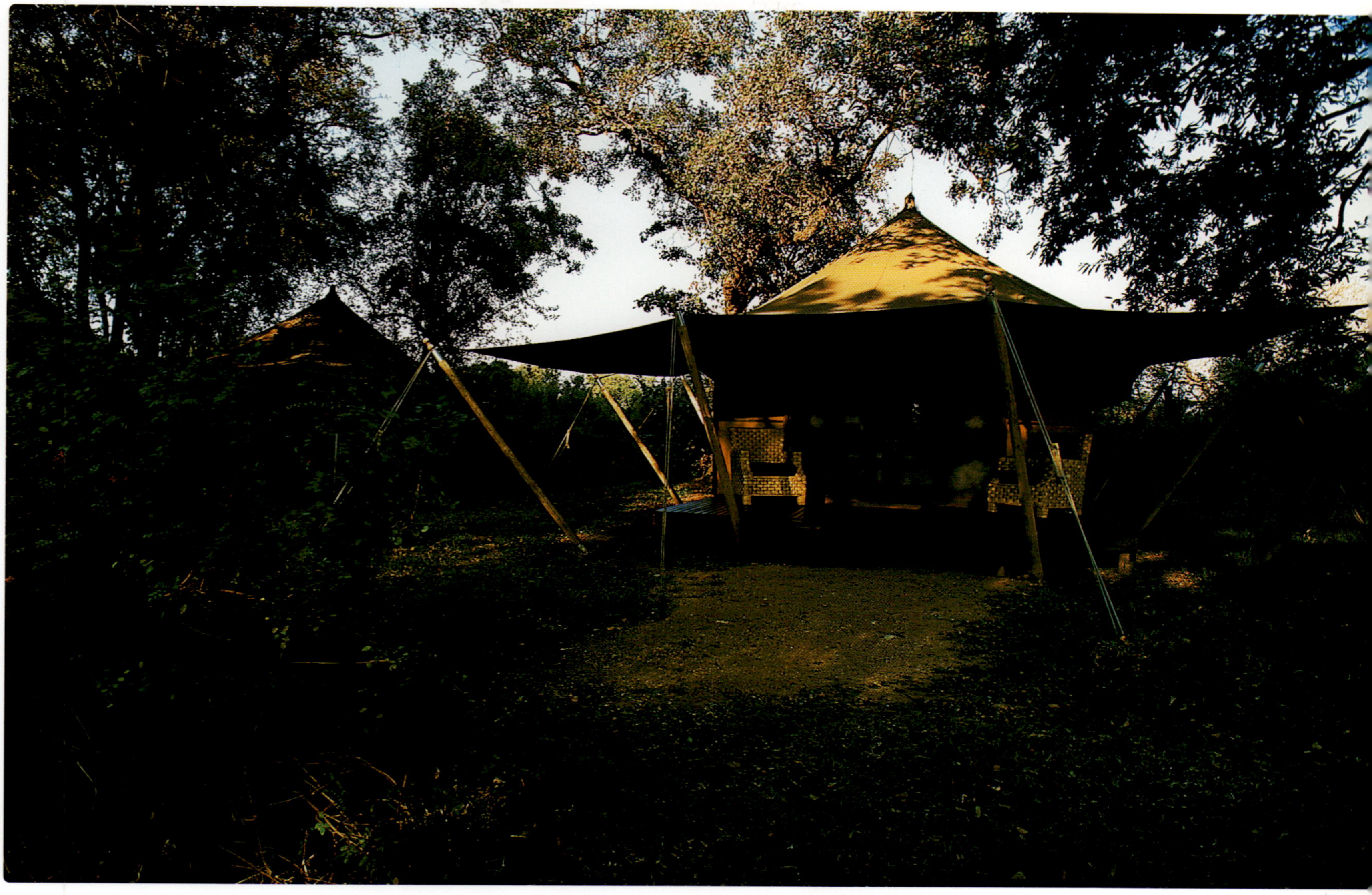

The private camps in the Kruger region are among the most exclusive in Africa. They have played a major role in establishing South Africa's reputation as a tourist destination. The Ngala camp, belonging to the Conservation Corporation, is one of the best. Each hut has its own swimming pool and comes with an all-terrain vehicle. The difference between the privately run and public parts of the Kruger Park is striking, not just in terms of the hotels, but also in terms of the atmosphere. The private camps are havens of calm and tranquility, while the camps in the state-run part of the park are much larger. Some are almost the size of small towns, such as Satara and Skukuza, with their own schools, hospitals, banks, churches, and sports centers.

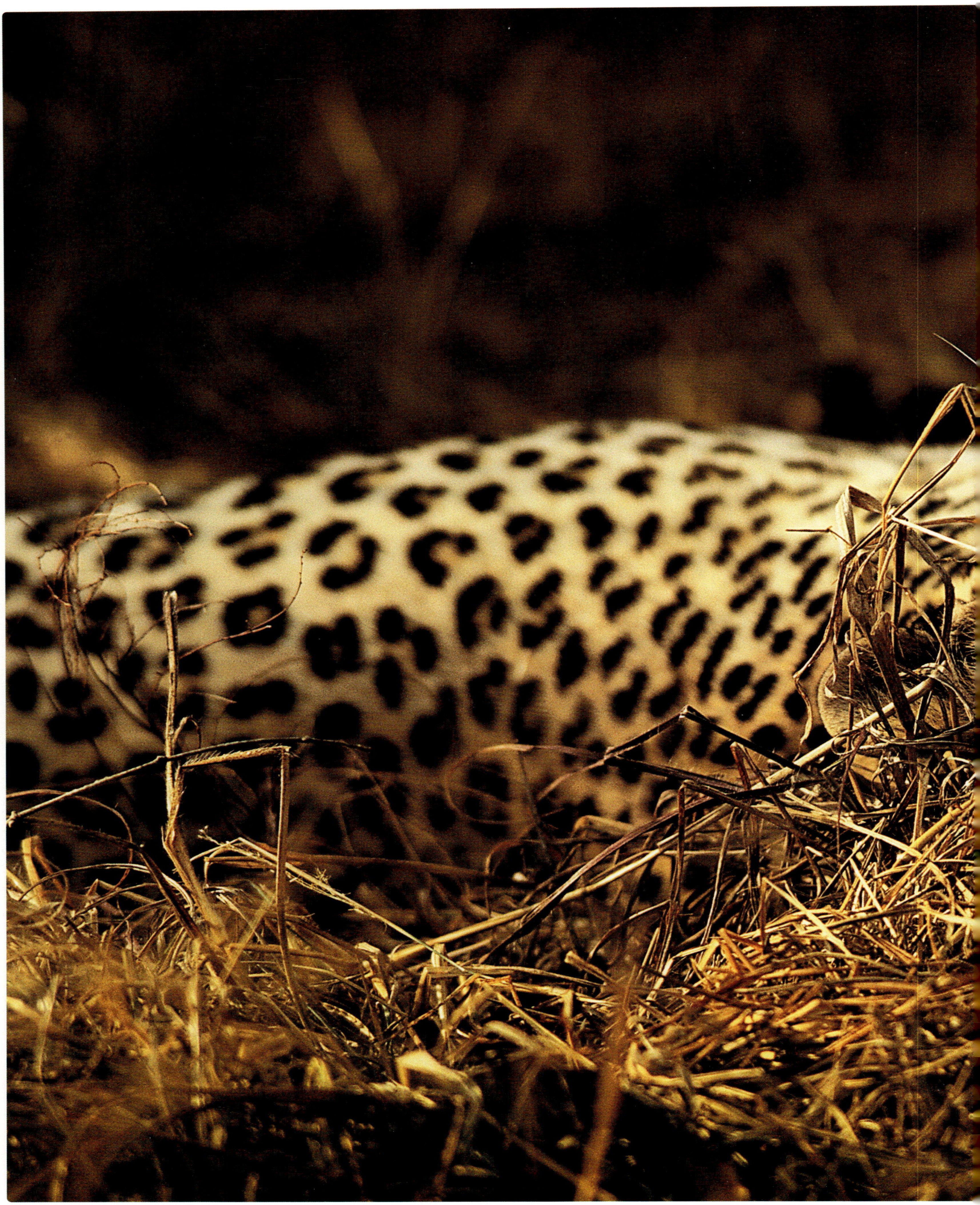

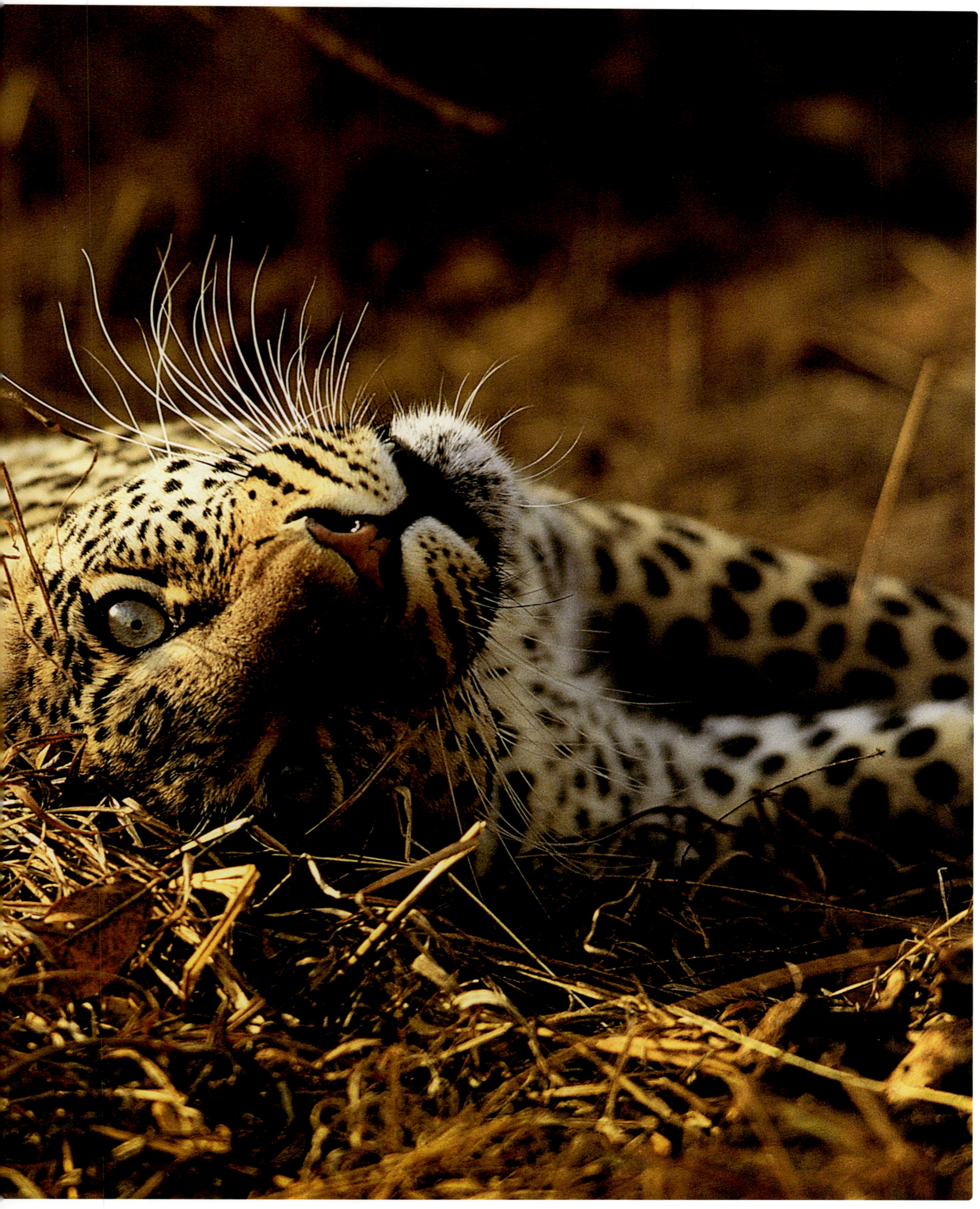

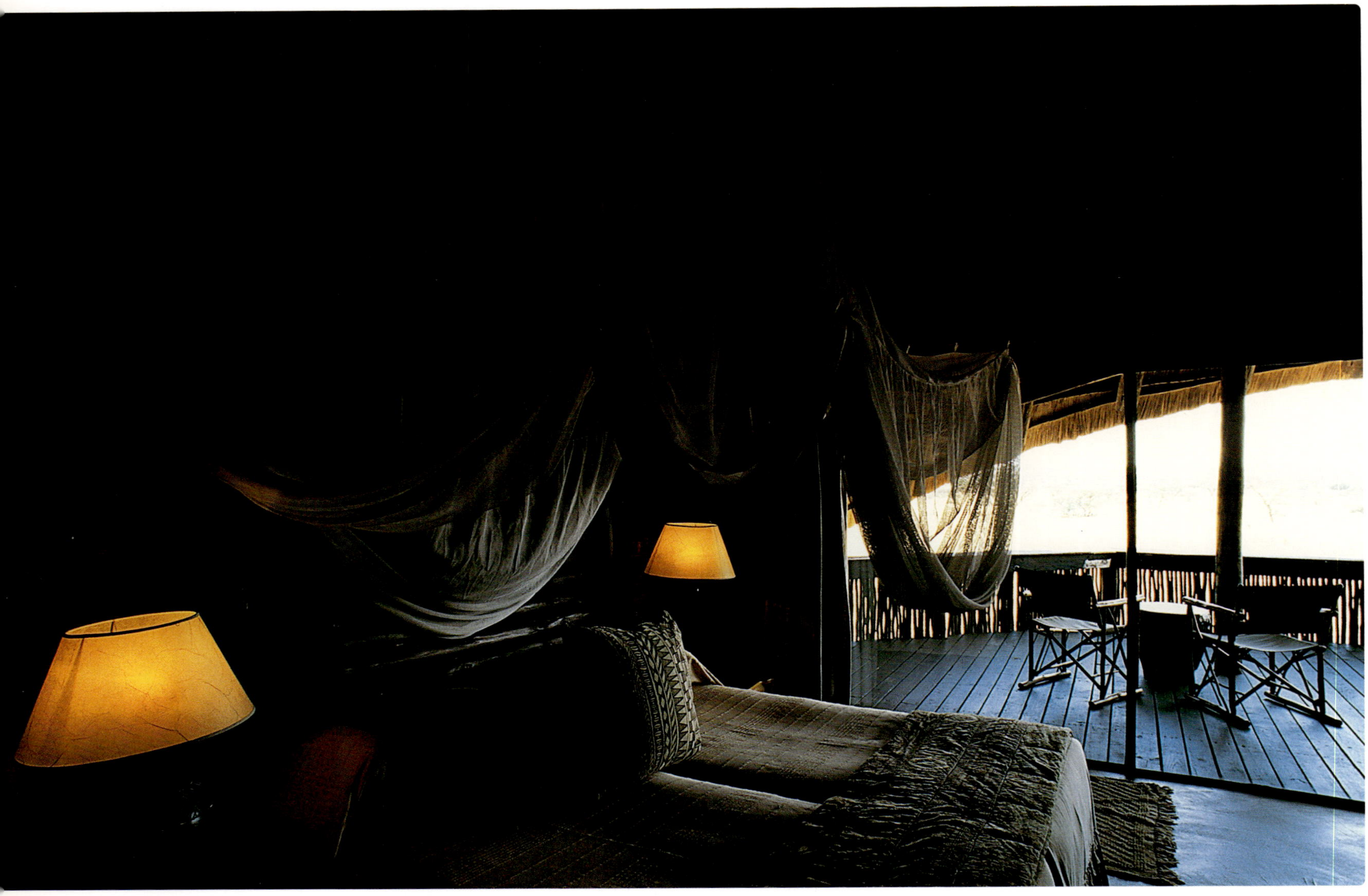

PRECEDING PAGES:

Leopards are timid creatures that are not easy to observe in the wild. We were only able to approach this one after following him for several days to allow him time to get used to our presence. This is the only way to get close to leopards, which are adept at using their spotted coats as camouflage in the dappled shadows of the long grass.

ABOVE:

Leaving the Kalahari Gemsbok Park behind and following the Kuruman River to the east, we drove 175 miles (280 kilometers) on the R31 road to the Tswalu Kalahari private game reserve. The reserve was bought by the Oppenheimer family in 1999 after the death of its founder Stephen Boler. The reserve now has a first-class hotel set in some 222,400 acres (90,000 hectares) of mountains and swathes of crimson desert sand. The hotel stands on land that was once roamed by San tribes. Twelve thousand animals have been successfully released into the wild here, including black rhinos, roan antelope, buffalo, cheetah, and sable.

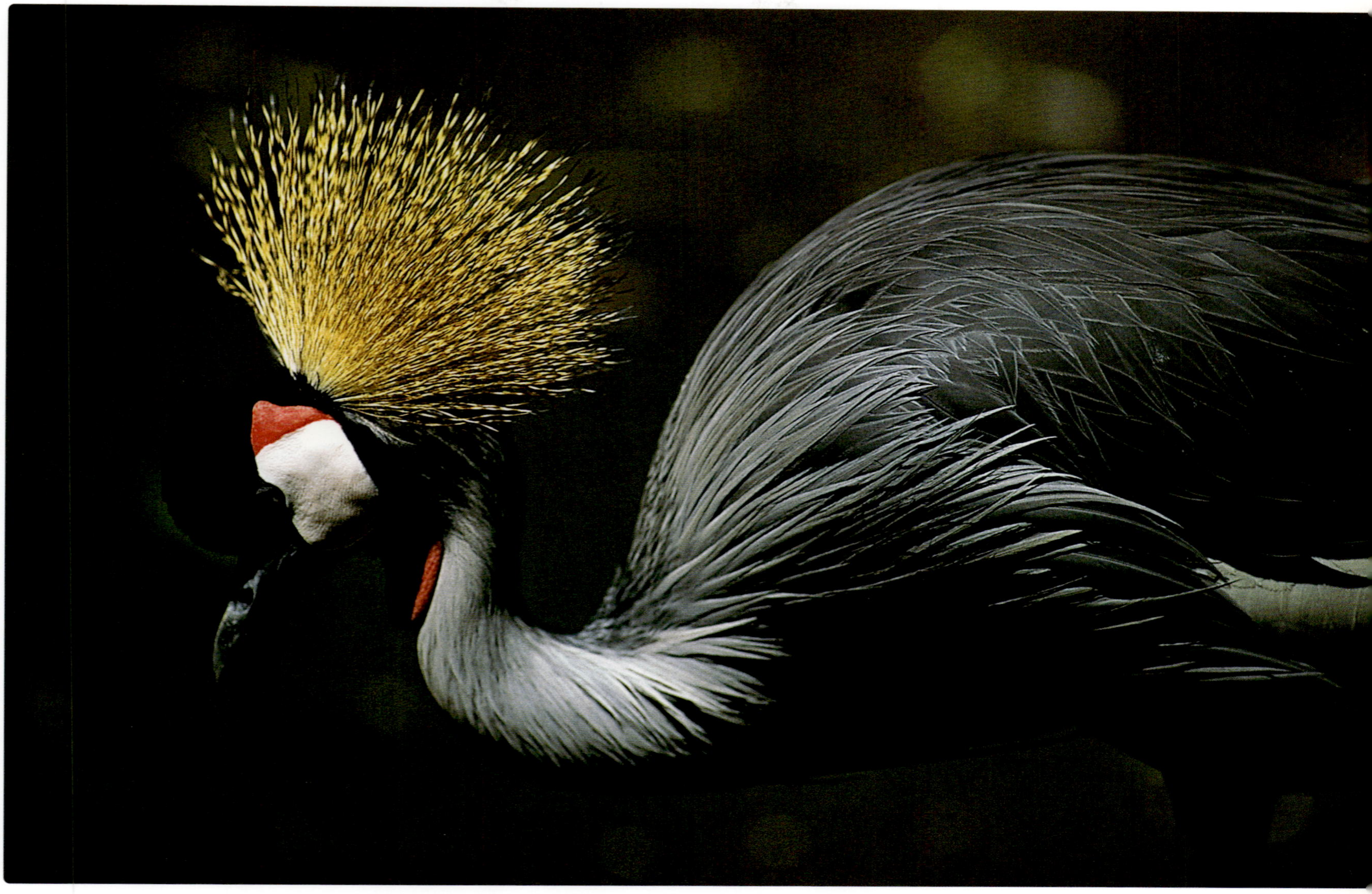

Crested crane are common in eastern South Africa. They are sedentary birds that are found in wetlands and dry areas alike. They are easily identified thanks to the crest of golden plumes that gives them a regal air, contrasting sharply with their sober gray plumage.

FACING PAGE:
The Garden Route along the eastern side of the Cape is perfect for visiting the coastal resorts. There are a few specialized game reserves in this part of the country, including the Buffalo Hills Park, which has a number of rhinos.

FOLLOWING PAGES:
Ostriches were hunted almost to extinction for their feathers and skin, used for leather, as well as for their meat. The best way to see ostriches up close is to visit an ostrich farm such as this one in the region of Oudtshoorn. The region owes much of its wealth to ostrich farming.

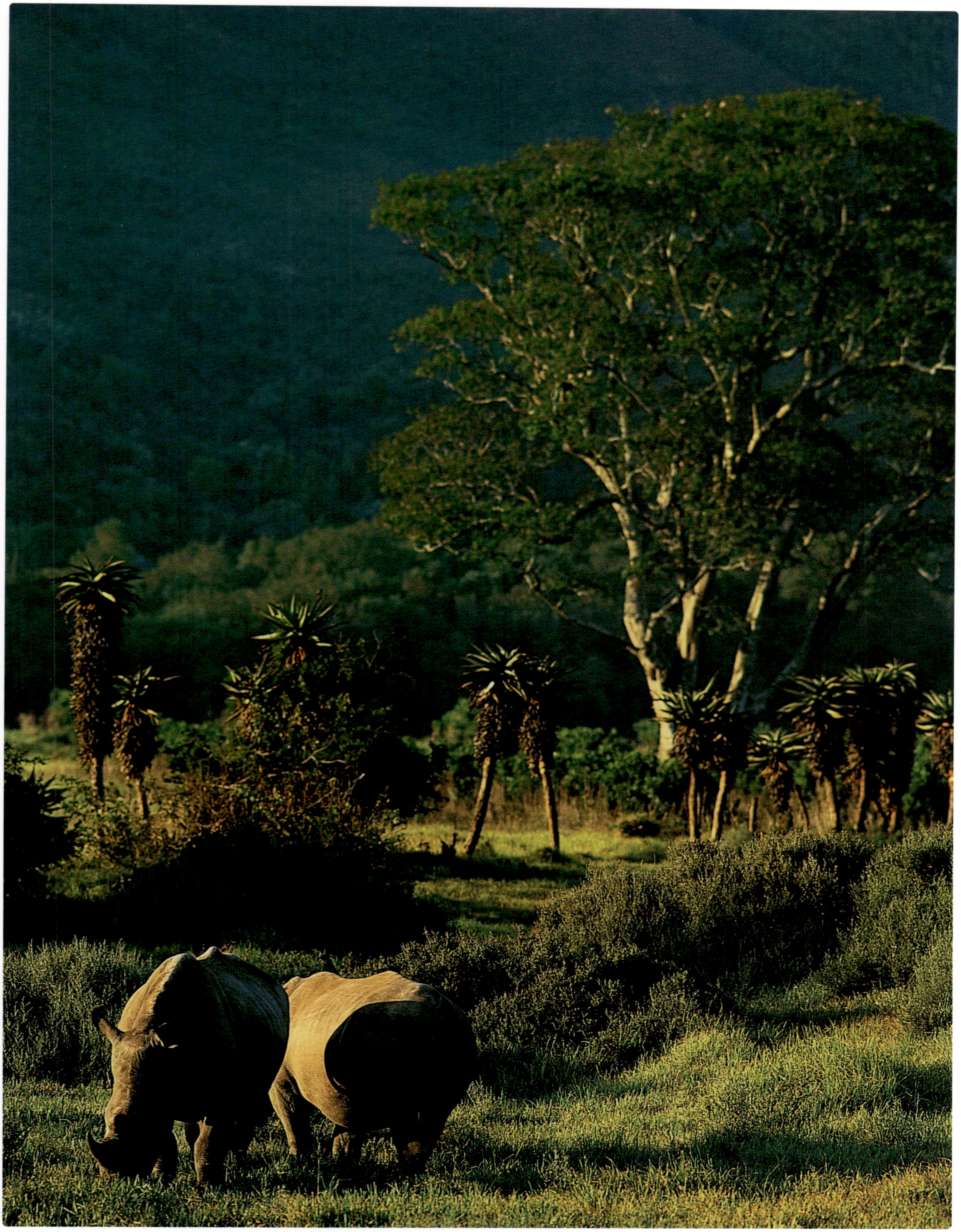

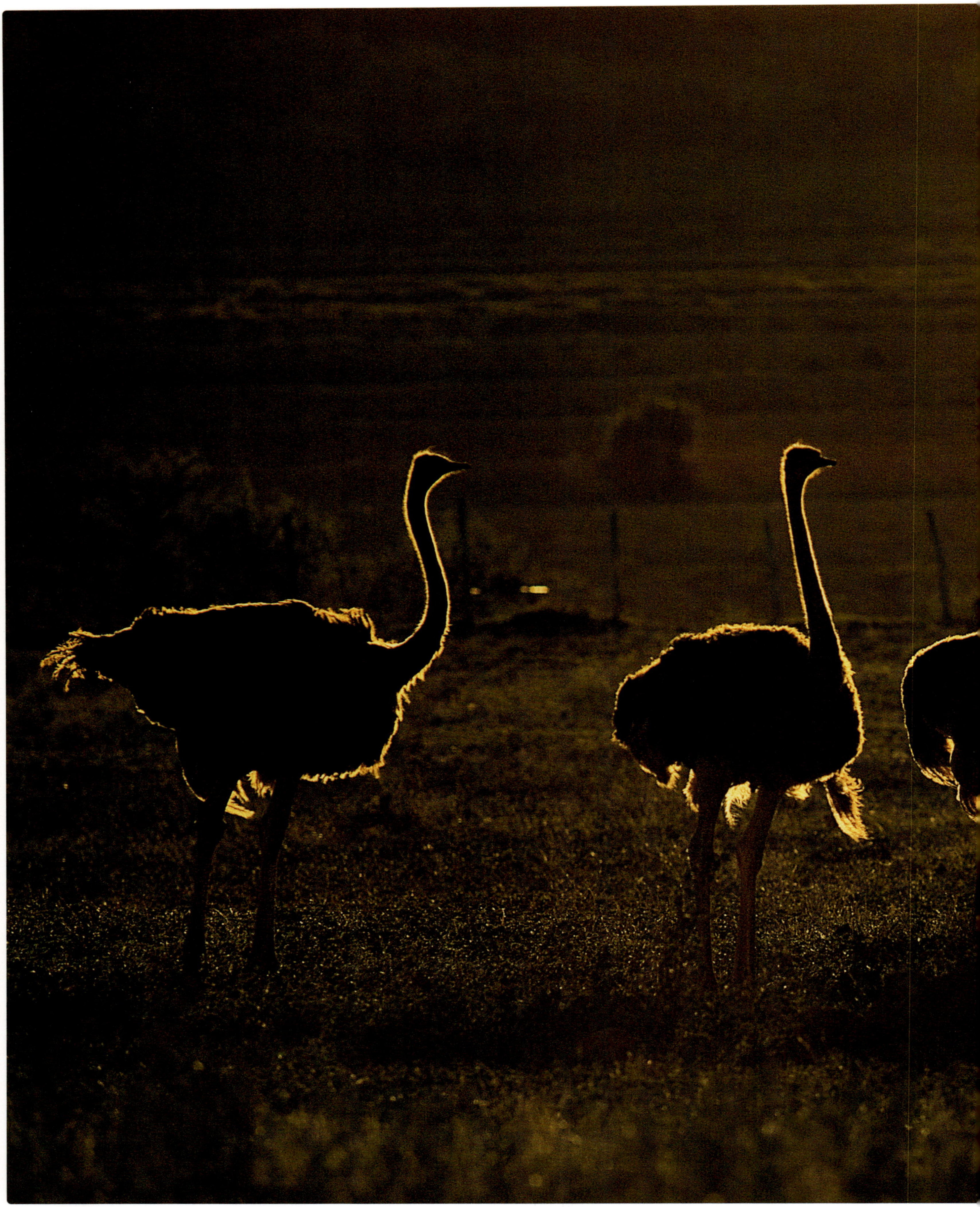

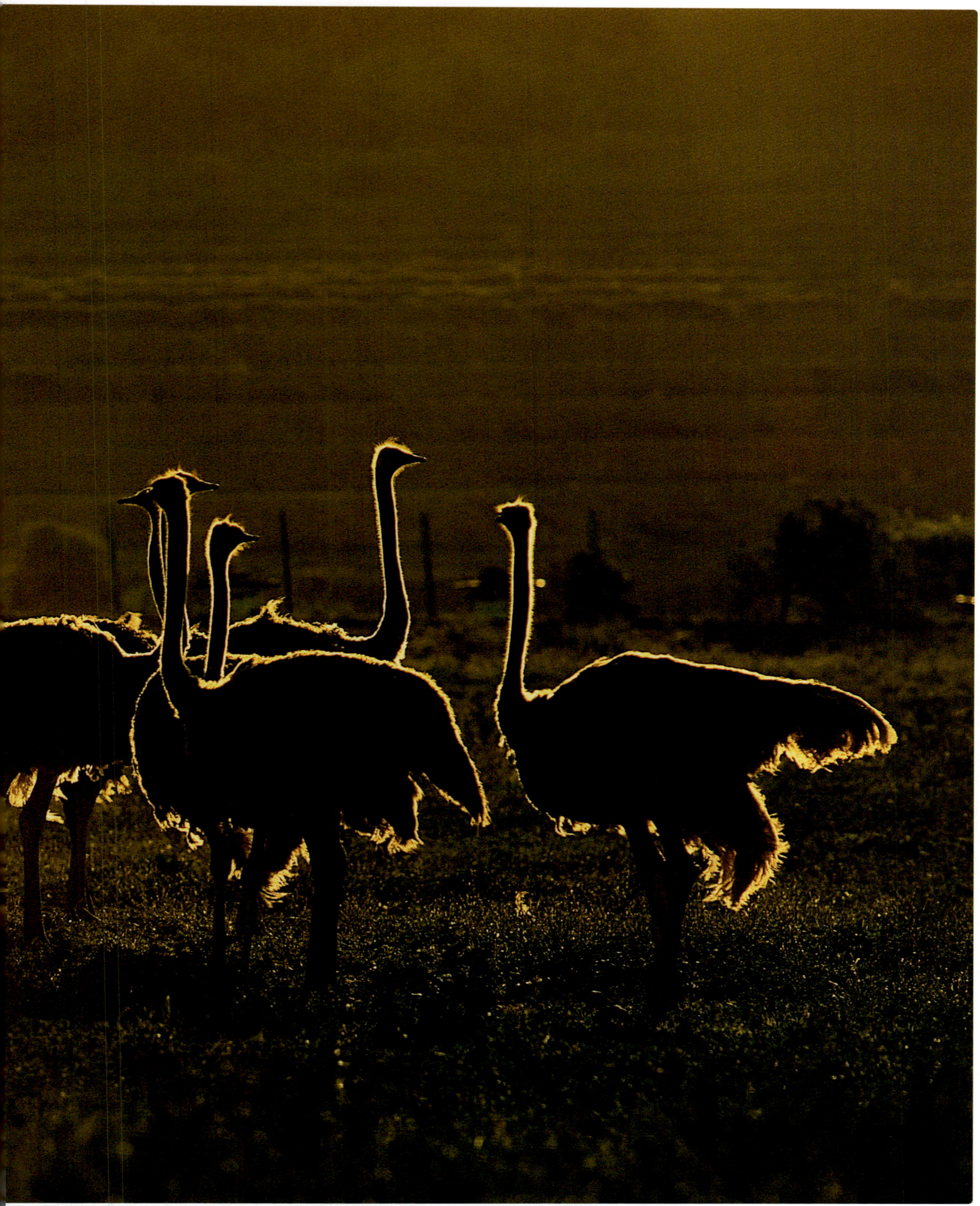

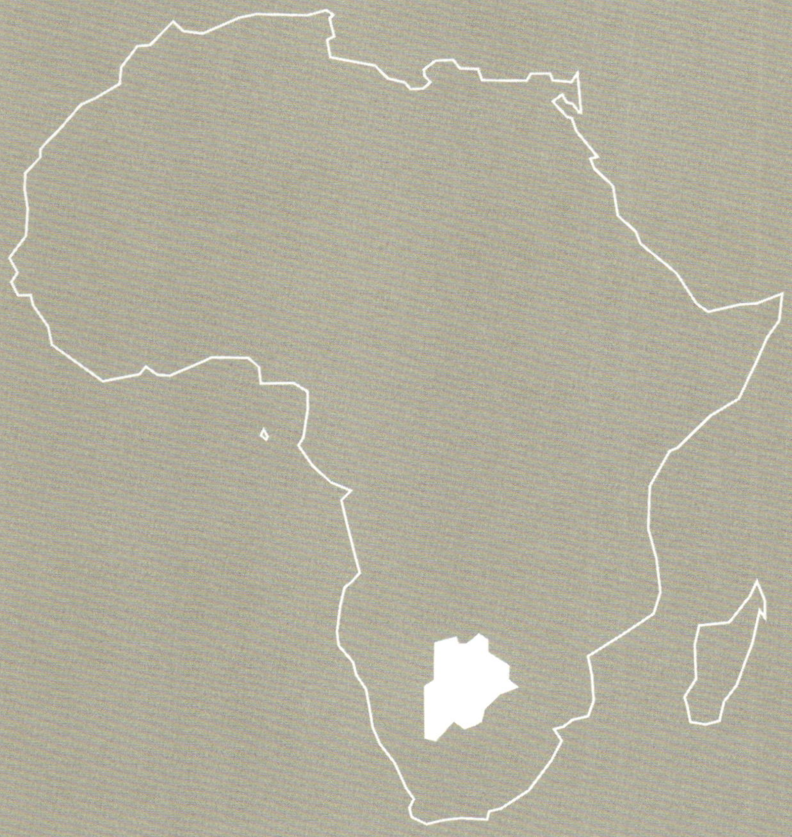

CHAPTER FOUR

BOTSWANA

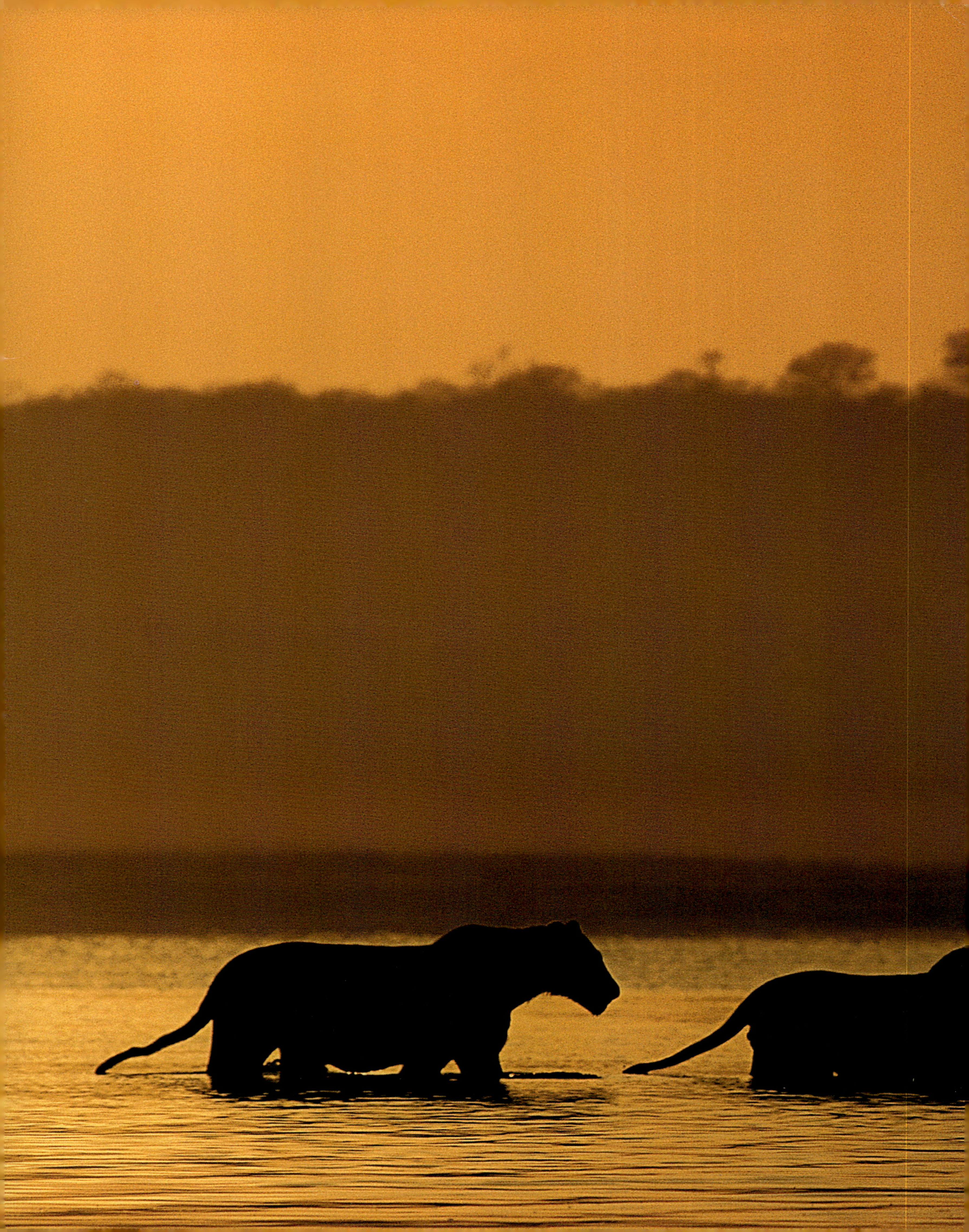

THE VAST EMPTINESS, SWEPT BY DUST-LADEN WINDS, SEEMS TO HAVE ABANDONED ITS GRIP ON LIFE. YET THERE, IN THE DISTANCE, BY THE TRUNK OF A MOPANE TREE, AN ELEPHANT PATIENTLY WAITS OUT THE HOTTEST HOURS OF THE DAY, USING ITS EARS TO FAN ITSELF WITH THE HOT, HEAVY AIR.

The tracks worn by generations of migrating animals are deserted. The waterholes have all dried up. All that remains are shallow dents in the ground, with occasional shrubs greedily sucking up the remaining drops of moisture from the parched earth. The scrubby bushes are dusty ocher. The soil looks crumbly like an ancient parchment. The vast emptiness, swept by dust-laden winds, seems to have abandoned its grip on life. Yet there, in the distance, by the trunk of a mopane tree, an elephant patiently waits out the hottest hours of the day, using its ears to fan itself with the hot, heavy air. It is waiting for the cool of evening to continue its route north, where the fresh green of the wetlands will bring refreshment. Here, the land is vast, open, and empty.

Bounded by Namibia, Zimbabwe, Zambia, and South Africa, a world of exuberant green. The earth is so extraordinarily rich that plants burst forth in magnificent profusion, reaching out their tendrils to embrace the land. Nature here is capricious, untamed, wild, high-spirited, lavish, unpredictable, infuriating. It is a verdant ocean, a kaleidoscope of mosses, emeralds, and verdigris. Botswana is a land of superlatives. Here, the nature reserves are not fenced in and closed off as they are in Kenya or South Africa, where an exploding population is putting increasing pressure on scarce resources. In Botswana, the open spaces reach all the way from the red sands of the Kalahari to the bottle-green waters of the Linyanti and Chobe rivers.

Botswana covers 52,433,280 square miles (135,801,650 square kilometers) with a population of just 1,600,000 inhabitants, most of whom live in the vicinity of the capital, Gaborone. Gaborone lies in the southeast of the country. It is rarely visited by tourists, most of whom arrive in the country either from Johannesburg or Victoria Falls and prefer the safari hot spot of Maun. Small bush planes leave Maun regularly, bound for the Okavango delta.

Tourists only come to Botswana for one thing. The Okavango is unique, and has made the country's fortune as a tourist destination. The inland delta, where the Okavango River pours its waters into the desert sands, is the largest in the world. The waters that fell as heavy rainfall on the high plateaus of Angola six months previously unfurl their might during the southern winter. The river divides into countless meanders and tributaries that nourish the fertile soil of Ngamiland, bringing exceptional beauty in their wake. Every winter, the whims of the floodwaters, dictated by the vegetation and the banks of soil deposited the previous year, carve the land into new and fantastic shapes. The river originally ran its course to the Atlantic Ocean, but its route was cut off some two million years ago, probably as the result of an earthquake. The river then poured its waters over the Linyanti basin, reaching as far as the Makgadikgadi plains, creating an inland lake the size of Ireland. Only in the last 1,500 years have the waters shrunk, due to climate change. Today it is clear that one day, the magnificent delta will dry up completely. After crossing the Panhandle channel, the river loses its way in a vast, incredible tangle of tortuous rivulets, impenetrable marshlands, ephemeral lakes, treacherous bogs, nameless islands topped with clumps of mopane trees and palms, and hundred-year-old anthills. Although the delta is fringed by desert, the waters are not sucked up by the desert sands. Ninety-four percent of the delta's waters evaporate through the process of plant transpiration. If there were a reliable way of measuring this vast, largely uncharted tract of land it would likely find that the permanent delta stretches some seven thousand square kilometers, covering up to three times more when in full spate, sometimes reaching the outskirts of Maun. The flow varies from 423 billion cubic feet (12 billion cubic meters) per year in 1996, to 1.236 trillion cubic feet (35 billion cubic meters) per year in 1984.

The delta can be roughly divided into four natural milieus. The Panhandle is a strip of land a few kilometers wide. The permanent wetlands are a vast stretch of watery emptiness interwoven with narrow channels fringed with papyrus. The seasonal wetlands vary from year to year. Then there are a number of scattered islands—no one knows how many, as the number changes from season to season. The largest is known as Chief's Island.

Some forty game lodges, all relatively small, have been built on the vast stretch of land watered by the Okavango. Each game lodge stands on a patch of privately owned land. They all have their own private airstrip and a fleet of four-wheel-drive vehicles. Most of the lodges propose a series of activities on dry land or on the waters of the delta, such as excursions in one of the camp vehicles or canoeing, offered by Chitabe, Duba Plains, Vumbura, and Moremi camps, among others. Some only offer land safaris, including the top-of-the-range Mombo and Chief's Island lodges, which are both in the heart of the Moremi reserve and are perfect for spotting rare species. A few lodges, such as Xaxaba, Xigera, and Jacana, are ideal for exploring the delta by boat. The romance of the earliest camps, offering little more than a night under canvas, has gradually given way to luxurious lodges that are ruinously expensive. Exclusivity comes at a price.

PRECEDING PAGES:
I had been watching the animals at dawn on the banks of the Chobe River for more than two months when one day, just as the first rays of the sun were piercing the darkness, I spotted three lionesses swimming towards the bank, chasing a herd of terrified buffalo plowing through the inky waters.

FACING PAGE:
Every game lodge in Africa has its own troop of primates to watch over it. Baboons are sharp, inquisitive, and endlessly amused by the antics of humans. Hidden in a tree or sunbathing on an anthill, this troop spied on us all day in the hope of snatching some food while our backs were turned.

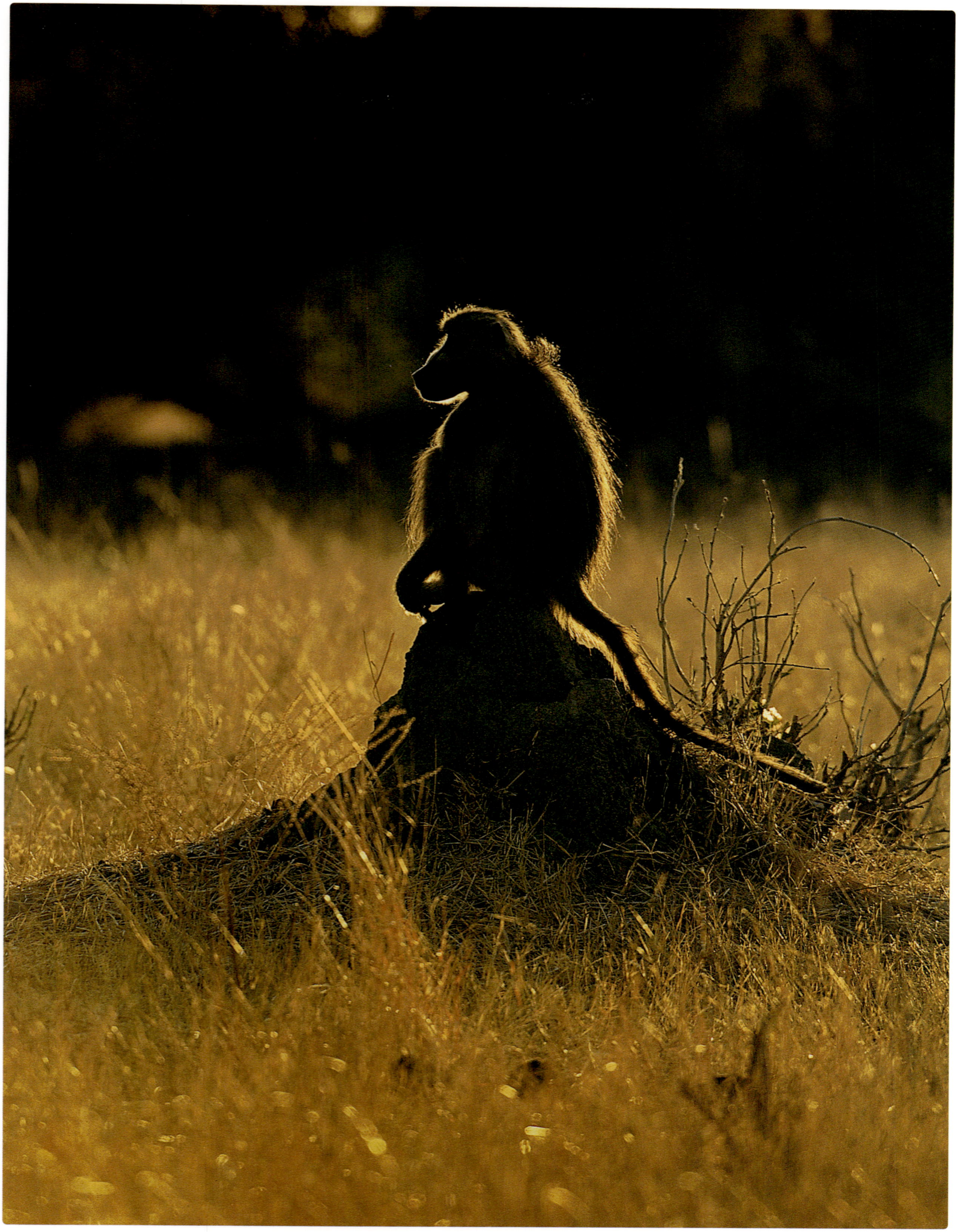

THE VAST, SILENT EMPTINESS OF THE LANDSCAPE IS AN EERIE YET STRANGELY MOVING SIGHT. THIS HARSHEST OF LANDS HAS BEEN CONQUERED ONLY BY THE SAN, AS THE BUSHMEN ARE PROPERLY KNOWN. THIS ARID PLAIN COVERS FOUR-FIFTHS OF THE COUNTRY'S SURFACE.

Private game reserves are not bound by the strict regulations governing the national parks, making it easier to get closer to the animals. There are no restrictions on where you can drive, no circuits to follow, no limited opening hours, no obligation to be out by sundown. Night drives are very popular.

Uncultivated land outside of the national parks is the responsibility of the Wildlife and National Parks body and the Tawana Land Board. These administrative bodies have divided the land into vast concessions, which are then rented to private companies on a fifteen-year lease. This system of temporary leases has proved unwieldy and complex to run, and the choice of company authorized to rent depends not only on ecological factors, but also social and economic ones, closing the market to all but the biggest investors.

The wandering course of the Chobe River is the country's second biggest source of fresh water, after the delta, of course. Actually, the Chobe is a river in name only. The rippling current is just an illusion created by the wind. The tributaries that feed the waters peter out at the Namibian border in the Linyanti marshes. Paradoxically, the waters now coursing between the banks come from further downstream. Thanks to a curious natural phenomenon, the flow of the Zambezi, blocked by a series of rapids near Kazungula, where four African countries—Namibia, Zambia, Zimbabwe, and Botswana—meet, backs up and pours into the bed of the Chobe. Some years, the waters reach several dozen miles to the west, creating an immense lake edged by an infinity of winding channels. The banks of the Chobe were formerly very rich in big game, and the region was very popular with British big game hunters in the early decades of the twentieth century. The indiscriminate slaughter of vast numbers of animals, particularly elephants, led to the first attempts to set up protected game reserves. In the 1930s, the district commissioner Colonel Charles Rey suggested the zone be declared a nature reserve. However, the plan only came to fruition in 1961, and it was not until 1968 that the 4,517 square miles (11,700 square kilometers) of the reserve were officially made a national park. The reserve is predominantly savanna grassland dotted with mopanes and acacias. The area surrounding Serondella is spectacularly beautiful. On a stretch of some twelve miles (twenty kilometers) along the riverbanks, there are literally hundreds of elephants. Unfortunately, the site is in danger of becoming overrun by tourists. The only lodge inside the park perimeter is the Chobe Game Lodge. The hotel is in a magnificent setting right in the heart of the park. The guests can be the first out on the mist-shrouded tracks and can enjoy evening boat trips along the river, although their peace may now be disturbed by the increasing numbers of motor launches from other hotels lying outside the park boundaries. The number of hotels on the outskirts of the park has shot up in recent years, increasingly putting pressure on the fragile equilibrium of the environment. The imposing Cresta Mowana hotel is the perfect example. However, some hotels do make an effort to respect the natural environment. The Impalila Lodge is one of these. It is a magical collection of comfortable huts discreetly tucked into the landscape, offering spectacular views of the rapids, just twenty minutes from Kasane by boat.

To the south of this delightful region, the plain stretches to the horizon, vast and empty, where the clouds scud across the sky without shedding a drop of rain. This is a semi-desert where water is a rare and precious commodity. The vast, silent emptiness of the landscape is an eerie yet strangely moving sight. This harshest of lands has been conquered only by the San, as the bushmen are properly known. This arid plain covers four-fifths of the country's surface. These are the great desert swathes of the Central Kalahari, Makgadikgadi, the Nxai Pan, and the Gembox Park. A few days here is a truly unforgettable experience. Nothing prepares you for the calm serenity of the ancient nomadic tribes who are now trying to adapt to modern life, sharing their ancestral tribal knowledge of the desert with the very few camps in the region, such as the legendary Jack's Camp or Deception Valley Lodge.

Botswana is now the third largest tourist destination in sub-Saharan Africa, after South Africa and Kenya. While the government seems perfectly open and transparent, it has recently come to light that the media has suffered a degree of censorship after revealing a series of scandals relating to the forced displacement of San tribes, backhanders from foreign companies, and issues of animal health. The country is still very much reliant on pastoral farming techniques and is finding it difficult to come to terms with the far-reaching changes required to compete in the international marketplace. Even the tourism industry, which has benefited from shrewd development and is therefore a major source of foreign revenue, has become the subject of controversy after certain political leaders, trained in the Soviet Union, demanded a return to a state-run economy. They may have a point. While the economy is growing, foreign investors are flocking to the country, and wealthy tourists are bringing in plenty of foreign currency, the people have seen little improvement in their daily lives, where, as elsewhere in Africa, AIDS is causing untold ravages.

FACING PAGE:
In the stunning Okavango delta, patches of lush grassland alternate with meandering backwaters that have regularly flooded the delta for thousands of years. Various species of mammals have traced an intricate labyrinth of paths through the reeds, linking islets where weary animals can rest in the shade.

FOLLOWING PAGES:
Botswana is the last remaining place on earth where you can see herds of many hundreds of buffaloes thundering through the marshlands of the delta. The herds mainly consist of females and calves. The only way to get an idea of the massive size of the herd is from an airplane.

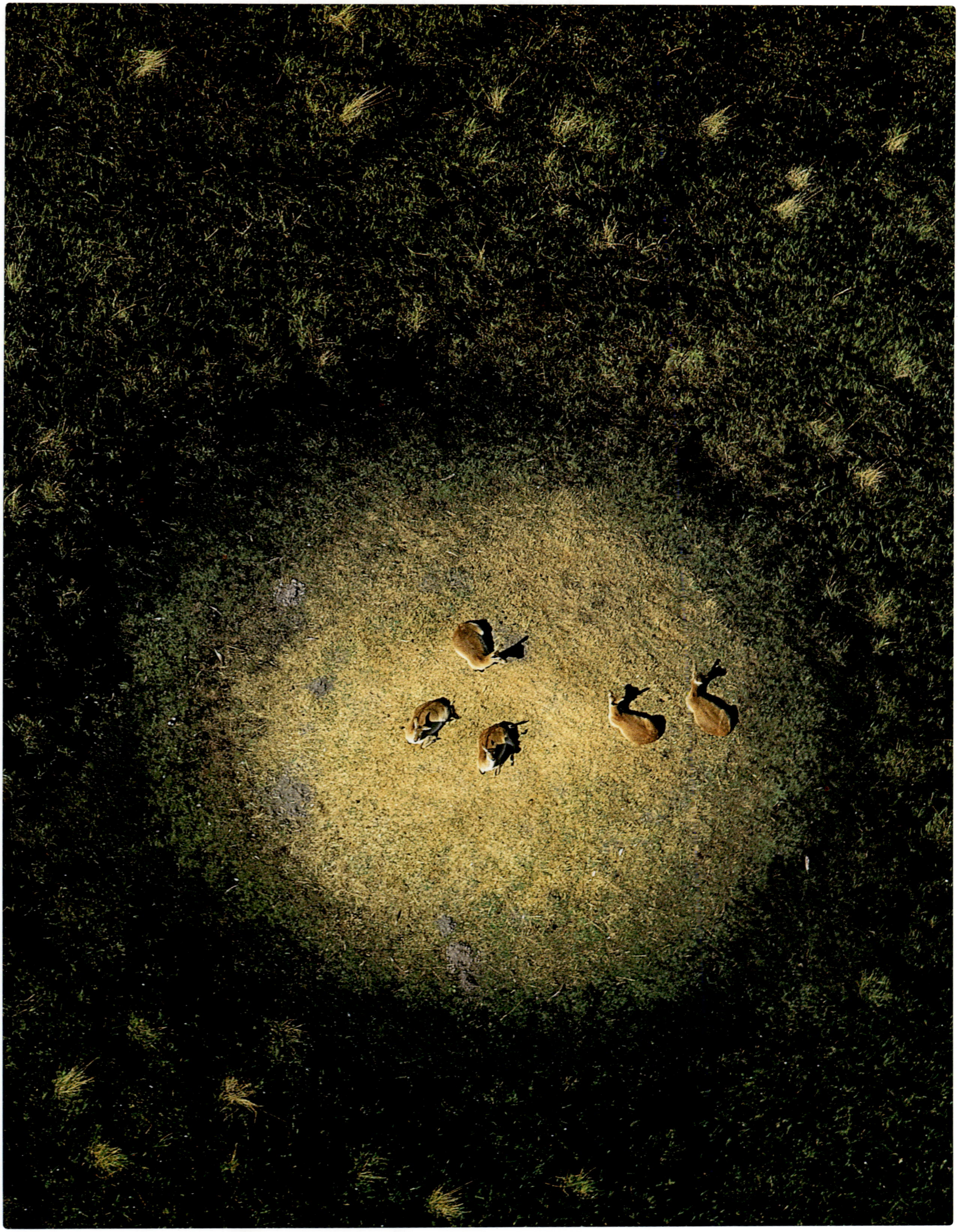

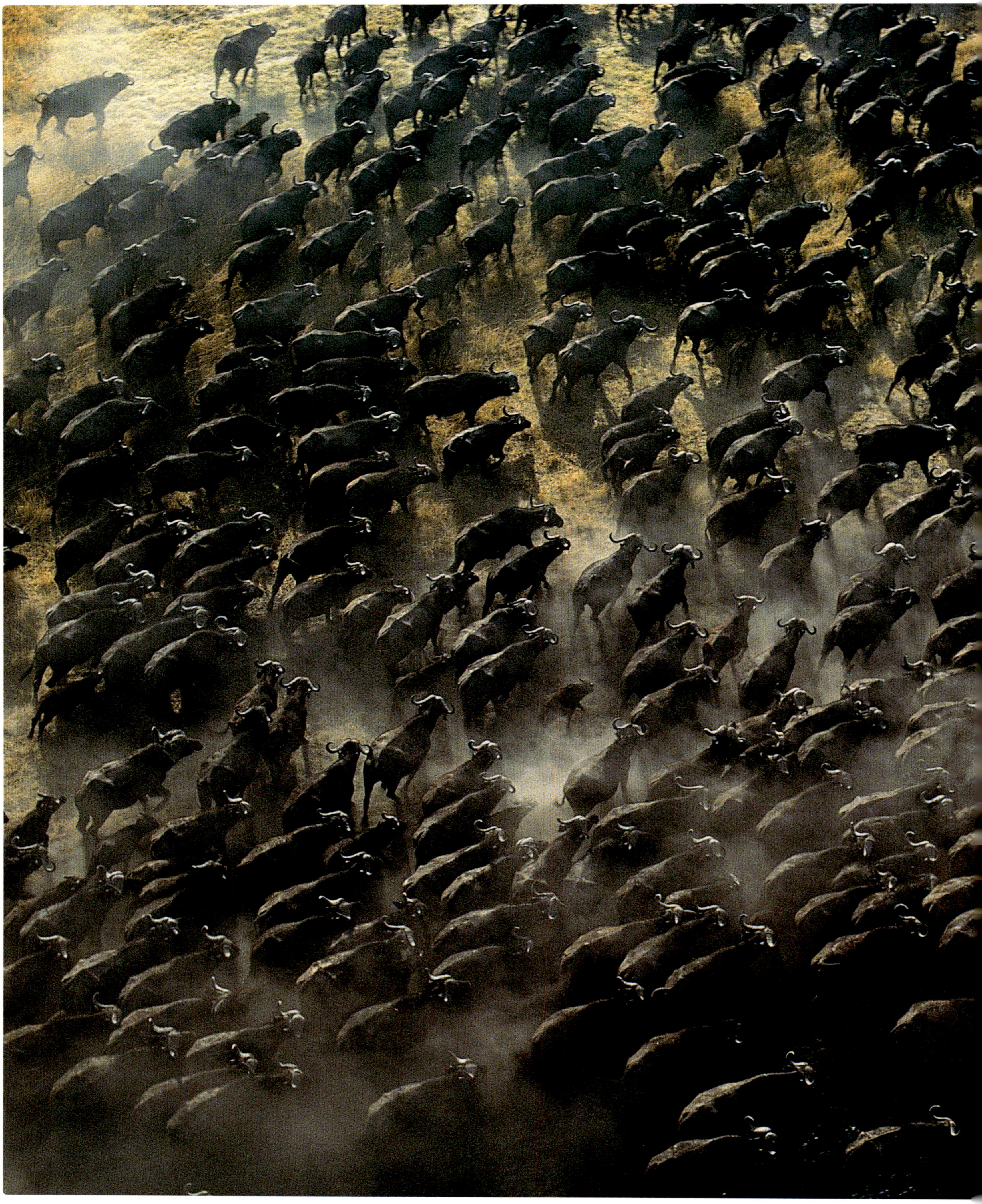

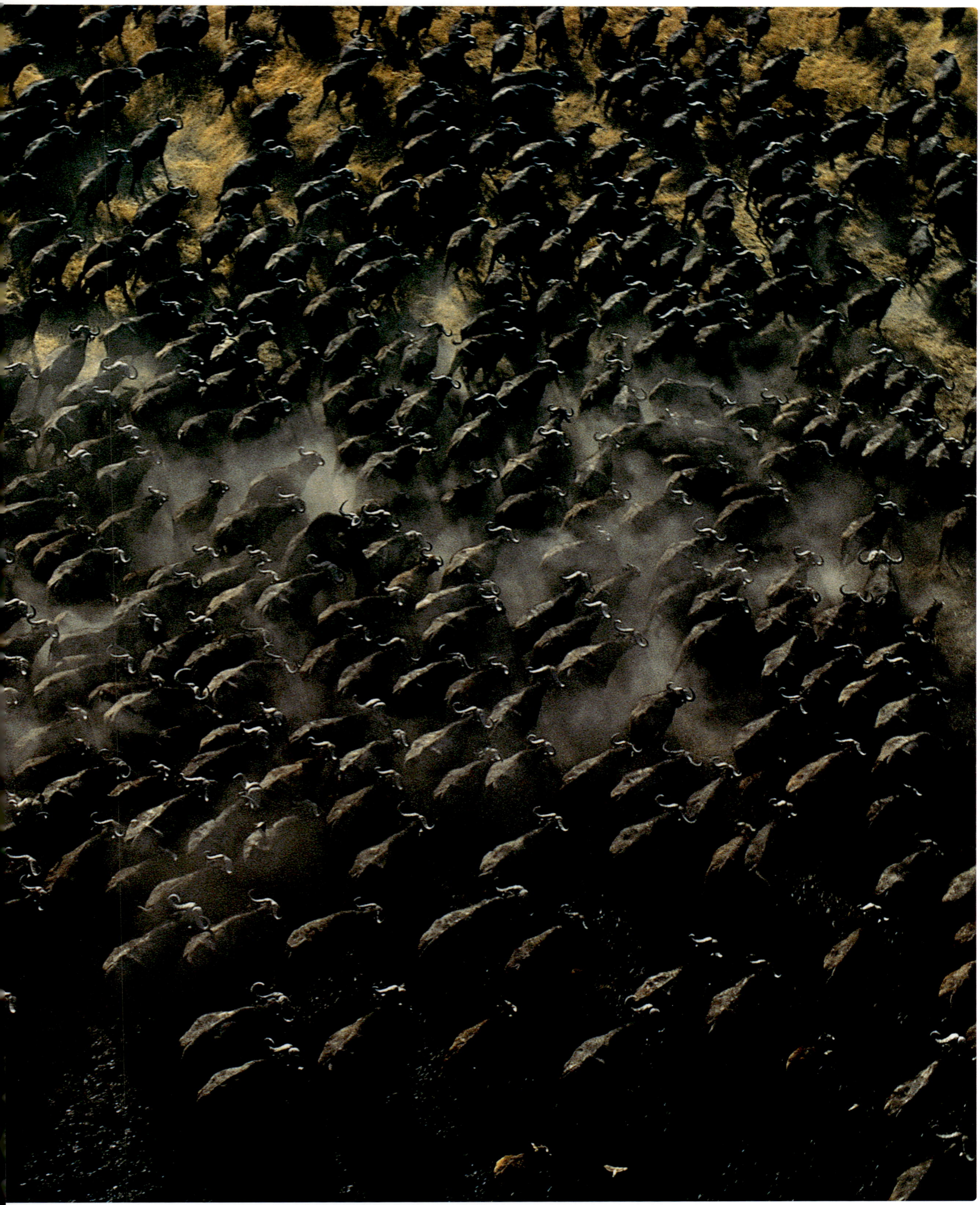

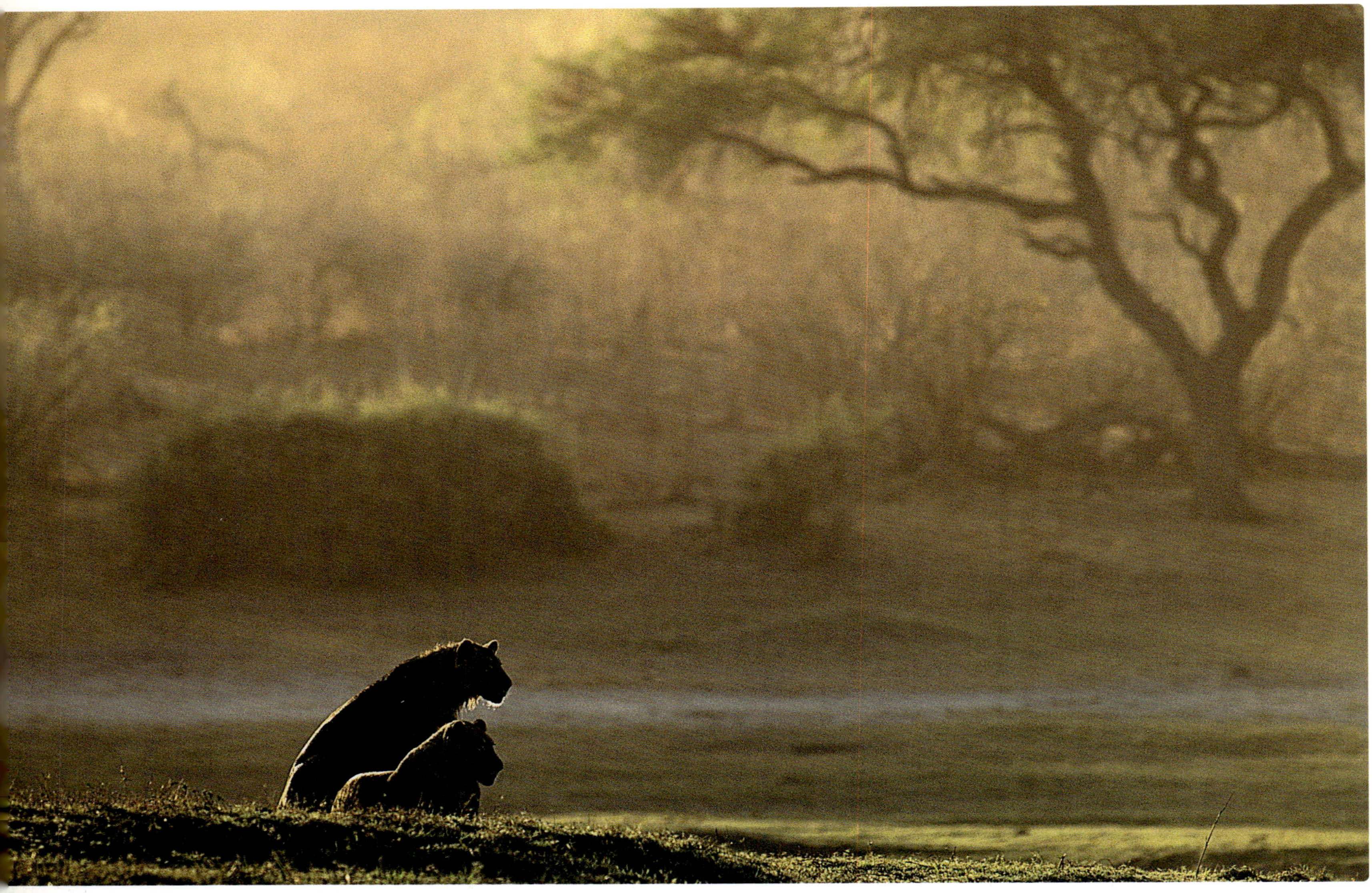

Dawn is the best time of day to see the big cats. I often saw these two lionesses slinking along as they hunted together in the gray early morning light. I nicknamed them Zoe and Chloe. On this occasion, they made short work of a warthog foolish enough to blunder across their path.

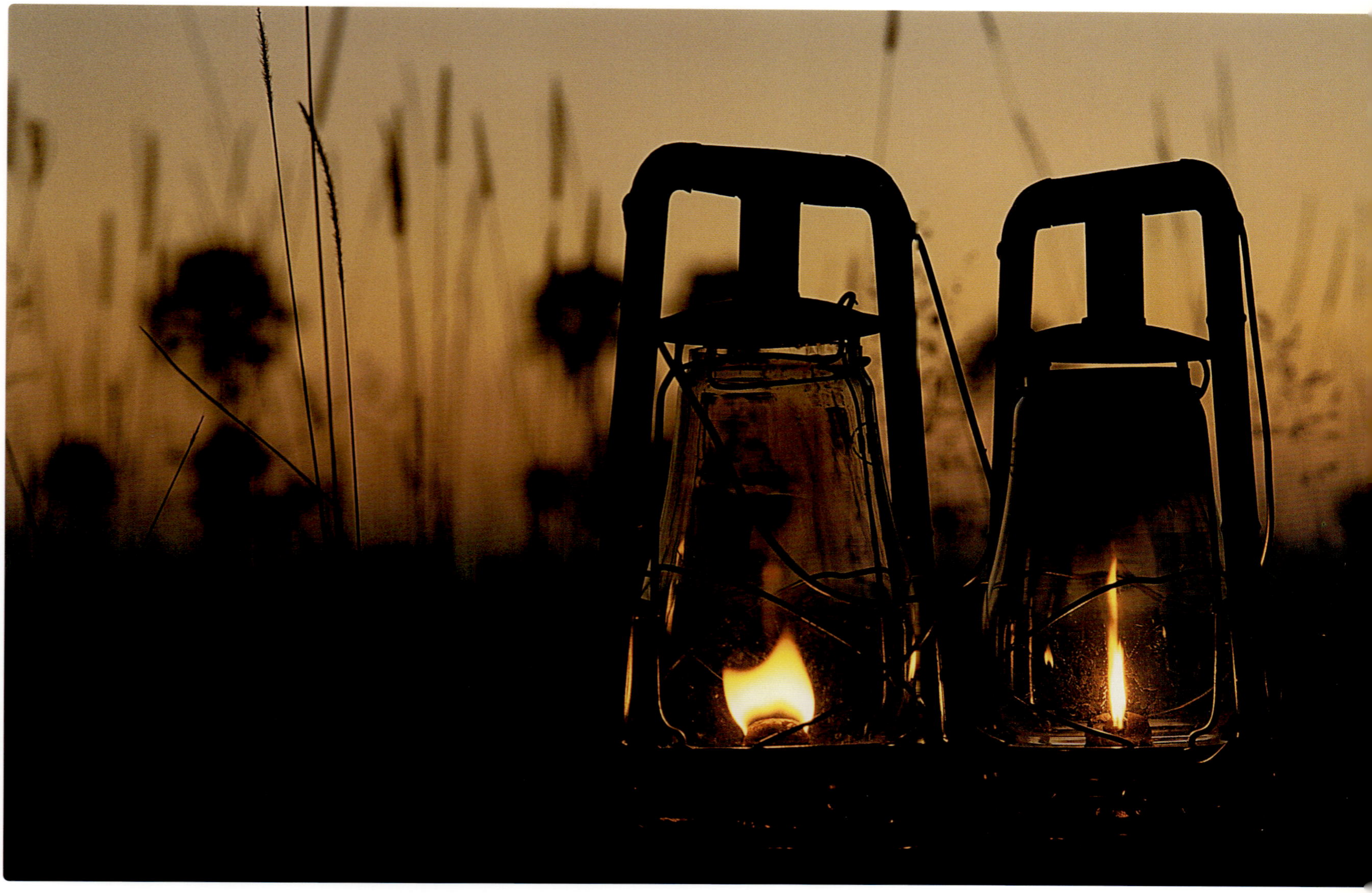

Old-fashioned oil lamps make a night on the savanna an unforgettable experience. Most game lodges have them in addition to electric lighting. The dreamily flickering light of the flame on the glass sides of the lamp casts eerie shadows along the paths, on the panels of the mosquito net, or on the tall grass of the Okavango wetlands.

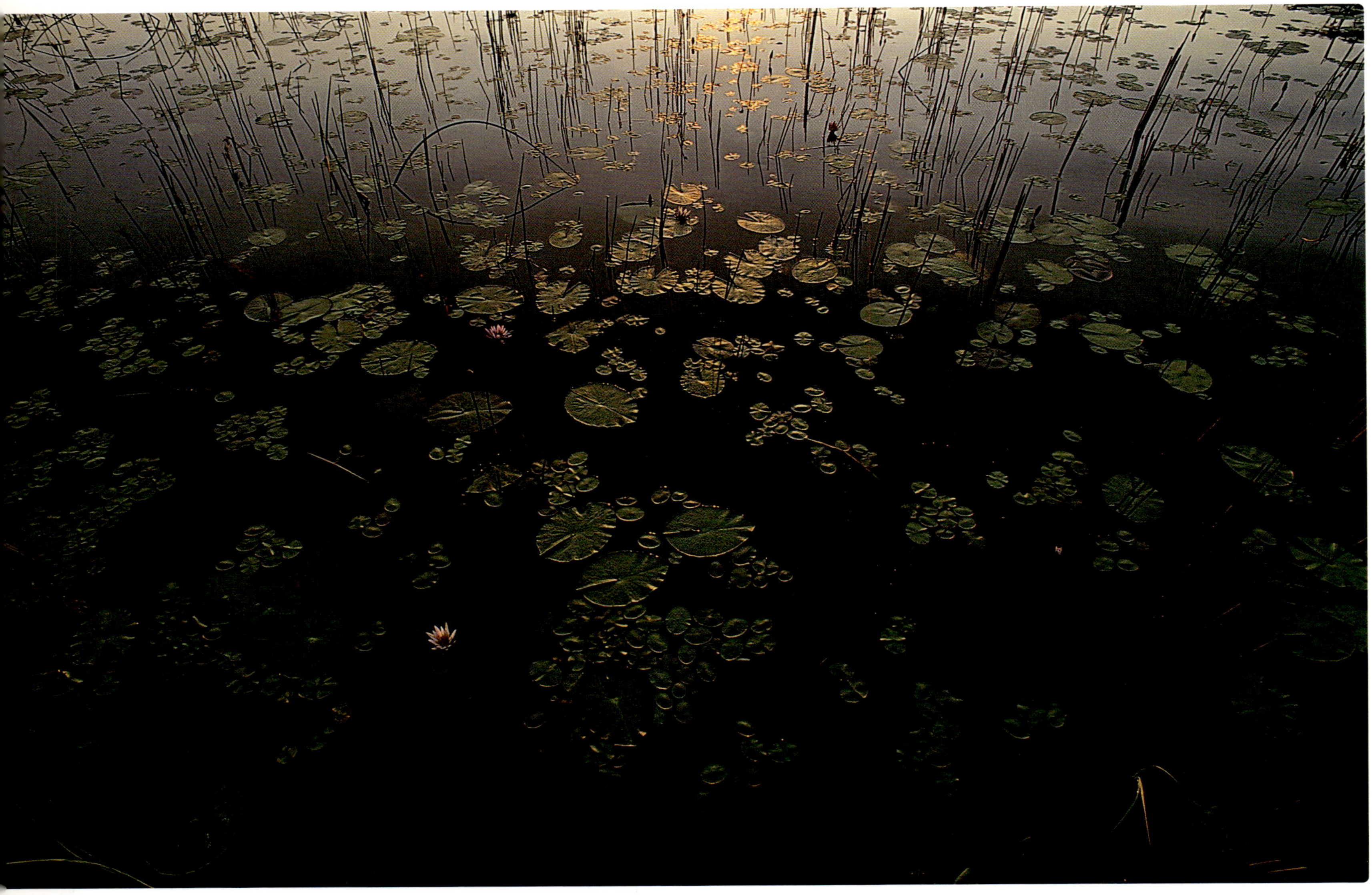

The broad, flat leaves of the water lilies at Xigera form a mosaic pattern on the waters of the Okavango. Our *moroko* glides through the tangle of leaves: the path we open is swallowed up again as soon as we pass. Occasionally we catch a glimpse of the striped silver back of a tiger fish.

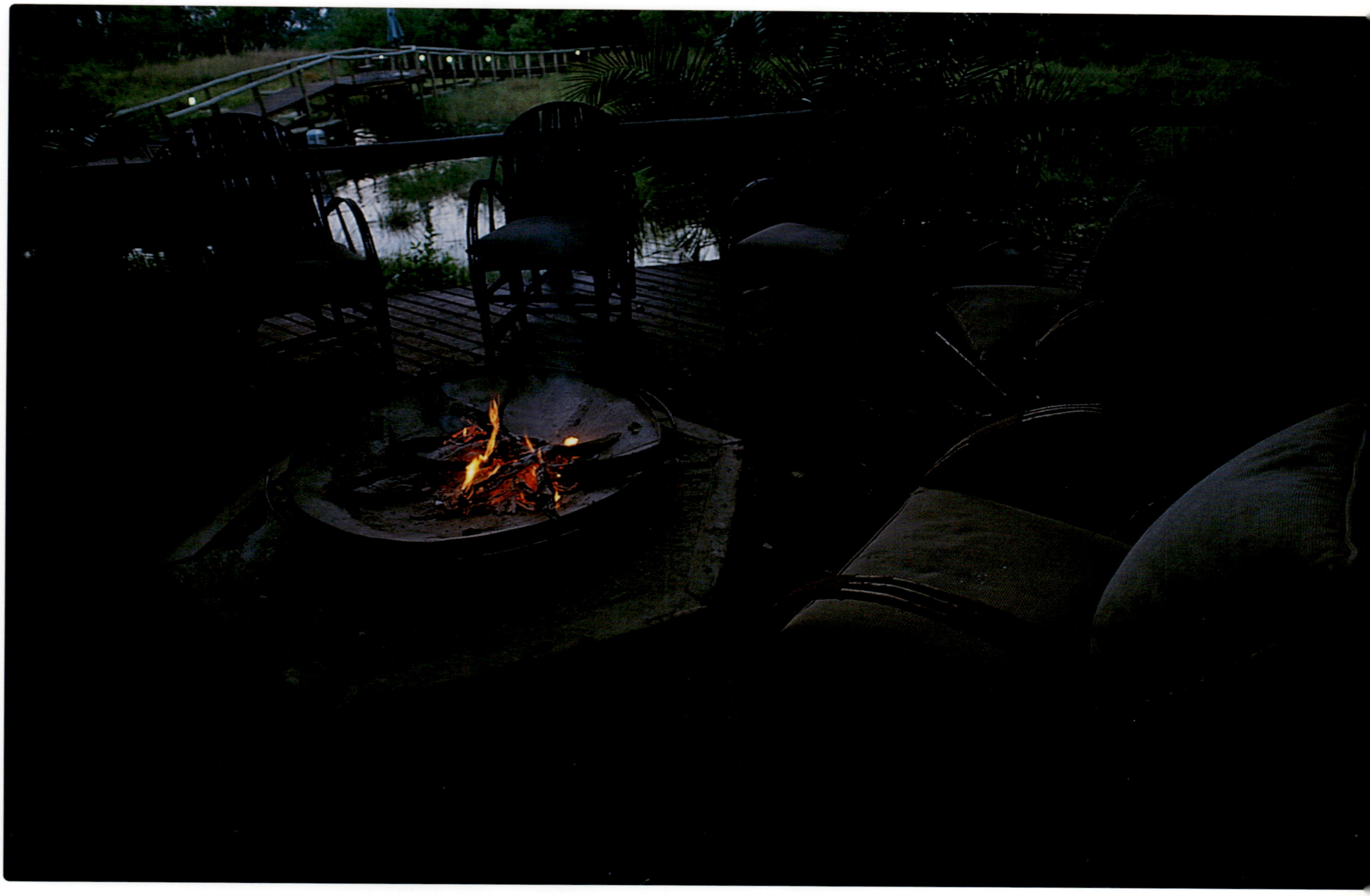

ABOVE:

Every evening, the rangers and visitors to the lodge gather round the campfire. Here, in Xigera, relaxing in a canvas or wicker chair, a cool drink close to hand, we swapped tall tales late into the night.

FOLLOWING PAGES:

A *moroko* is a simple form of canoe carved from a tree trunk. It is by far the best way to get close to the birds that flock to the Okavango delta. Gliding silently along a canal in Xaxaba, you might come across a family of elephants bathing, a crocodile hunting, or a sitatunga antelope.

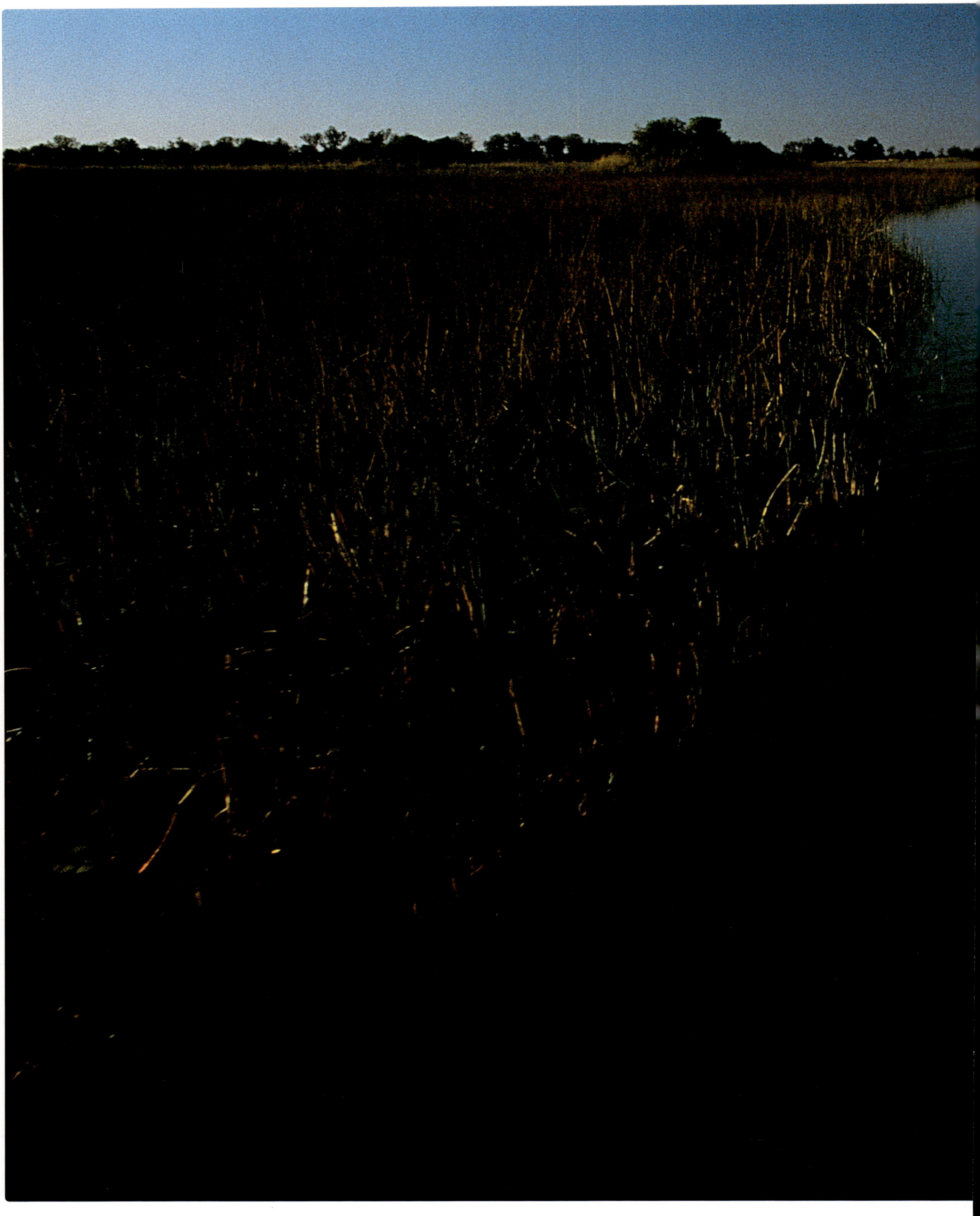

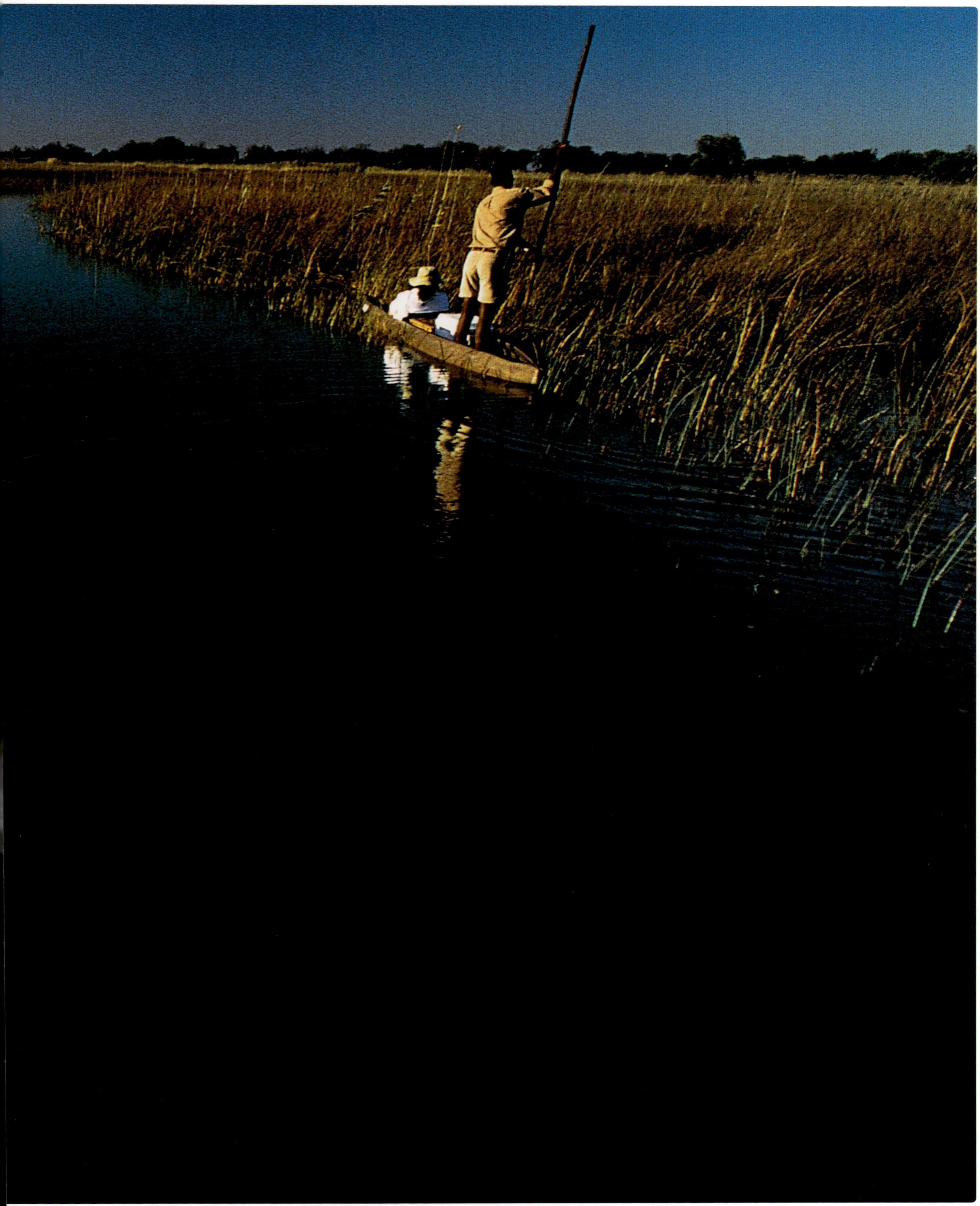

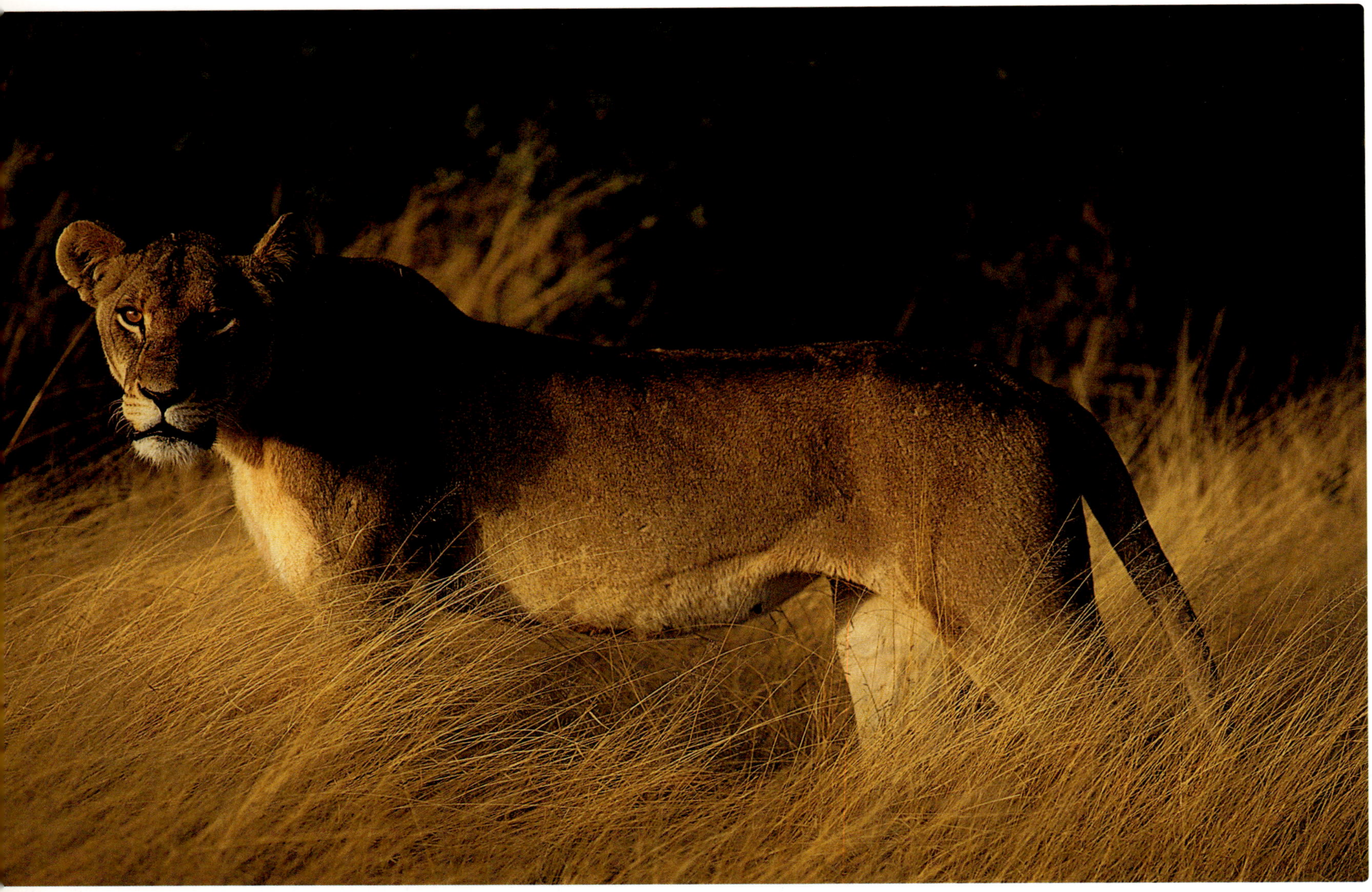

Lions are actually rather inefficient hunters. Most of the time, they feed on kills stolen from hyenas, leopards, and cheetahs. This lioness was about to set off hunting, having carefully hidden her cub, and obviously felt uneasy about our presence.

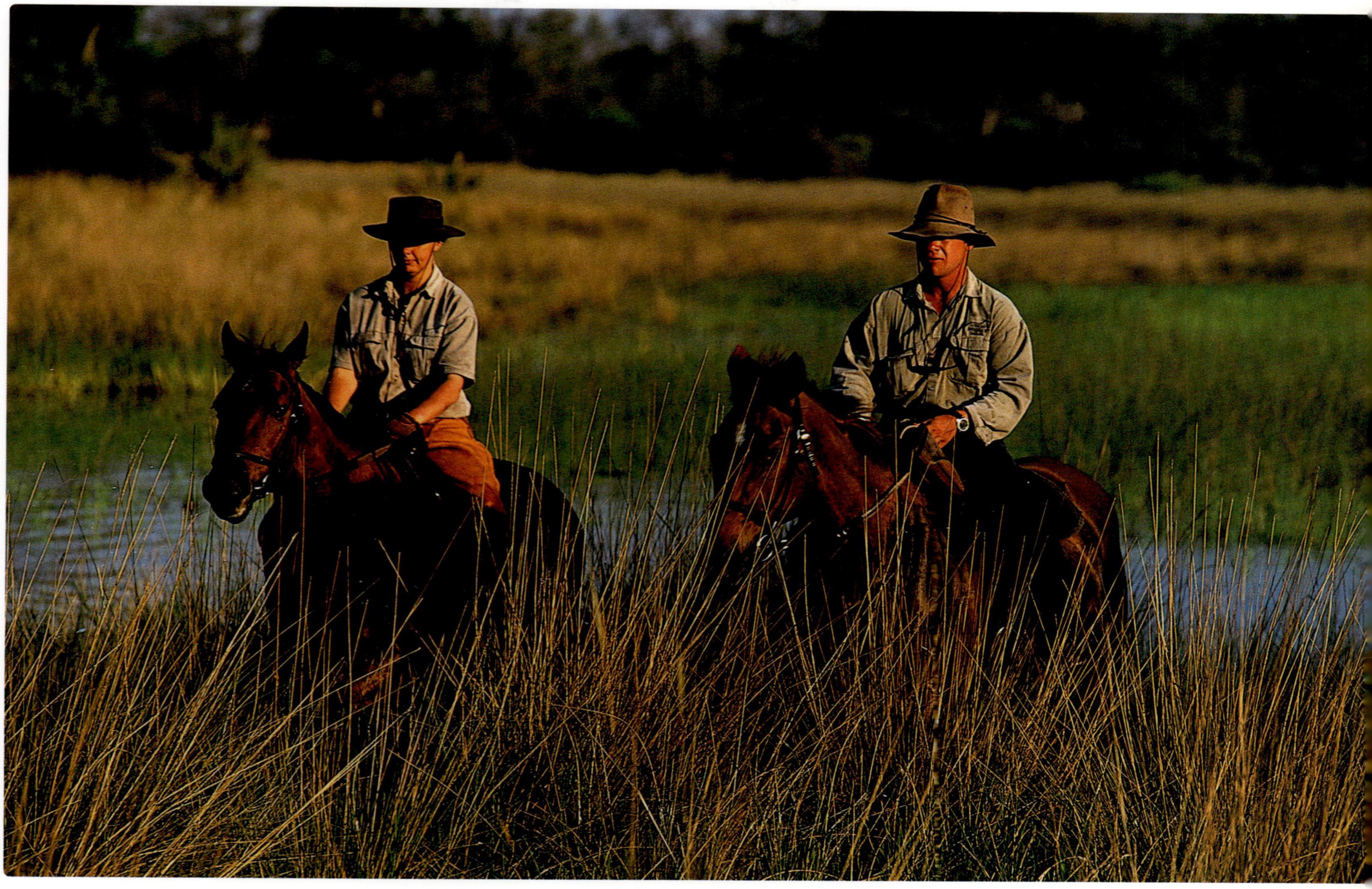

Surprising though it may seem, one of the best ways to travel in the delta is on horseback. Horses are perfectly adapted to the wetlands. Few things in life can be more pleasurable than galloping through the marshlands, getting up close to the herds of zebra, buffaloes, and elephants. The ideal safari outfit is a light fleece (it can be chilly in the mornings) and a cotton shirt and trousers, preferably green or khaki. You probably won't need a huge number of pockets. A few accessories are truly indispensable: walking boots, a canvas sun hat, sunglasses, and some mosquito repellent.

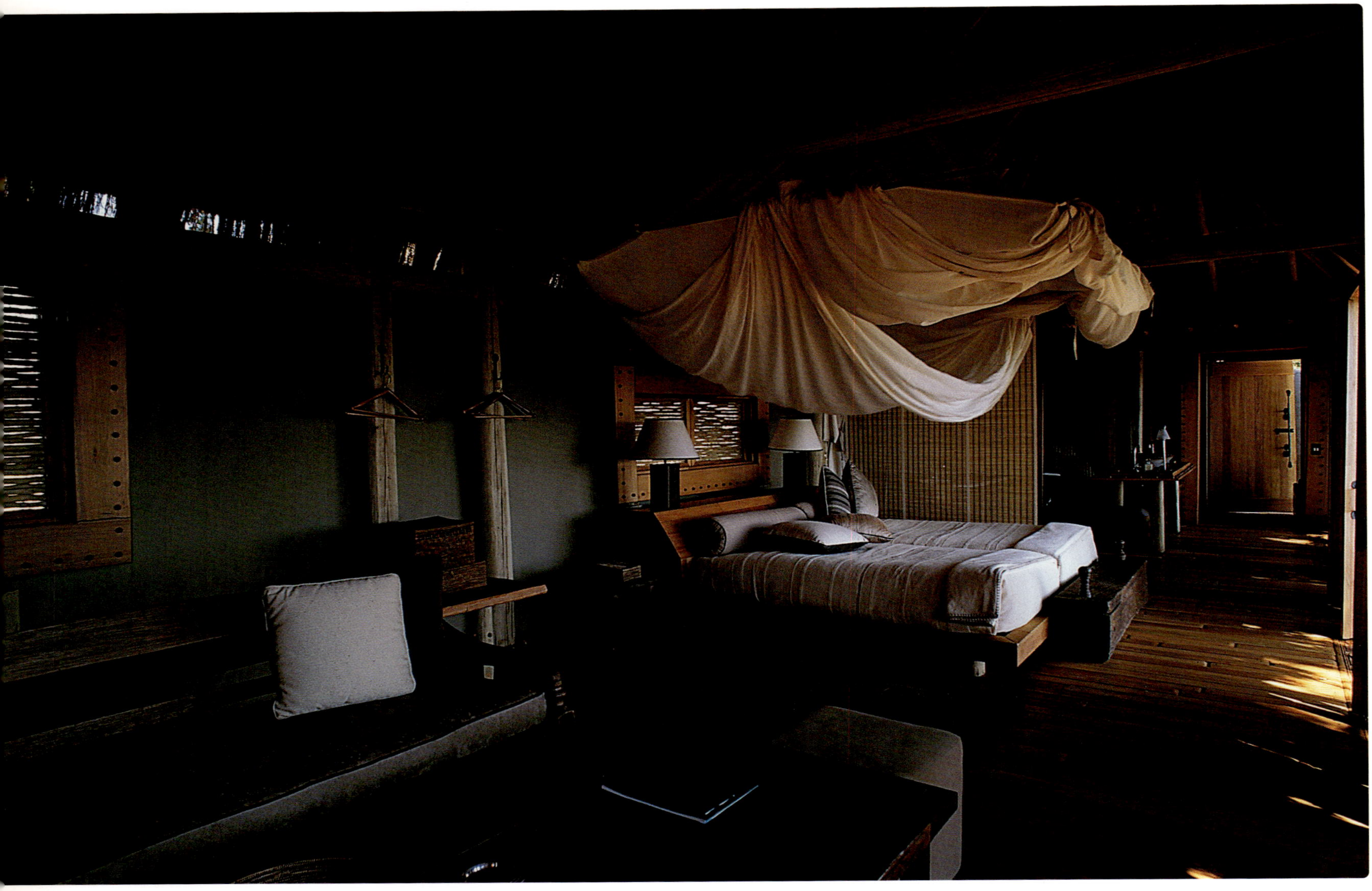

Little by little, the canvas tents of the early game lodges have been replaced by luxurious, air-conditioned cabins. Camps such as Jao, Mombo, and Abu are among the most exclusive in Botswana, catering for a decidedly well-heeled clientele.

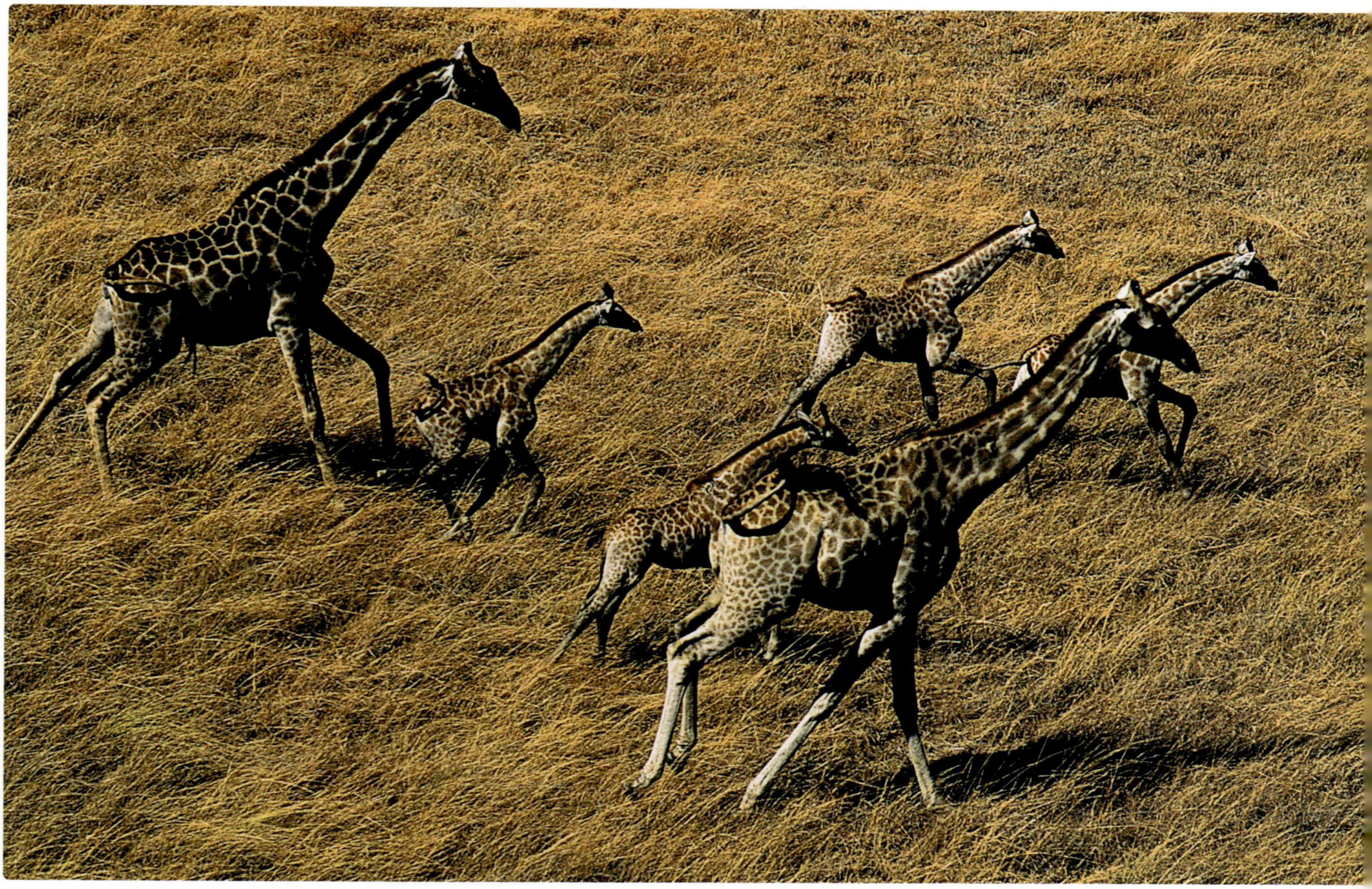

On average giraffes are fifteen feet (five meters) tall and weigh 1,500 pounds (700 kilograms). Their height means they can see danger coming many miles away. Once the risk has been spotted, they stand perfectly still for a while before deciding to canter elegantly away at speeds of up to, and even over, thirty miles per hour.

The lion is truly king of the beasts. He regally waits for his pride of lionesses to bring down their prey before moving in and feasting on the kill. However, if pushed by hunger, he can easily bring down a cob antelope with a single blow of his paw.

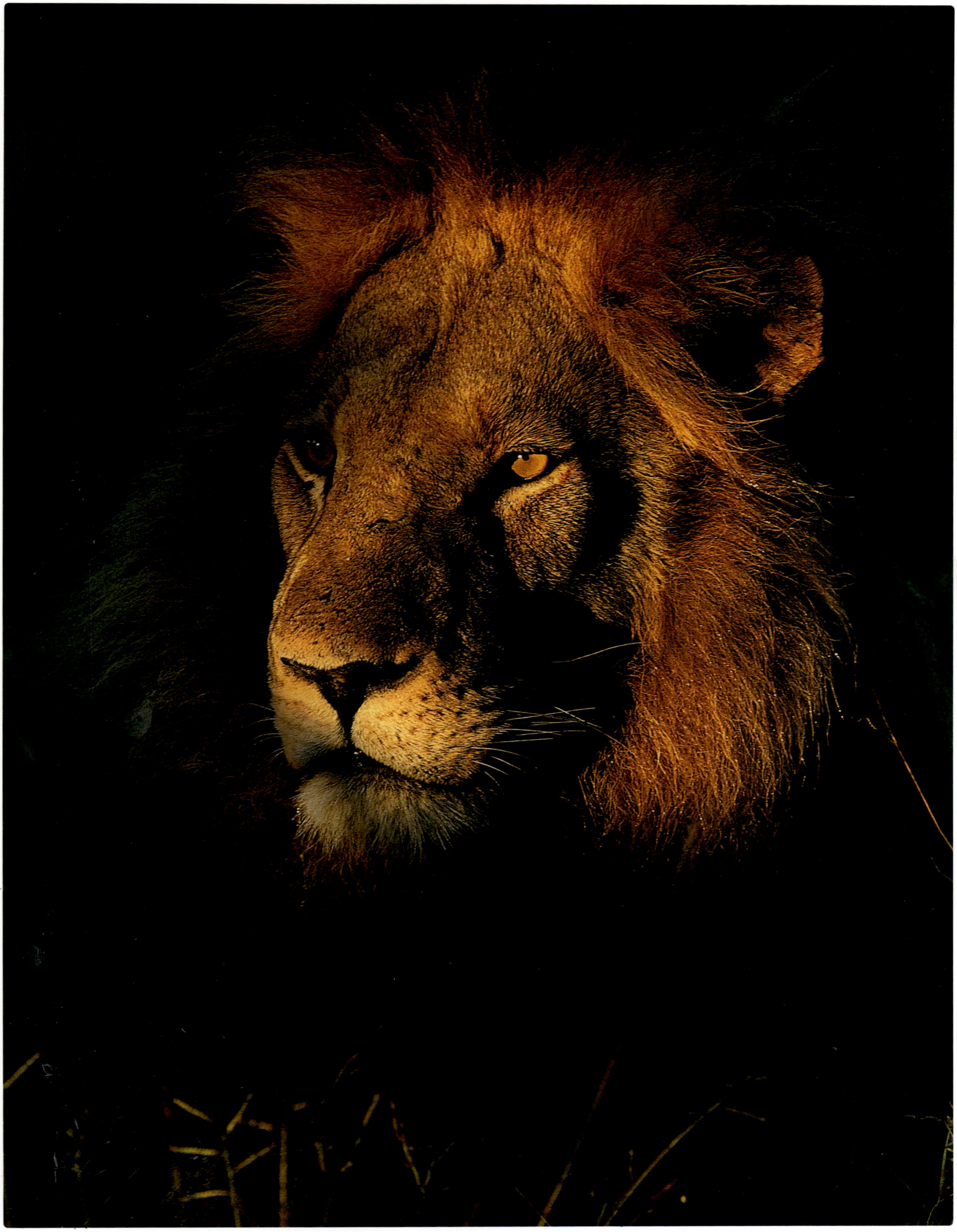

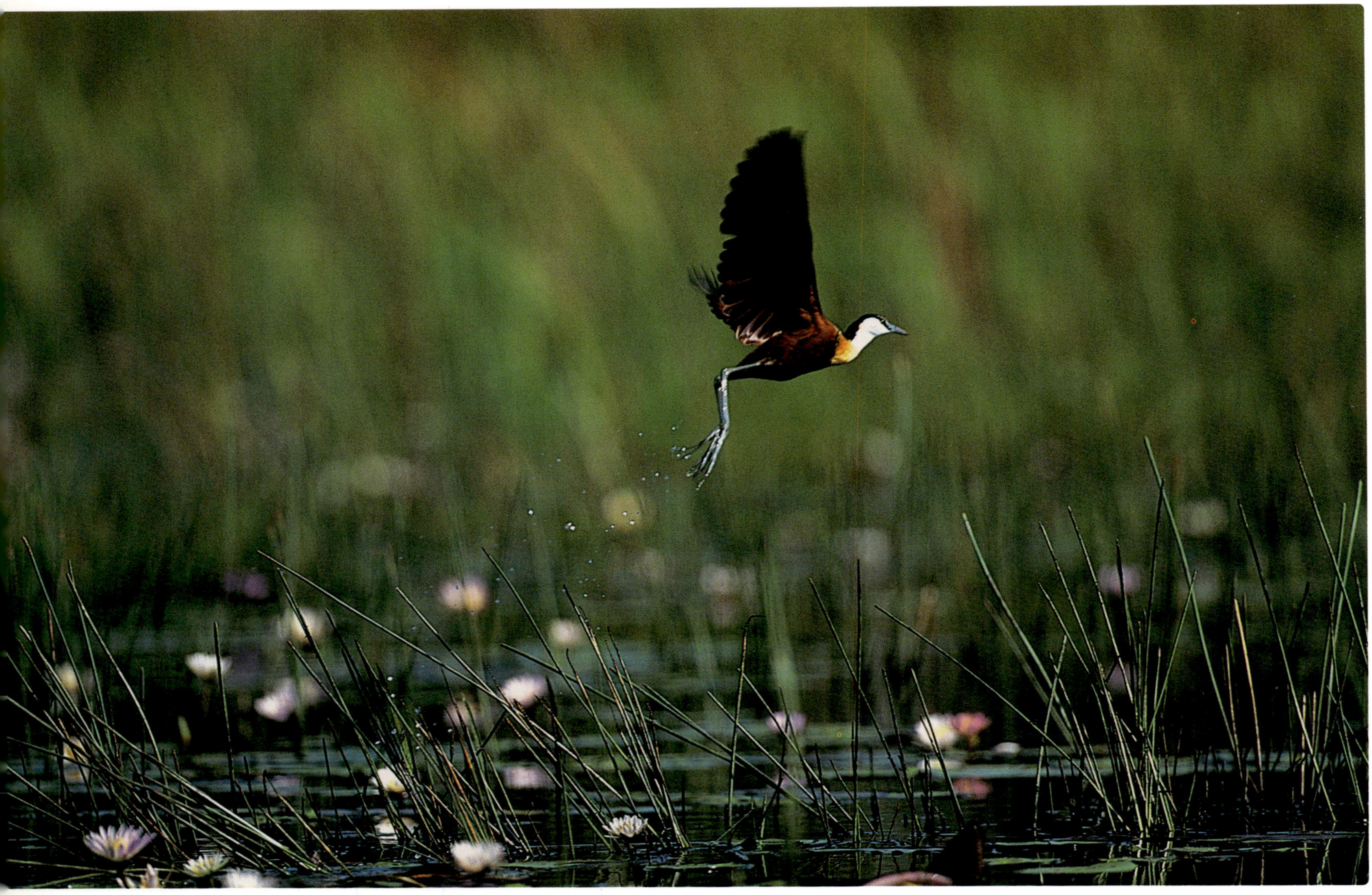

Jacanas are charming, inquisitive, comical birds. They are instantly recognizable thanks to the four outlandishly long toes on each foot that enable them to strut across swathes of lily pads. If disturbed, they will fly off, feet dangling, uttering their distinctive cry of "ik ik ik ik ik."

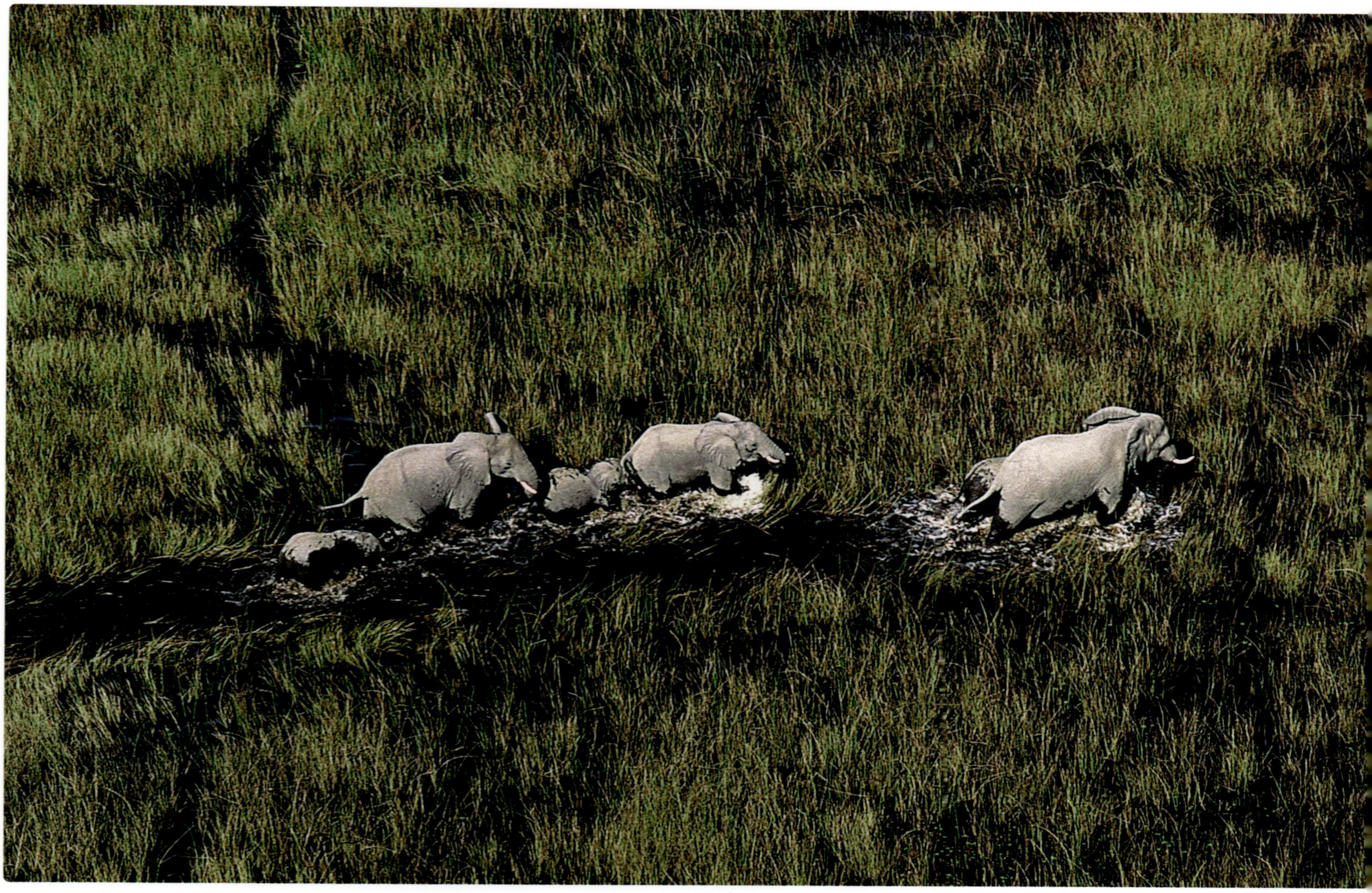

Nowhere else on earth is it possible to see elephants roaming free like in Botswana. Their domain seems unbounded. Yet here, as elsewhere, their kingdom is shrinking day by day as farmland encroaches on the wetlands.

FACING PAGE:

The black egret has developed a rather unusual fishing technique. It folds its wings above its head like a parasol, enticing the fish to seek refuge in the shaded patch of water and nibble on its yellow toes, which look like worms.

FOLLOWING PAGES:

The Okavango delta is a fabulously beautiful landscape of clumps of lush grass, fields of water lilies shot through here and there with the bold colors of water hyacinths, acres of papyrus and ferns tucked in meanders of the river, stretches of crystal-clear water, clusters of phoenix palms and aloes, fertile peat bogs, meadows of flowering grasses, winding rivulets, brackish ponds bordered by shores of black sand, fallen tree trunks covered in emerald moss. The vast area is crisscrossed with countless tracks worn by migrating herds of zebras, antelopes, wildebeest, elephants, buffaloes, and giraffes.

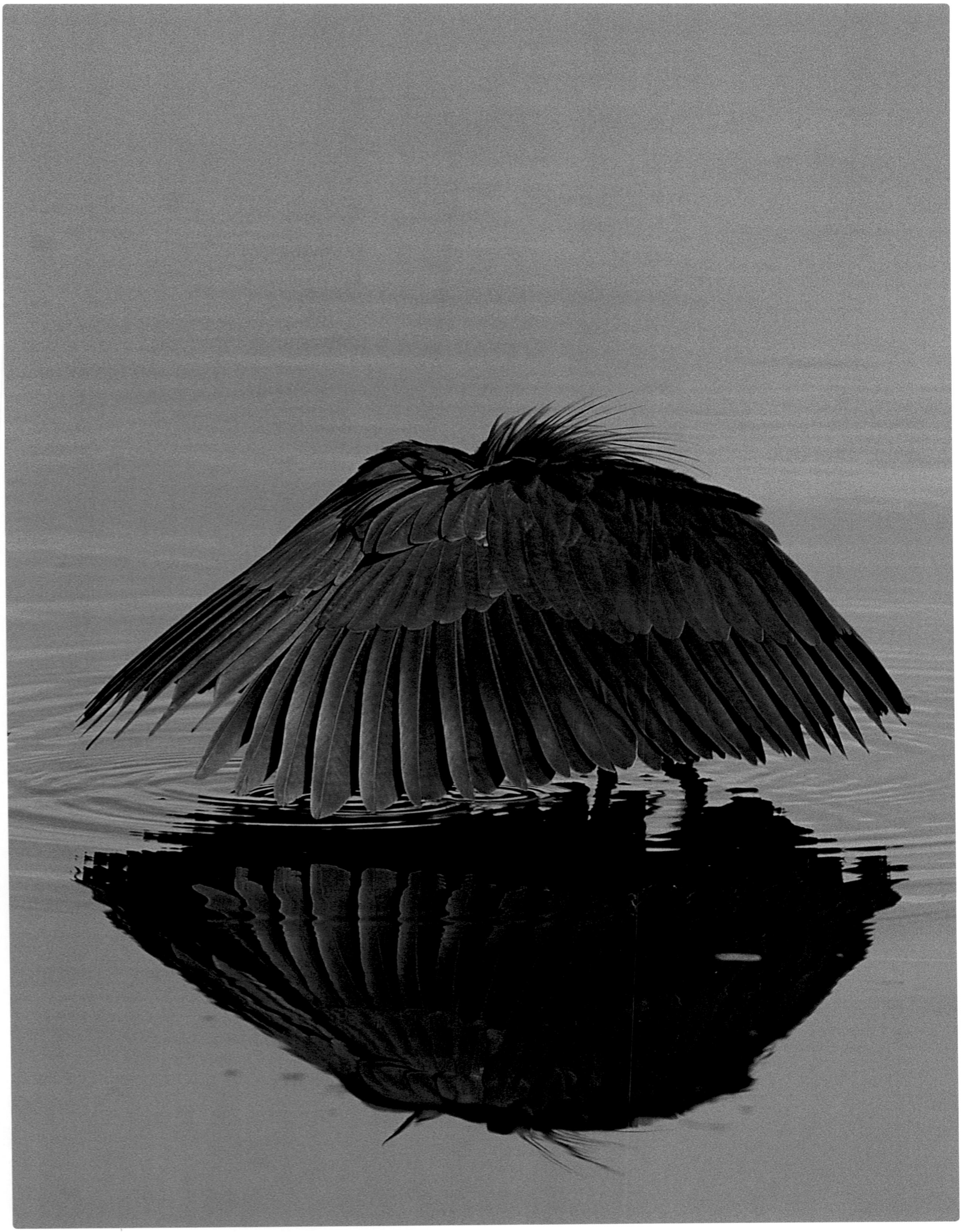

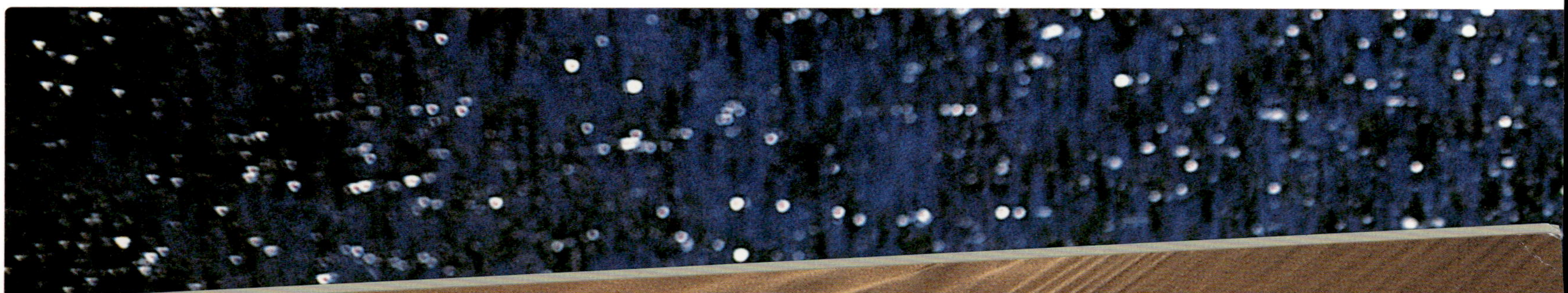
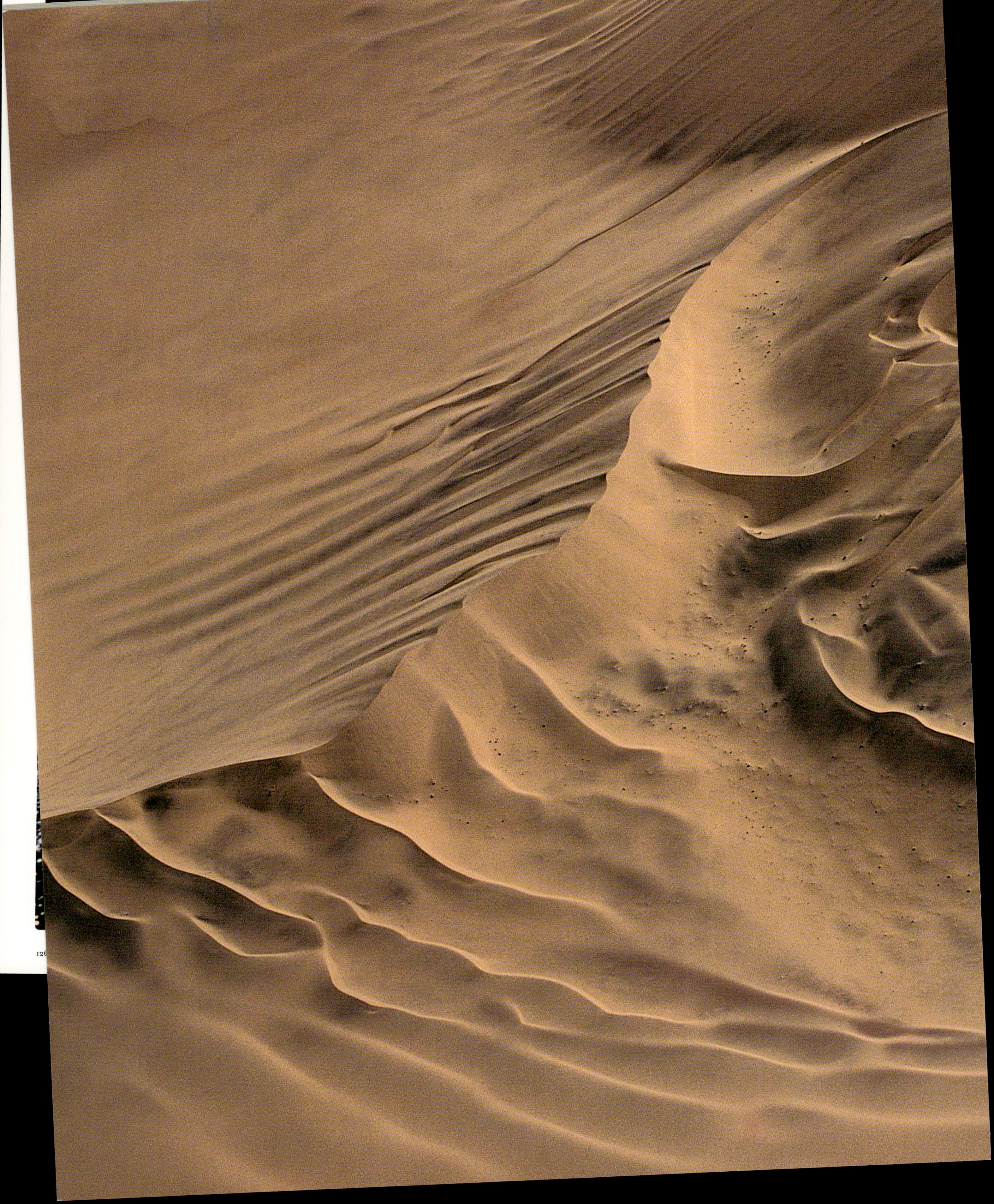

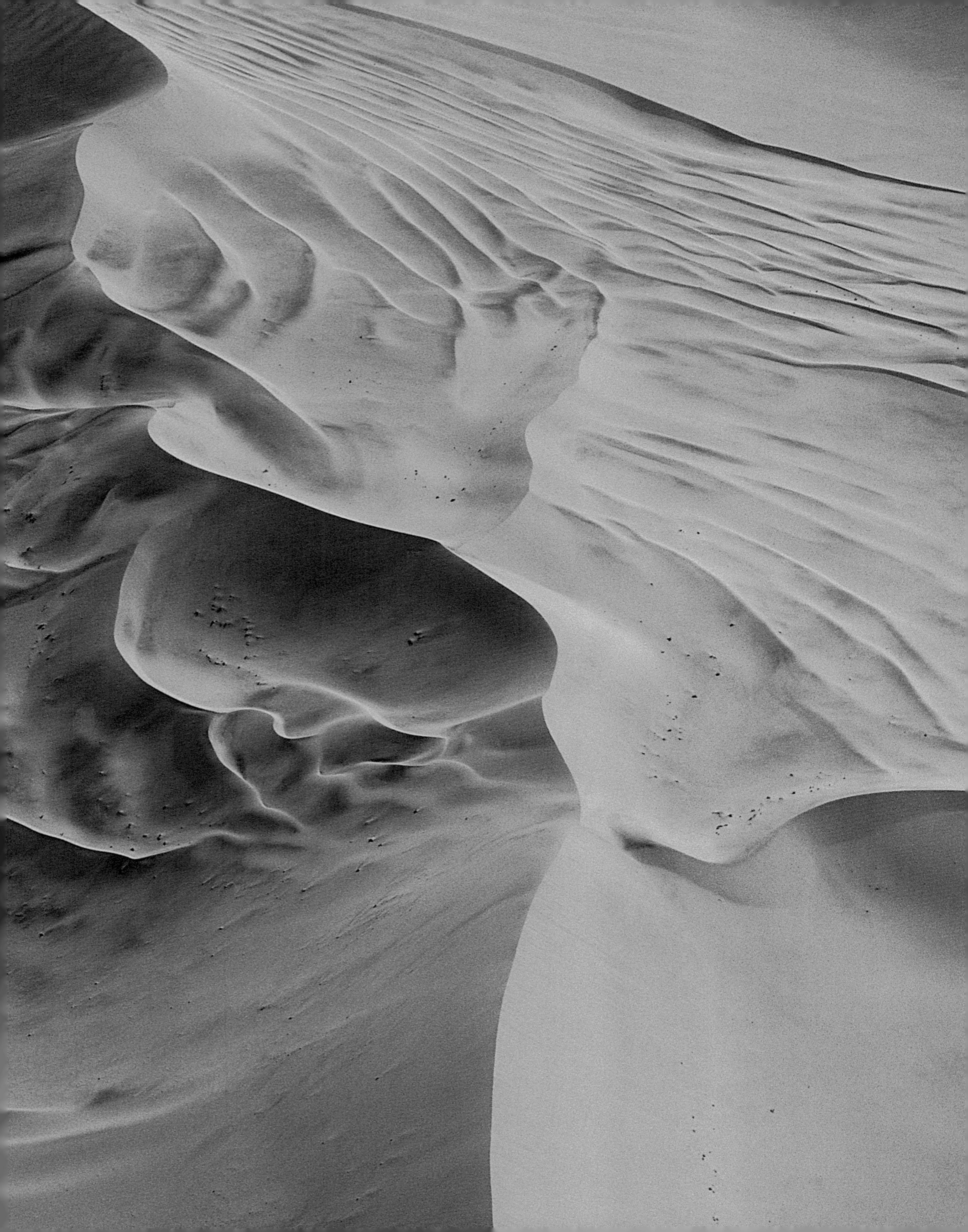

THE WINDS THAT HOWL IN OFF THE ATLANTIC HAVE SCULPTED THE WORLD'S HIGHEST SAND DUNES IN SOSSUSVLEI. AT SUNDOWN, THE HARMONIOUS CURVES OF THE LAND ARE SUFFUSED WITH OCHER AND HONEY TONES WITH OCCASIONAL METALLIC GLINTS.

The scorched, arid, empty landscapes of Namibia appear at first sight unrelentingly hostile. Yet it is the very desolation of the wastes of desert that gives the country its remarkable rugged beauty. The harsh poetry of the bare rocks against the blazing sky gradually weaves a potent spell. The flora and fauna of Namibia are equally remarkable—mammals, reptiles, and insects that have evolved over millennia to become perfectly adapted to desert life, trees with round bellies like pregnant women and a tangle of branches that seem to be holding up the endless expanse of the sky.

Namibia is a vast country of 318,500 square miles (824,790 square kilometers), as large as France and Italy put together, but with a population of just 1,700,000. Here, unspoiled nature reigns supreme. The immense tracts of arid bush, dunes, and rocky outcrops are home to many species of animal, but the very vastness of the country means that you may go many hours without seeing any. Here more than elsewhere, safaris demand time and patience. The most striking feature of the Namibian landscape is the sheer scale of its geography. From the vast, gaping gash of the Fish River Canyon in the south to the endless sweep of the dunes further north, Namibia is a land where the earth is twisted into arabesques alternating with sharp angles. The only way to get an idea of the true scale and the rugged beauty of the country is by plane. As the plane climbs away from the capital, Windhoek, flying over the modern buildings of the university, nature spreads her sumptuous palette of colors below. Naukluft National Park is still an hour's flight away, but the views are already spectacular. The curves of long-dry riverbeds, the shallow dips of former lakes, and the jagged lines where the earth was torn apart by earthquakes countless millennia ago, present a harmonious spectacle of pinks, browns, ochers, and dusty purples that meld into the pitiless blue of the sky. This must be what the earth looked like when it was still a new planet, eons before the first men walked upright on its surface. The Namibian highlands seem to be trying on a series of shapes and colors for size. The land seems to be in a state of flux. On the horizon, I can make out a desert of reds and yellows that seem in places to blend together, in others to clash angrily. Now we are approaching the park, but there is no sign of a fence or perimeter to indicate where it begins and ends.

Naukluft National Park covers an area of 8,800 square miles (23,000 square kilometers) stretching from Swakopmund to Lüderitz. The park is bathed in a faintly eerie, dreamlike atmosphere, haunted by the invisible yet incredibly powerful presence of untold wealth in the form of the diamond lodes that lie beneath the surface. The winds that howl in off the Atlantic have sculpted the world's highest sand dunes in Sossusvlei. At sundown, the harmonious curves of the land are suffused with ocher and honey tones with occasional metallic glints. A few years ago, before the Karos Hotel—now called the Sossusvlei Lodge—began bringing in increasing numbers of tourists, the park rules were less strict and it was possible to stay overnight, watching the bat-eared foxes at play before settling to admire the sunrise from the summit of the highest dunes. Nowadays, the only way to see this magnificent spectacle is from a hot-air balloon. Gliding silently over the dunes at daybreak is an unforgettable experience. But the best way to get really close to the Namibian wildlife, including the oryx, represented on the country's national coat of arms, is on foot. The oryx is a large antelope standing some four feet (1.2 meters) tall, with a gray-beige coat marked with a dark stripe across its flanks, a black-and-white muzzle, large ears, and elegant white markings on its legs that make it look as if it is wearing spats. Its most striking feature, however, is its pair of long, curving horns. The oryx is mainly active at dawn and dusk. It has an extremely slow metabolism, spending most of the day standing perfectly still to conserve energy. Like other desert antelopes, the oryx has evolved a remarkable system for maintaining a constant body temperature, which means it does not lose any of the precious water sucked drop by drop from leaves, fruits, and buried roots in sweat.

The other truly remarkable inhabitant of the Namibian dunes is the desert elephant. These live much further north, in the Skeleton Coast Park, one of the most inhospitable places on earth. The Skeleton Coast is a strip of land along the Atlantic seaboard measuring 310 miles (five hundred kilometers) long and twenty-five miles (forty kilometers) wide. It is an untamed expanse of dunes that are much more recent but also much closer together than those in Naukluft. The zone reaches from the Ugab valley to the Angolan border. The sands of the desert sweep into the cold waters of the Atlantic, and, paradoxically, are often veiled in thick fogs that roll in off the ocean. The Skeleton Coast takes its name from the countless ships that have come to grief off the treacherous coasts. The sands are strewn with rusting hulks,

PRECEDING PAGE:
The Skeleton Coast is a unique, otherworldly place, where the sands, veiled in fog, are swept by the wind into an infinite pattern of curves and peaks to create a swirling harmony of color.

FACING PAGE:
The best way to explore the vast wilderness of Namibia is by air. Many local companies now specialize in air safaris.

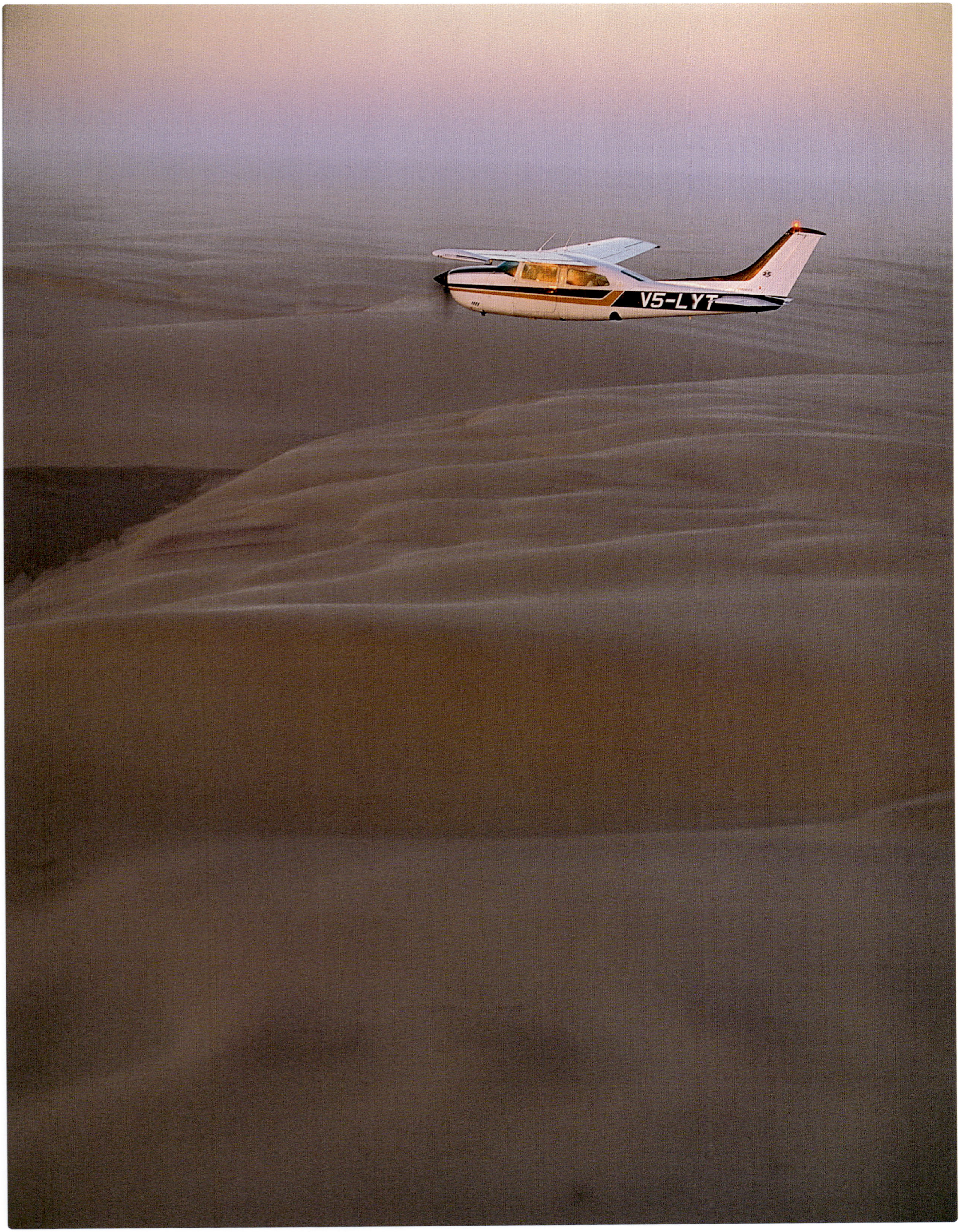
V5-LYT

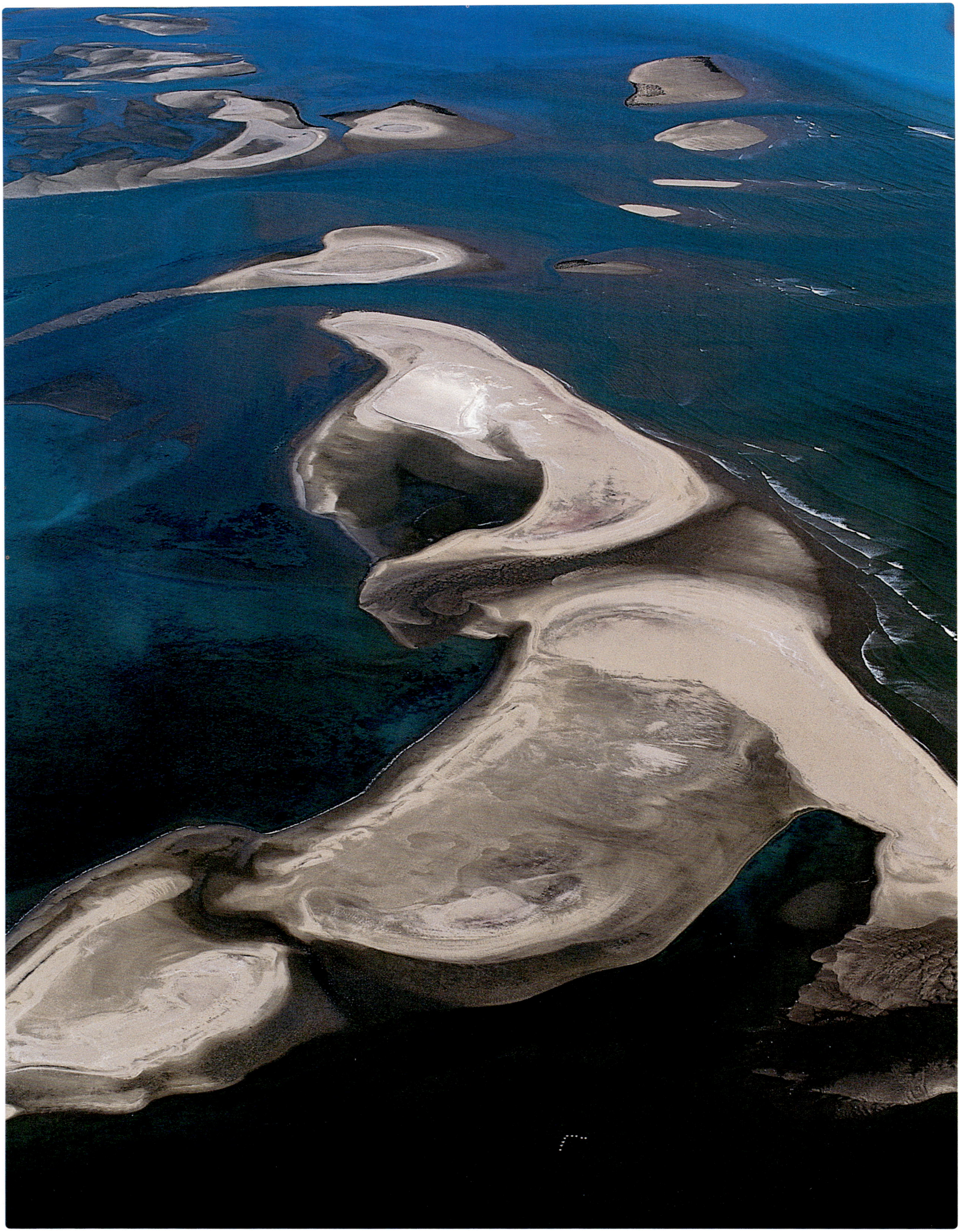

bleached whale skeletons, and piles of driftwood. Some specialist magazines would have you believe that the desert elephants live in these unforgiving surroundings. Actually, they prefer the green valleys of the rivers Hanib, Gotanum, Hanamib, Hoarusib, and Khumib that curve across the park and are also home to giraffes, rhinoceros, springboks, and oryx. Desert elephants are said to have shorter legs and more splayed feet than African elephants, but in fact there is much doubt as to whether the Namibian elephants truly constitute a separate species. The only real difference is the great care the desert elephant takes when feeding from the withered branches of the few desert trees that are its principal source of nourishment. While it is not unknown to encounter elephants in the heart of the dunes, it is a rare occurrence. Elephants generally only venture into the true desert to cross from one valley to another in periods of drought. To be sure of encountering a herd of elephants, the best way is to fly along the river valleys. Louw Schoeman has been organizing air safaris since 1977, and has inspired many other companies to offer the same service. The magnificent, solitary wastelands of the Skeleton Coast now draw visitors from all over the world, although the cost of such an expedition is prohibitive. Accommodation is also scarce in the region, although Wilderness Safaris now have a superb camp of six comfortable and roomy tents in the lands of the Himba tribespeople. This is the best place to start from to visit the seal colonies along the coast—you may see a jackal or two on the prowl for fresh meat—the valleys with their springboks, hyenas, giraffes, and elephants, the temporary villages set up by the nomadic tribes, and the magnificent rock formations sculpted into fantastic shapes by the combined action of wind and sun.

While these parks are the most spectacular in terms of the natural landscapes, the best place to see animals is without a doubt Etosha. Until 1956, Etosha National Park covered nearly 38,610 square miles (100,000 square kilometers). Today, the park is much smaller, but still covers 8,600 square miles (22,270 square kilometers), a quarter of which is the Etosha Pan, a vast, desolate, salt-encrusted plain where you can often see mirages dancing in the sky. Legend has it that the region was home to a tribe that was attacked by pitiless enemies who killed every man and child. One of the surviving women wept a lake of tears, which then evaporated, leaving a desert of salt known locally as the lake of the weeping mother. More prosaically, the zone is also known as the great white place—the literal translation of Etosha. The mysterious poetry of the landscape is due to a change in the course of the waters of the Kunene River when the land was pushed upwards, forcing the river further west. The Etosha Lookout gives a particularly clear idea of the effect this geological change had on the local environment. From the lookout, you might see the elegant silhouette of an oryx or an elephant wandering across the bleached white surface of the pan. The best way to be sure of seeing animals is to wait for a few hours by one of the watering holes, where many different species come to slake their thirst. At the watering holes, you will see species side by side that normally live quite separately. There is an established hierarchy of species for drinking at the watering holes, with smaller species making way for larger ones. Warthogs, impalas, kudus, oryx, elands, zebras, cobs, giraffes, rhinoceroses, and elephants come to drink, watched by lions too tired and hot to hunt. Not a breath of wind stirs the air and the temperature is well over 104°F (40°C) during the day. The big cats spend most of the daylight hours asleep. They only begin to hunt at dusk, when tourists leave the watering holes to return to their lodges. It is strictly forbidden to remain after dark. However, a number of lodges such as Halali, Namutoni, and Okaukuejo are located in the heart of the park, near the watering holes. The most interesting private game reserve in the vicinity is Ongava, measuring just 115 square miles (three hundred square kilometers), but with a wealth of wildlife including lions and rhinos. The only species not found here is the elephant. The owners tried to introduce a few, but they quickly found their way back to their old stamping ground in the neighboring park.

THE MYSTERIOUS POETRY OF THE LANDSCAPE IS DUE TO A CHANGE IN THE COURSE OF THE WATERS OF THE KUNENE RIVER WHEN THE LAND WAS PUSHED UPWARDS, FORCING THE RIVER FURTHER WEST. THE ETOSHA LOOKOUT GIVES A PARTICULARLY CLEAR IDEA OF THE EFFECT THIS GEOLOGICAL CHANGE HAD ON THE LOCAL ENVIRONMENT. FROM THE LOOKOUT, YOU MIGHT SEE THE ELEGANT SILHOUETTE OF AN ORYX OR AN ELEPHANT WANDERING ACROSS THE BLEACHED WHITE SURFACE OF THE PAN.

However huge and spectacular are Namibia's many parks, none can compare with the ones in the Caprivi Strip. The landscape here is quite different from the rest of the country. The thin strip of land, 310 miles (five hundred kilometers) in length and varying between twenty and sixty-three miles (thirty-two and a hundred kilometers) wide, seems to have been added

FACING PAGE:
Pelican Point, jutting out to the south of Walvis Bay, is a spit of sand formed by the sediment churned up by the Kuiseb River. It forms a natural barrier that is home to thousands of seagulls, cormorants, pelicans, and flamingos.

THE IMMENSE, UNTAMED EXPANSES OF NAMIBIA ARE A UNIQUELY RICH WILDERNESS, MAKING THE COUNTRY ONE OF THE MOST ENCHANTING AND FASCINATING IN THE WHOLE OF AFRICA.

on as an afterthought. In fact, historically speaking, this is almost the case. The strip resembles an arrowhead pointing towards the Victoria Falls, bordered by Angola and Zambia on the northern side and Botswana to the south. Originally, this strip of land was part of the British protectorate of Bechuanaland, now Botswana. It was handed over to the Germans when the colonies were carved up at the Berlin Conference in July 1890, then brought back under British control as part of Bechuanaland at the start of the Second World War. Finally, it was attached to Namibia. Today, the zone is the scene of sporadic outbreaks of fighting between the army and rebel troops. It is a wild, lawless area. While the situation has calmed down a great deal since the beginning of a fragile peace in Angola, the Caprivi Strip remains a risky place because of the appalling poverty of the displaced Angolans who have been known to attack and rob tourists. But it is a haven of outstanding natural beauty with excellent hotels, and the region is beginning to attract more and more tourists. Maybe this will help it overcome its troubled history. The Impalila Lodge, twenty minutes by boat from Chobe National Park, is spectacularly lovely. Its wooden chalets are built on stilts overlooking the lush greenery by the river. The air is full of birdsong and the roaring of the waters as they pour over Mombova rapids on the Zambezi River. This is the very furthest tip of the Caprivi Strip, far from the trouble spots further west, practically at the point where Namibia, Zambia, Botswana, and Zimbabwe meet. The equally delightful Suswe Lodge is forty minutes by plane from Kasane. The six huts, each with their own pool, are in the heart of the swamplands of the Bwabwata Reserve, famed for its elephants, lechwes, hippopotamuses, and leopards. Lianshulu Lodge is much better known. It is the ideal base for exploring Mudumu National Park and discovering the Lizauli people who live on the fringes of the park and who play an important role in developing the tourist trade and in local conservation, vital for their future survival as a tribe. Their participation represents a considerable benefit for the tour organizers while at the same time allowing the villagers to earn a much better living than they ever could with the back-breaking labor of their traditional fishing and farming.

The economic potential represented by the wealth of Namibian wildlife has not escaped the notice of many Afrikaner farmers. More and more are deciding to convert their vast farmlands into animal reserves, making the best of the fact that they can never hope to keep out all the baboons, mongoose, kudus, springboks, oryx, hyenas, giraffes, zebras, elephants, rhinos, caracals, cheetahs, and leopards that freely cross over from the official game reserves into private farmlands. Some landowners have even decided that simply fencing in their land to keep in the wild animals is not enough. A market has sprung up in South Africa selling wild animals to these would-be rangers. In the worst cases, rhinos, lions, and leopards are kept in entirely unsuitable conditions to attract tourists who, for the most part, do not know any better. However, foreign investors have recognized the damage such unscrupulous activities are doing to Namibia's reputation as a tourist destination and such practices should be stamped out in the future.

Based at the Okonjima guest farm, founded by Wayne and Lise Hanssen in 1990, the Africat Foundation is a non-governmental organization dedicated to protecting Africa's big cats. It focuses most of its efforts on leopards and cheetahs, which are still relatively common in Namibia, although the demands of the European fur trade in the 1960s and 1970s decimated the two species. While the fur trade is now heavily regulated, the big cats are still under attack by the region's farmers, who do not hesitate to shoot animals perceived to be threatening their livestock, despite the fact that research by the foundation indicates that such uncontrolled culling actually does more harm than good. When a dominant male is killed, for example, a number of young males move into the territory and attacks on livestock increase as a result. The example of the Hanssens has been taken up by Tommy and Uwe Hoth, who have also set up their own wildlife reserve, not far from Okonjima, on the southeastern fringes of Etosha National Park. They aim to protect the environment by encouraging sustainable tourism and hope to succeed in increasing the lion population, now estimated at just 350 individuals—a drop of fifty percent in just twenty-five years. The biggest problem is that the lions often crawl under the electric fences where warthogs have burrowed a passage, only to be shot by the owner of the neighboring land who fears for the safety of his livestock.

The immense, untamed expanses of Namibia are a uniquely rich wilderness, making the country one of the most enchanting and fascinating in the whole of Africa.

FACING PAGE:
The air is so dry in the Sandwich Harbor region that water evaporates extremely quickly, making the waters of the bay very saline. Tiny marine crustaceans proliferate, providing easy pickings for the wading birds.

FOLLOWING PAGES:
Desiccated, scorched, and bleached by the sun, the Namib Rand is a majestic yet austere landscape that is best seen from a hot-air balloon, particularly at daybreak, just as the first rays of the morning begin to caress the ground.

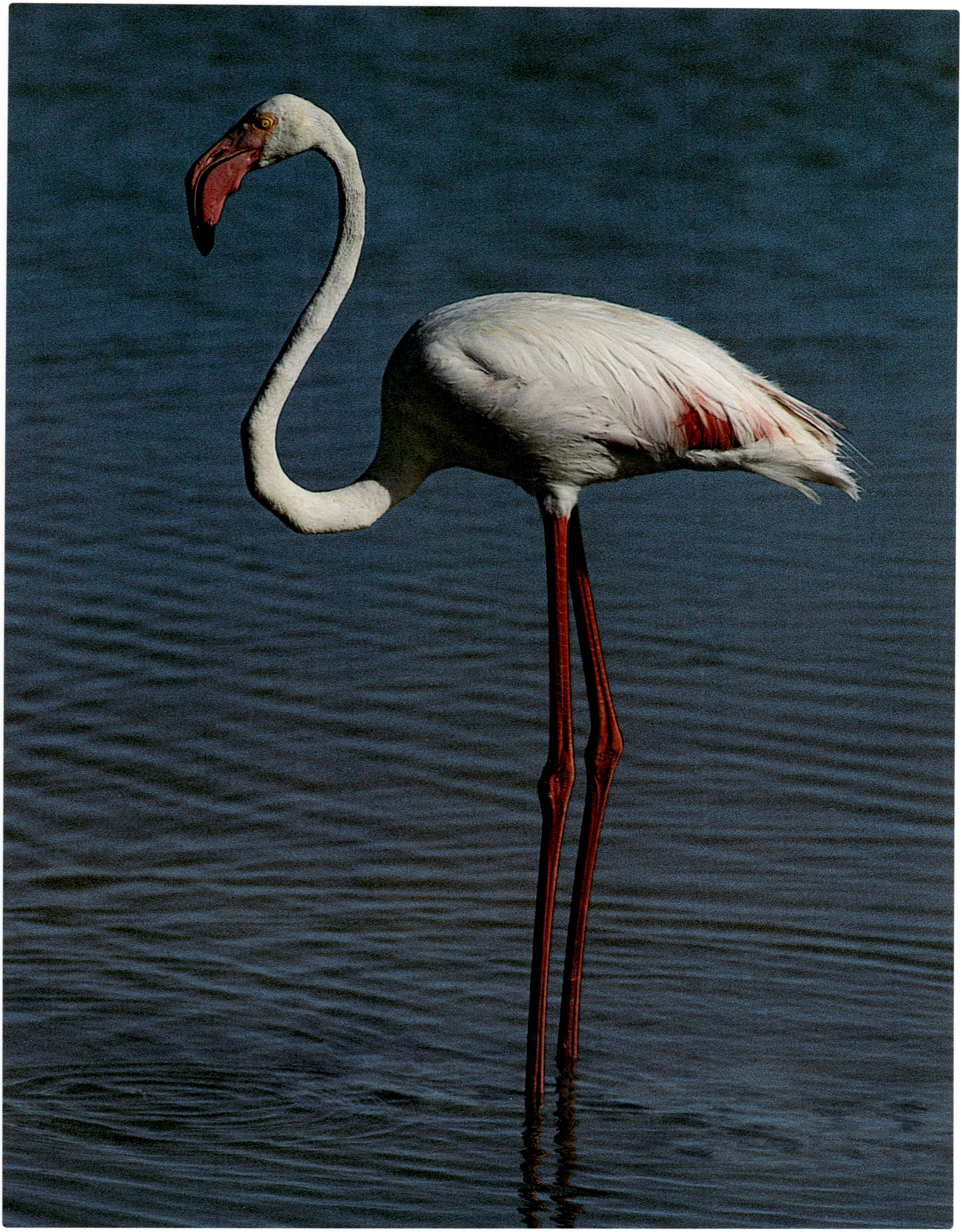

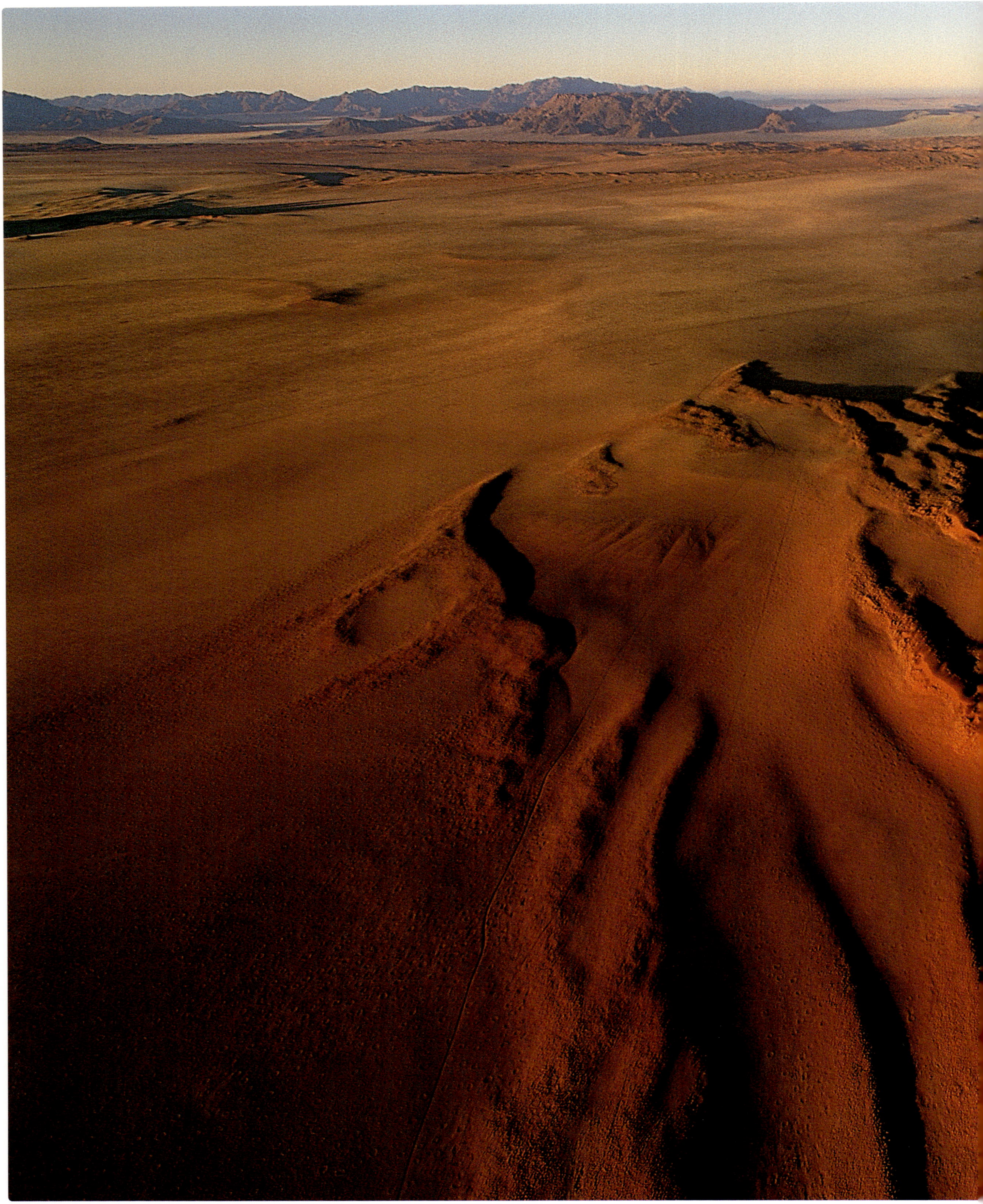

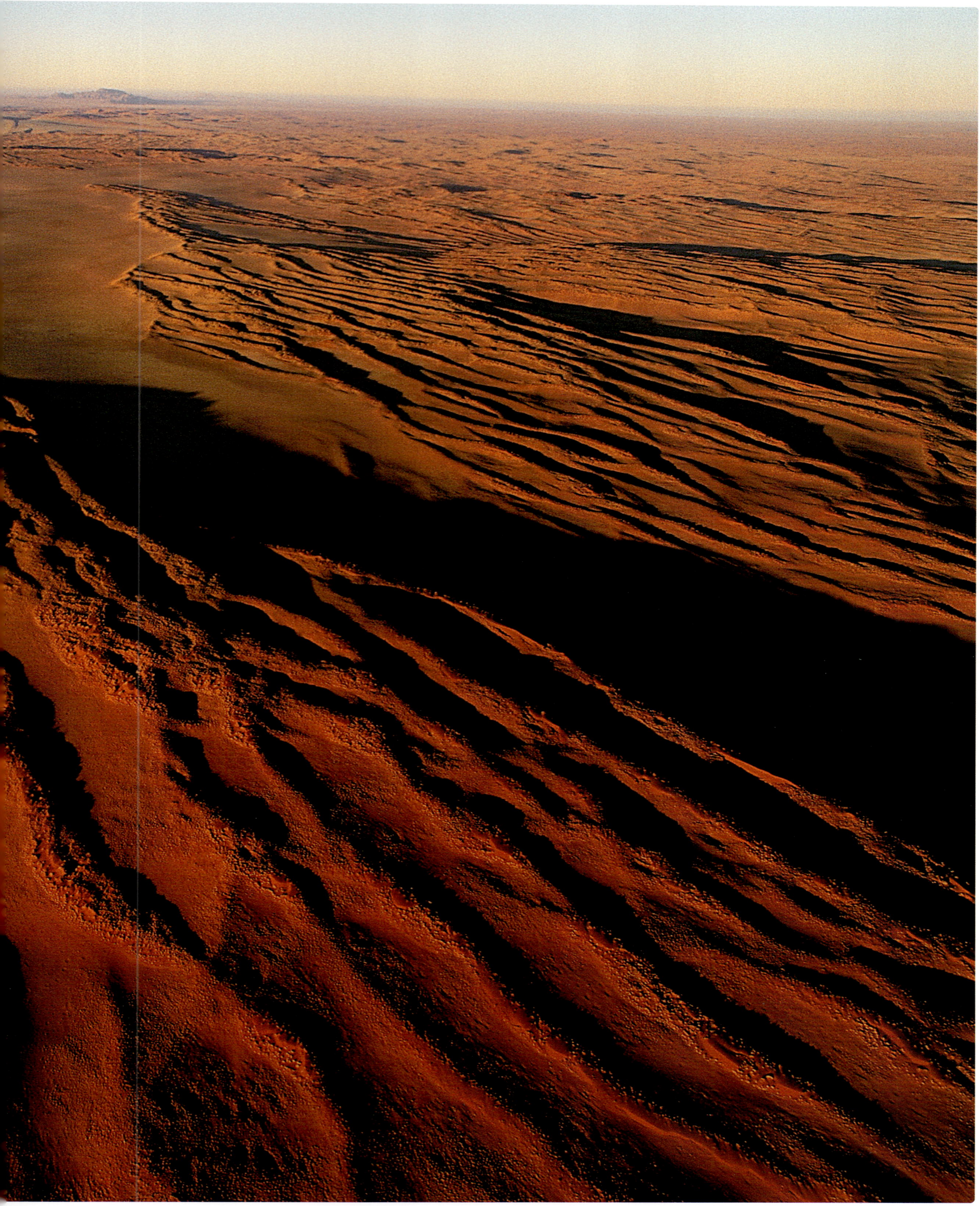

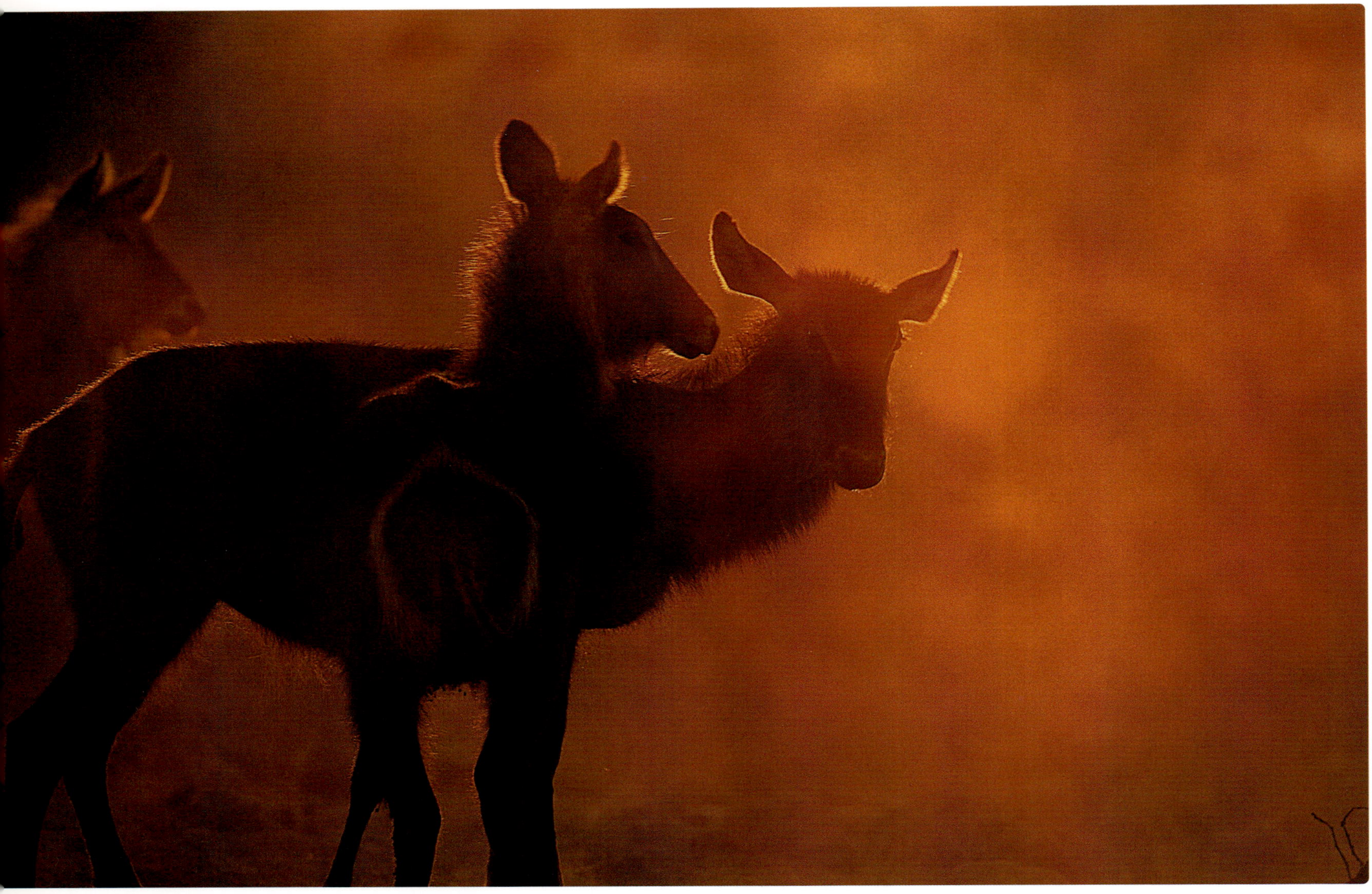

Contrary to what its name suggests, the waterbuck does not spend all of its time in the water, although it will seek refuge there in case of danger. It is more commonly found in undergrowth, as here in Ongava. There are three game lodges, including Ongava Tented Camp, in the Ongava reserve. They are excellent for animal-watching and for enjoying magnificent sunsets in superbly tranquil surroundings.

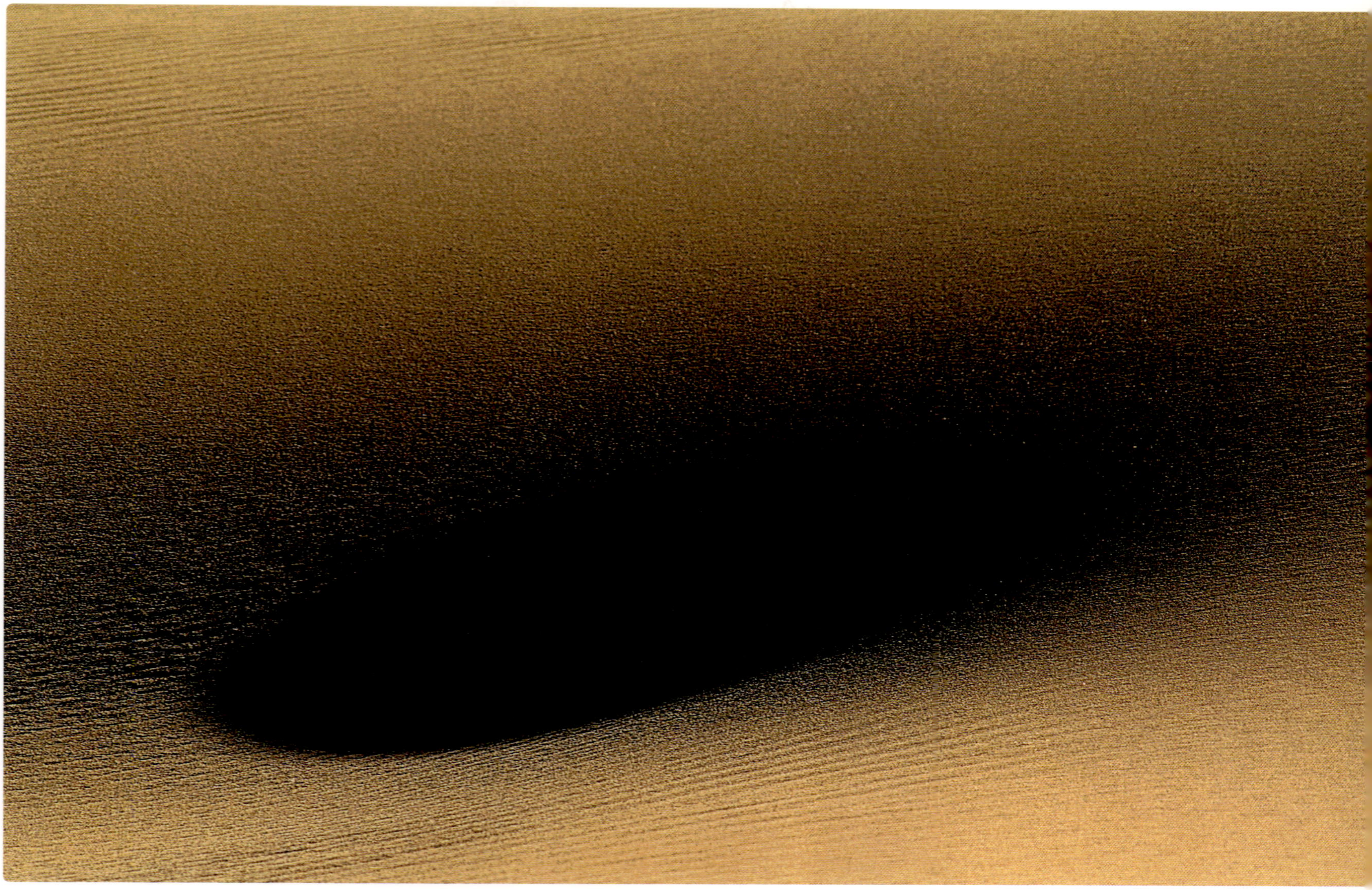

The sands of the Namib Eand have a harsh and savage beauty all their own. This is the oldest desert on the planet. It is a strangely troubling place—a sort of gateway to a lost paradise.

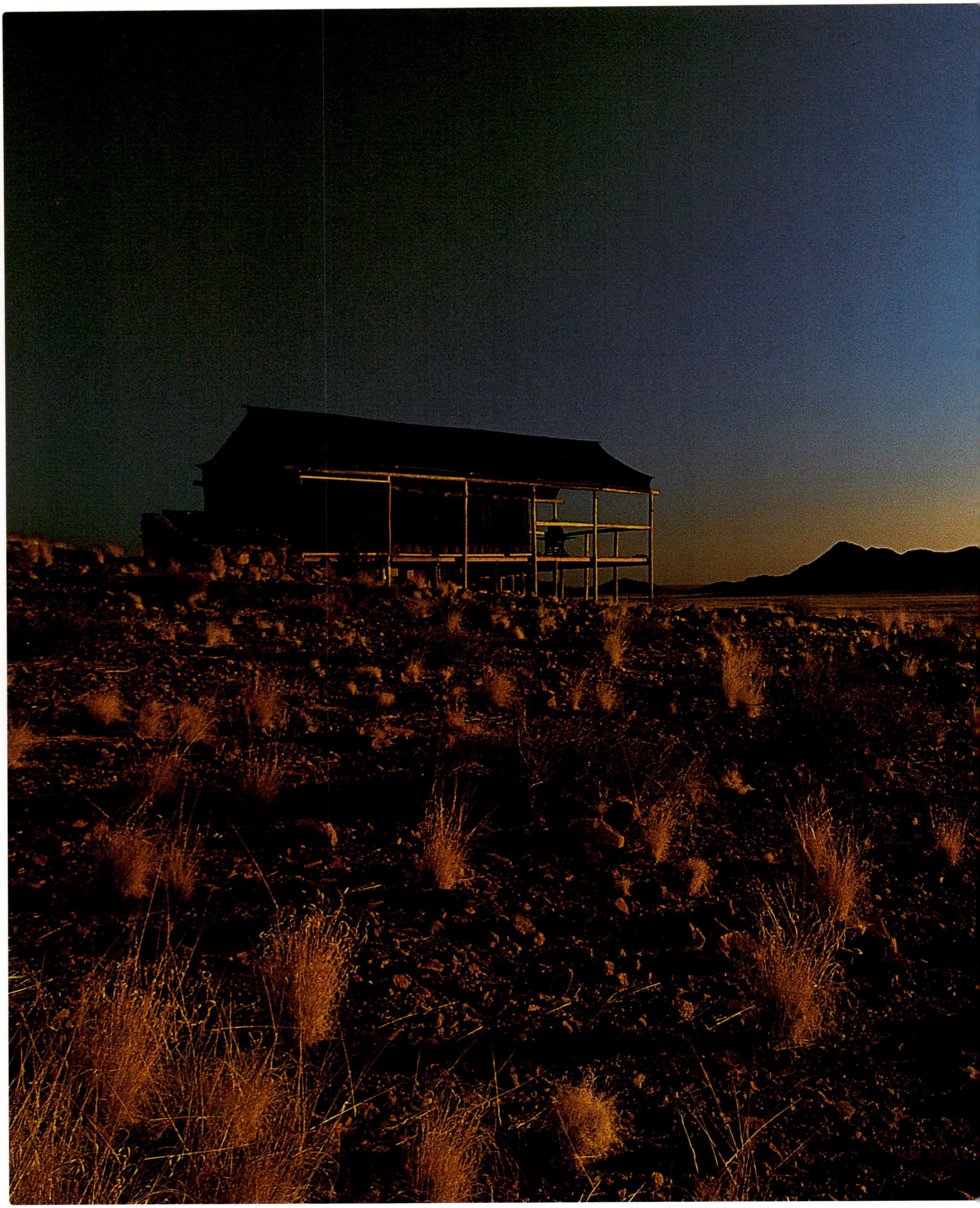

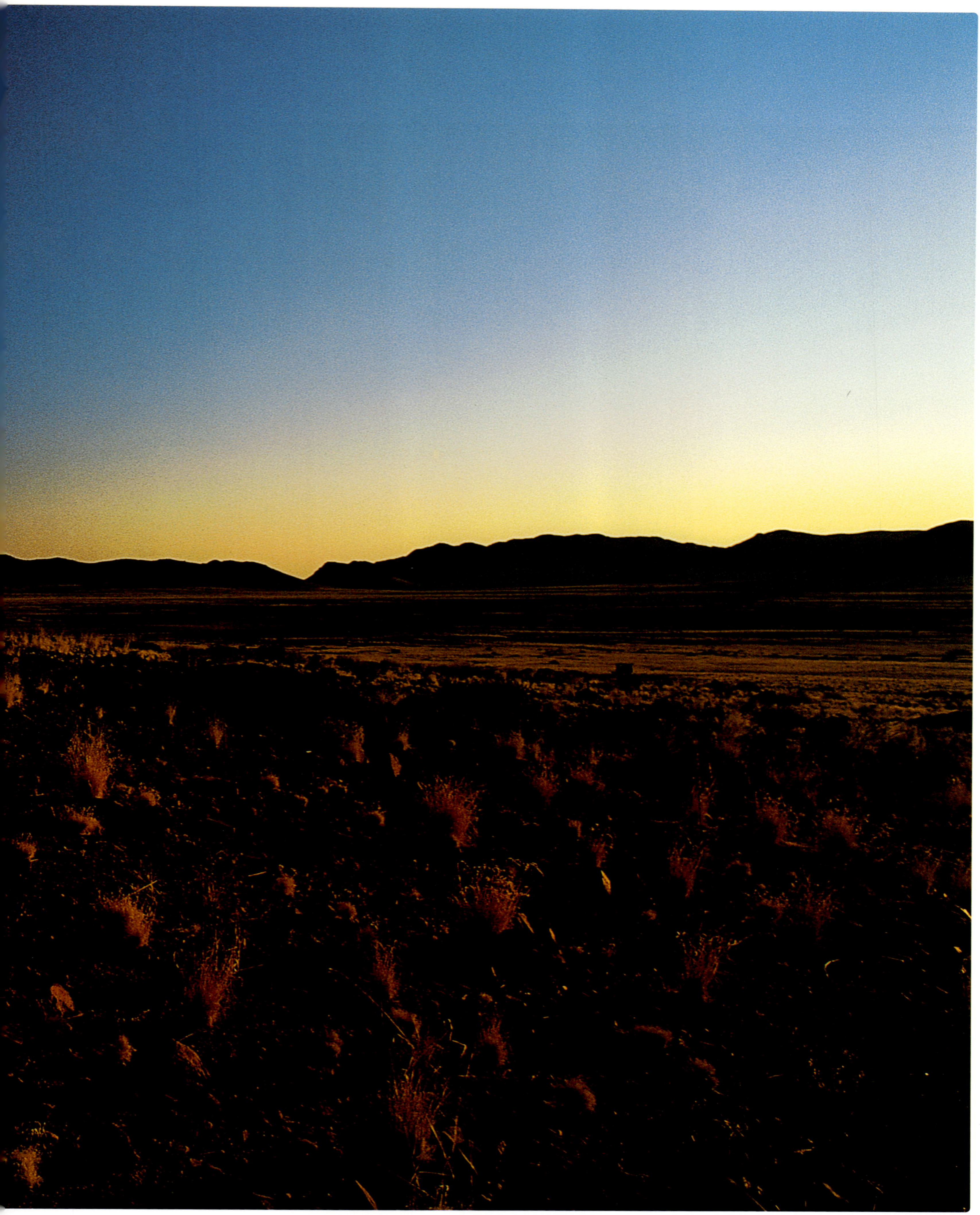

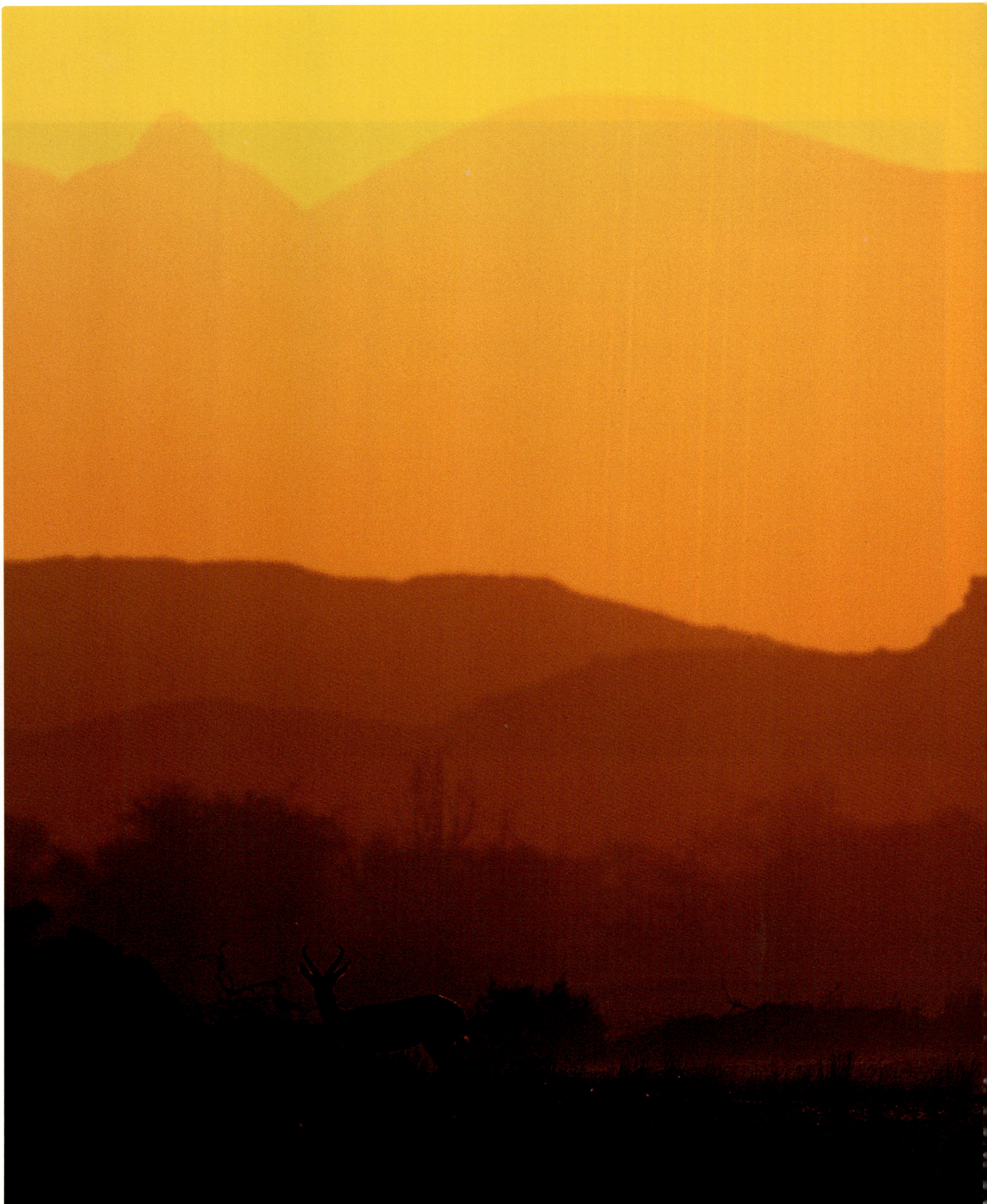

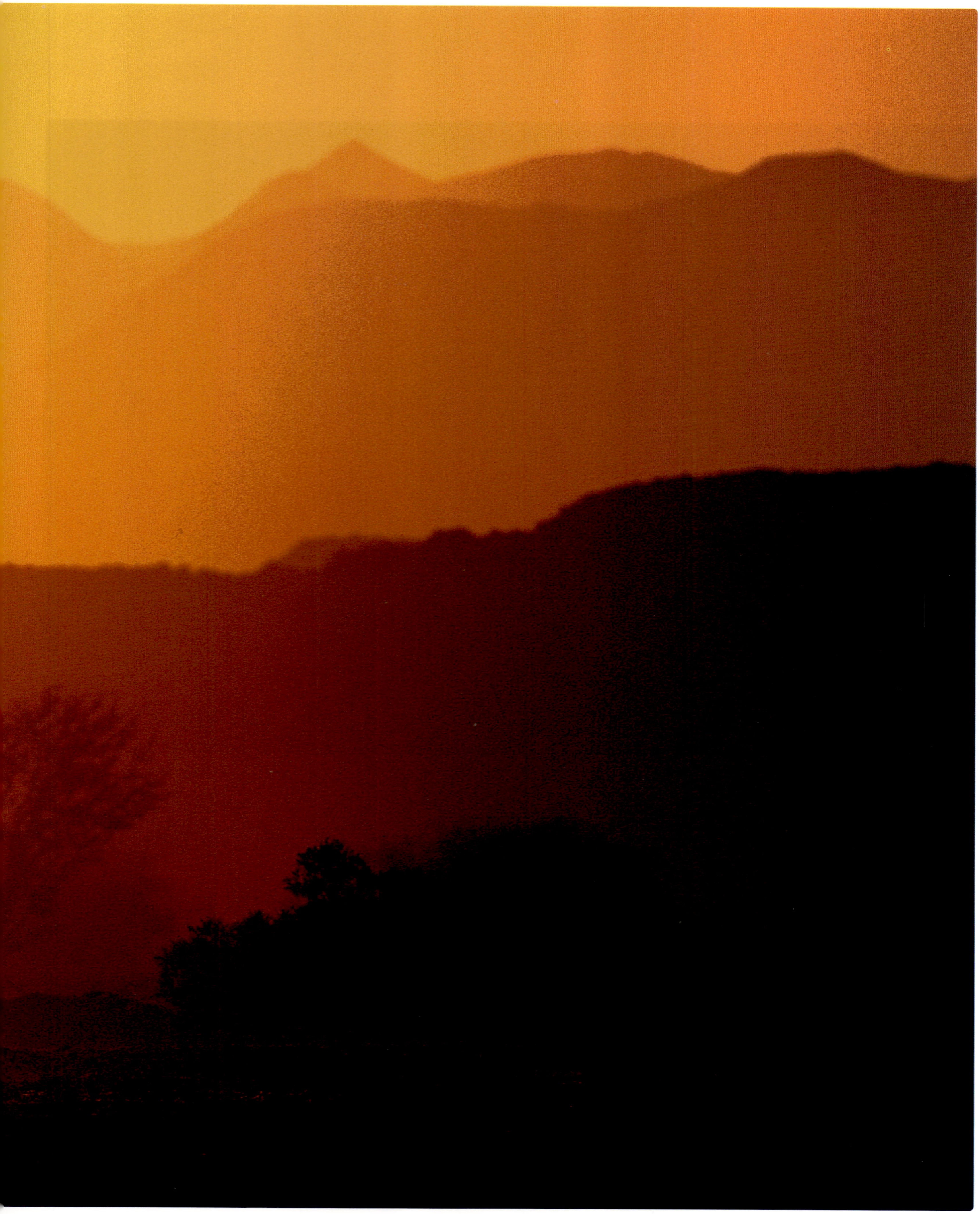

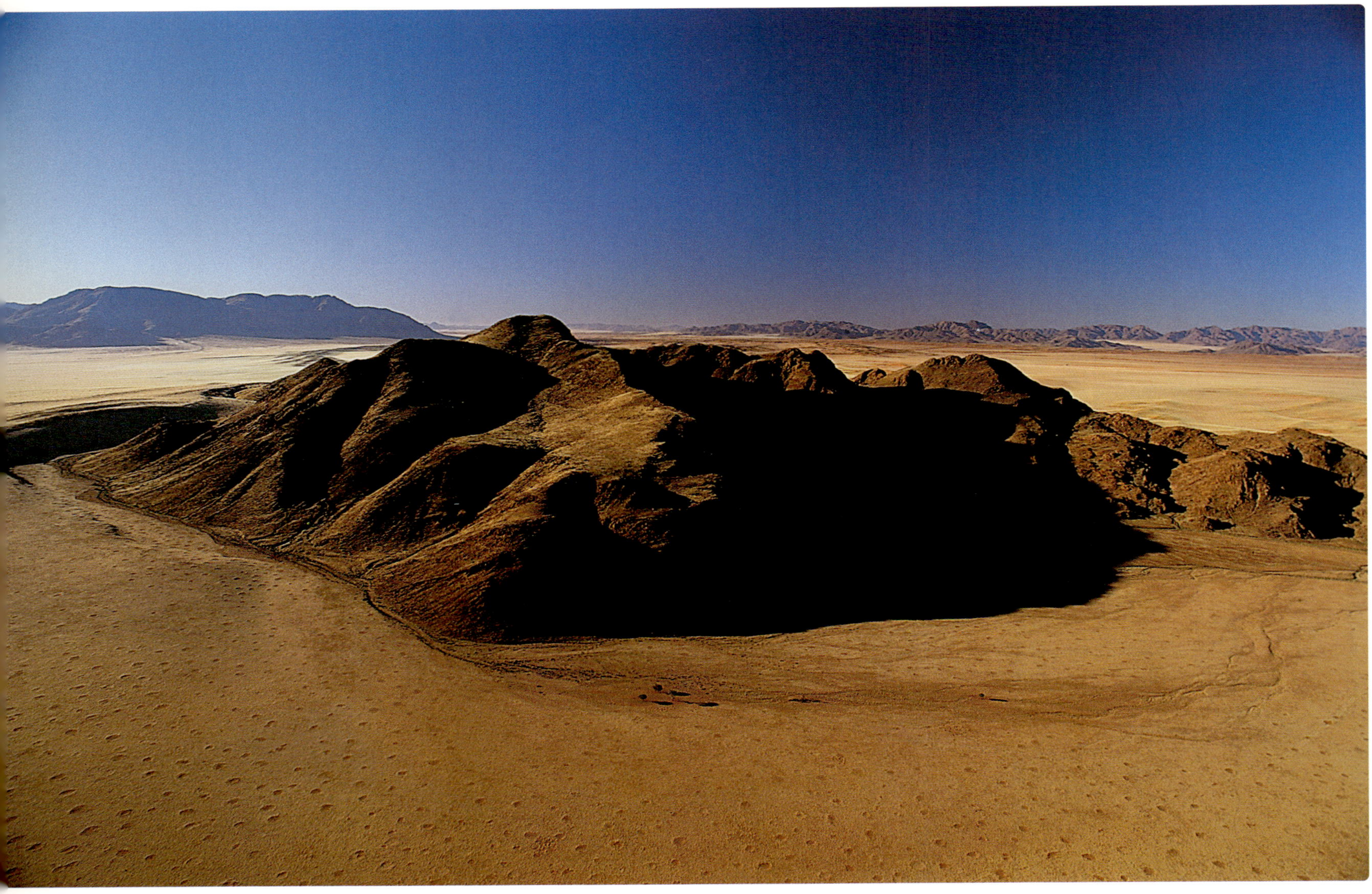

ABOVE:
Mwisho is like something out of a painting by Salvador Dalí, with strange shapes draped across the naked desert sands. I took this photograph during a balloon trip with Eric Hessemans.

FACING PAGE:
Namibian trees dig their roots into the bare sand and rock. In Etosha, west of Okaukuejo, the forest of moringa trees is said to be haunted.

FOLLOWING PAGES:
Fairy rings like these, known locally as *heuveltjies*, are found both in the Namib Rand and in the north of the country. Many theories have been put forward to explain their formation, but none have so far managed to convince the scientific community.

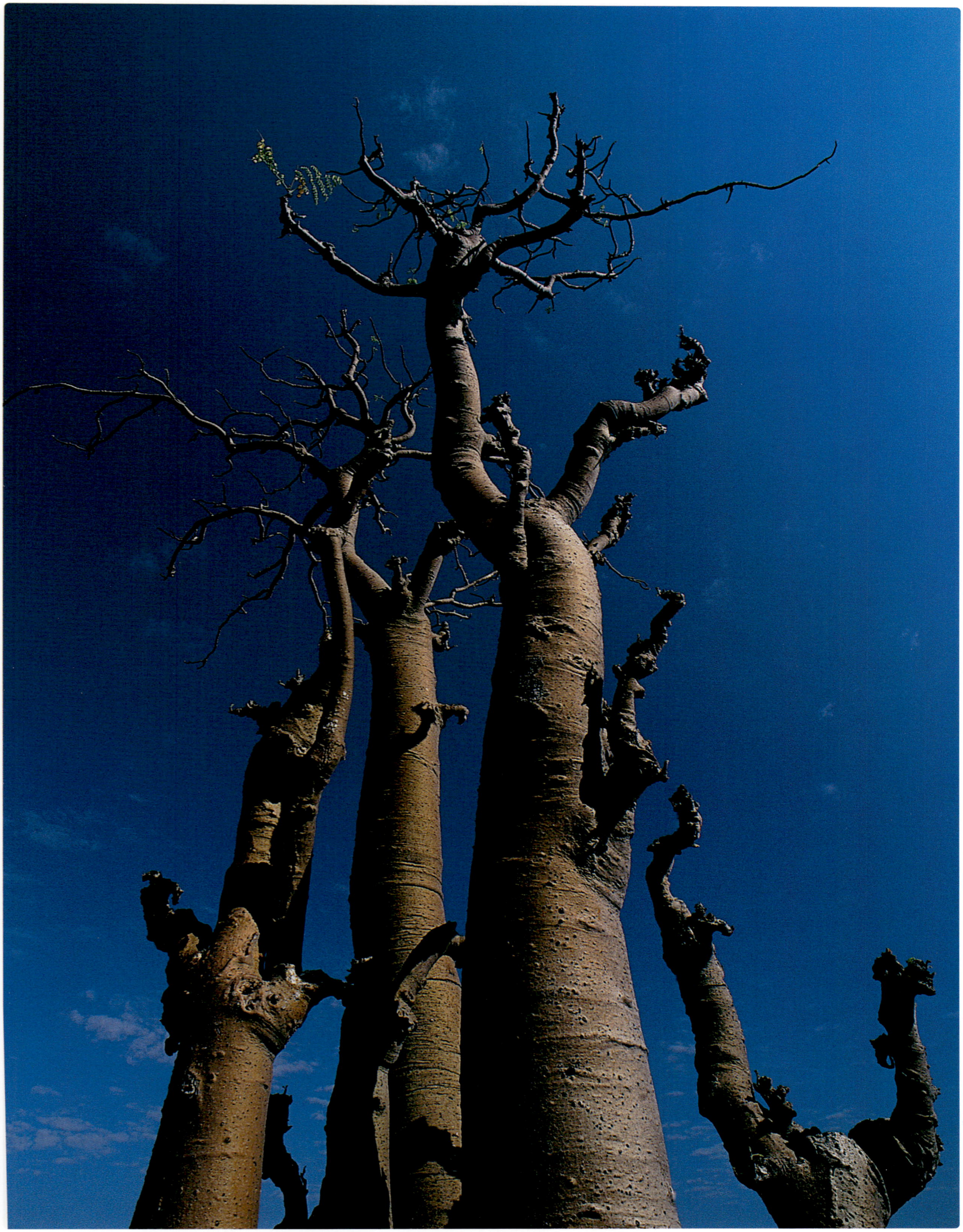

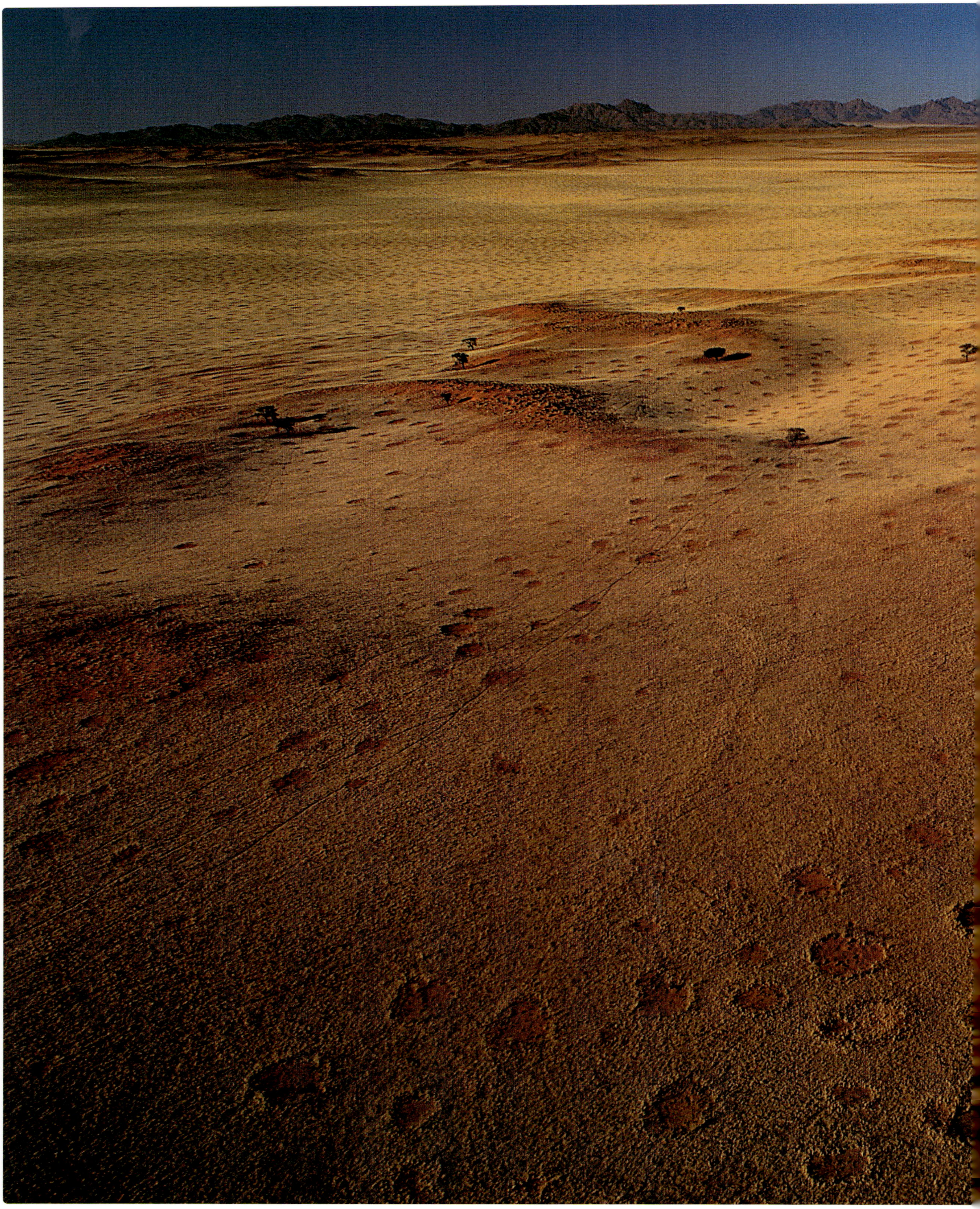

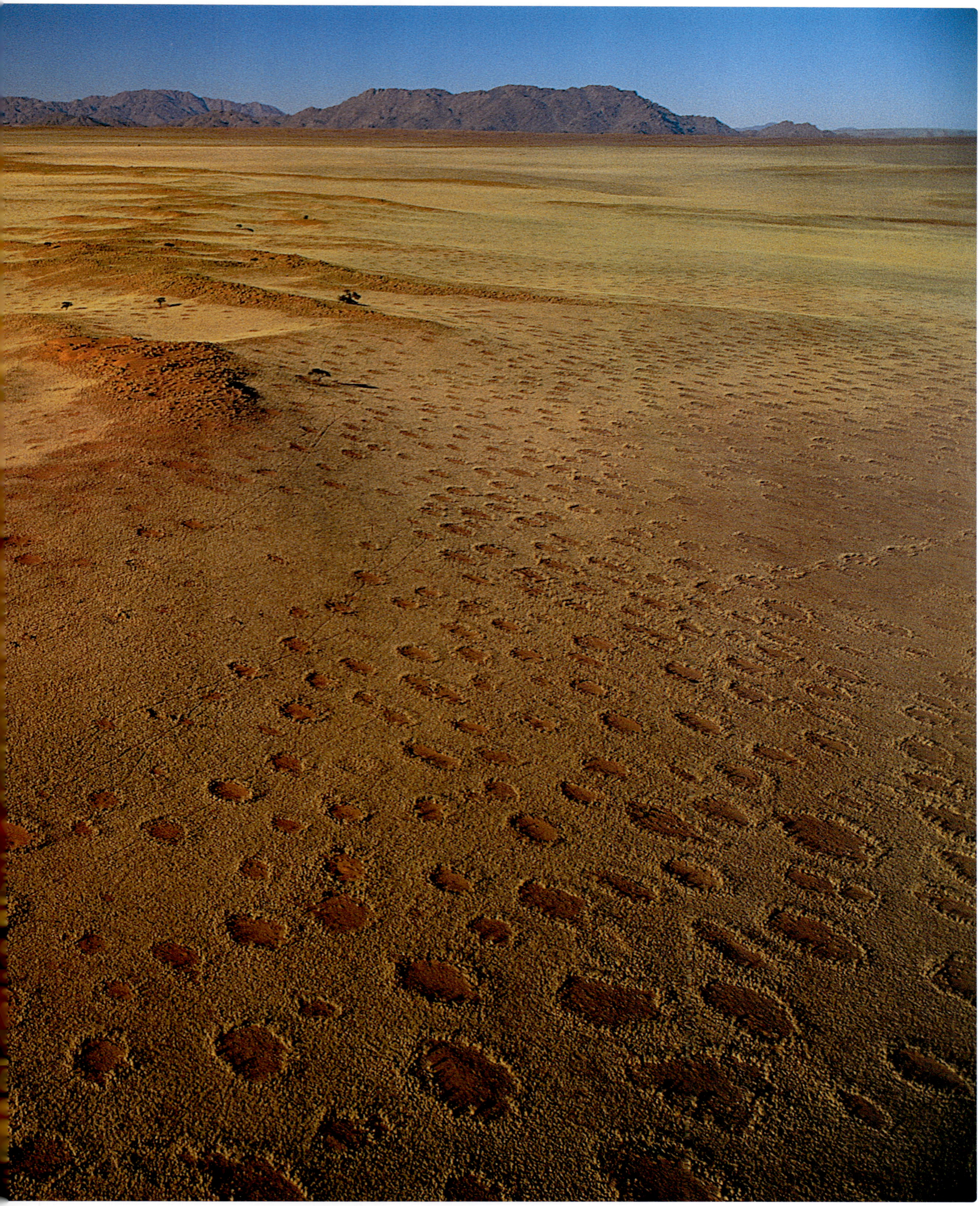

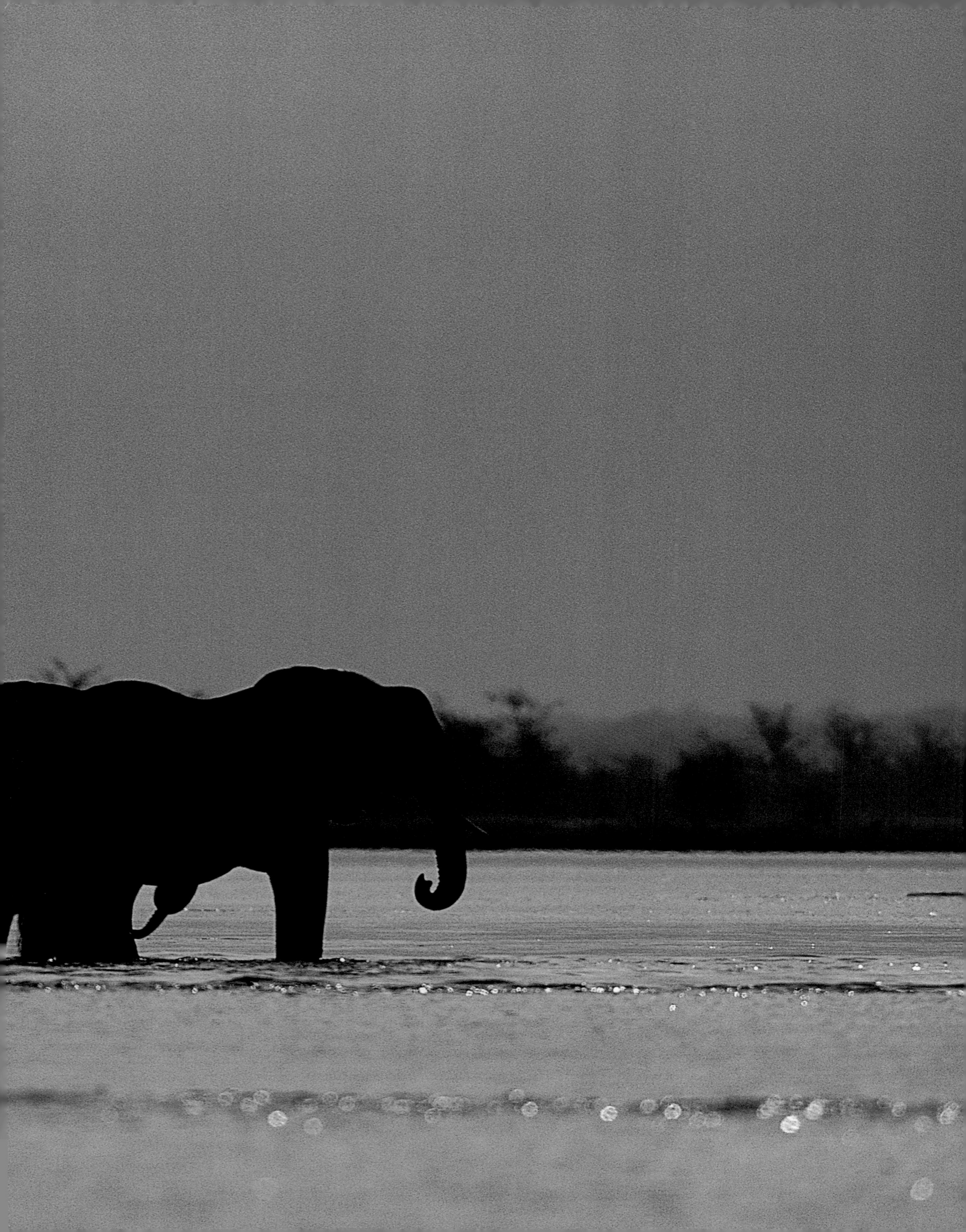

IN ZAMBIA, MORE THAN IN ANY OTHER SAFARI DESTINATION, YOU WILL FIND YOURSELF LISTENING TO HEAR WHAT NATURE HAS TO SAY. THE SMALLEST NOISE—A CRACKING TWIG, A RUSTLE IN THE LEAVES—IS A POSSIBLE INDICATION OF SECRET LIFE THAT WILL BE REVEALED ONLY TO THOSE WHO HAVE THE PATIENCE TO SEEK IT OUT.

A number of elegant canvas-backed chairs stand round the wood fire that will burn slowly all night to keep the wild animals at bay. The flickering flames cast eerie shadows over the trees and termite hills. The wind rustles the branches, while in the distance a fish-eagle utters its piercing cry. A kettle sings cheerily on the fire, reminding us that soon we will have to return to our daily lives. But for the moment, the magic of the African night reigns supreme.

A safari in Zambia is always an adventure. The camps are rough and ready—some might say under-equipped—but this creates an authentic taste of Africa, which more than makes up for any lack of comfort. Here you will find no crowded minibuses guided by radio to the nearest lion kill, no vast, soulless hotels, and no tourist circuits. The animals are truly wild, not semi-domesticated by daily visits from hordes of tourists. Zambia offers delightful little family-run camps that are still true to the spirit of their founders. Here, it is up to the visitor to adapt to the local rules, and not vice versa. In Zambia, more than in any other safari destination, you will find yourself listening to hear what nature has to say. The smallest noise—a cracking twig, a rustle in the leaves—is a possible indication of secret life that will be revealed only to those who have the patience to seek it out. In the Zambian savanna, the skies are as rich as the earth. Over four hundred species of birds live in the grasslands, providing a riot of color and sound. It is a shame that so many people ignore this astonishingly rich bird life in favor of the big five that everyone hopes to see. The birds of the savanna have developed a remarkable range of calls that are instantly recognizable to expert ornithologists. The strident, mocking whistle of the African starling, which resembles a blackbird with a metallic sheen to its feathers, is omnipresent to the point of being irritating. The lilac-breasted roller has a whole range of cries at its disposal to mark out its territory. The best singers are undoubtedly the rufous-naped larks, which repeat musical phrases of four or five notes, often for many minutes on end. English-speaking birdwatchers have compared this song to the phrase "hope you can see me," to which the crescendo of guttural cries of the arrow-marked babblers replies in chorus.

The constant chattering of the black-eyed bulbul that lives in groups in the undergrowth is less musical, but the powerful rhythm of their song is just as evocative. Birdwatchers say their song sounds as if the bird is ordering the listener to "wait a bit" and to "come back to Calcutta." Heuglin's robins are quite the philosopher, urging ornithologists to "think of it, think of it" in a variety of tones, which change according to the time of year, from an almost jazzy sound to whistles, alternating modulations and accelerating as the inspiration takes them. They often indulge in duos, singing from early dawn, rivaling the common whitethroat's scratchy song and the red-backed scrub robins who sing in a repetitive twitter that breaks off now and then in strident clicks. Unusually, these birds warn of approaching danger by raising their tails absolutely vertically.

The wealth of Zambia's open country—most of which is protected wilderness—is just as impressive as its bird life. The country has a population density of just fifteen people per square kilometer, and some thirty percent of the country, or 86,870 square miles (225,000 square kilometers)—roughly the size of the United Kingdom—has protected status as game reserves. However, a certain number of these game parks are extremely difficult to get to and to explore and several do not offer accommodation. The Zambian wilderness is very much off the beaten track. Zambian game parks are the perfect place for keen adventurers who want to experience safaris as they were a few decades ago,—before the modern tourist industry got hold of the idea. While the three main parks—the Lower Zambezi, Kafue, and South Luangwa—offer relatively comfortable overnight facilities, the Zambian tourist industry is still in its infancy, which means that anyone looking for a unique safari experience off the beaten track has come to the right place.

The South Luangwa park has fifteen or so camps where tourists can stay, making it the most visited game reserve in the country. The wealth of wildlife certainly makes a visit here worthwhile. Although Zambia does not have perhaps quite so many different species to offer as South Africa, it is still a good place to see wildebeest, zebras, warthogs, elephants, hyenas, leopards, lions, cheetahs, monitor lizards, crocodiles, and hippos. Large numbers of hippos often gather in the Luangwa and Zambezi rivers, making the waters boil and froth. The South Luangwa National Park is an excellent place to explore in the company of an experienced ranger, particularly in the Tafika private reserve, which lies alongside the national park. A walking safari in the tall grass which reaches high above your head is always full of suspense and

PRECEDING PAGES:
Elephants crossing the shallow waters of the Zambezi. Note the dominant female at the head of the herd and the way adults make sure the baby elephants are well surrounded to protect them from crocodiles.

FACING PAGE:
The Armchair Falls pound over the rocks between Knife Edge in Zambia and Danger Point in Zimbabwe. Despite the ever-increasing number of tourists, the site of Victoria Falls is still relatively unspoiled on both sides of the Zambia-Zimbabwe border.

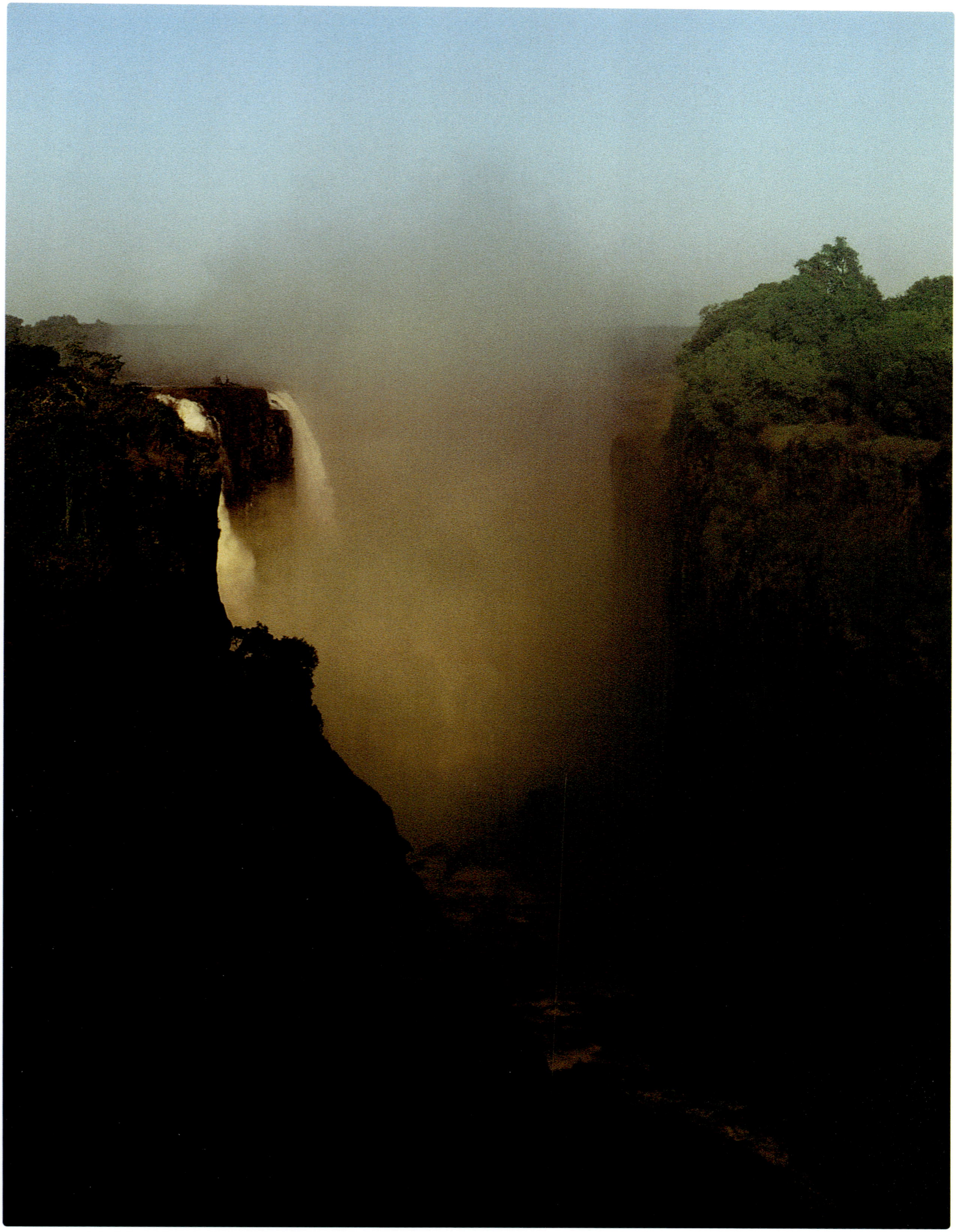

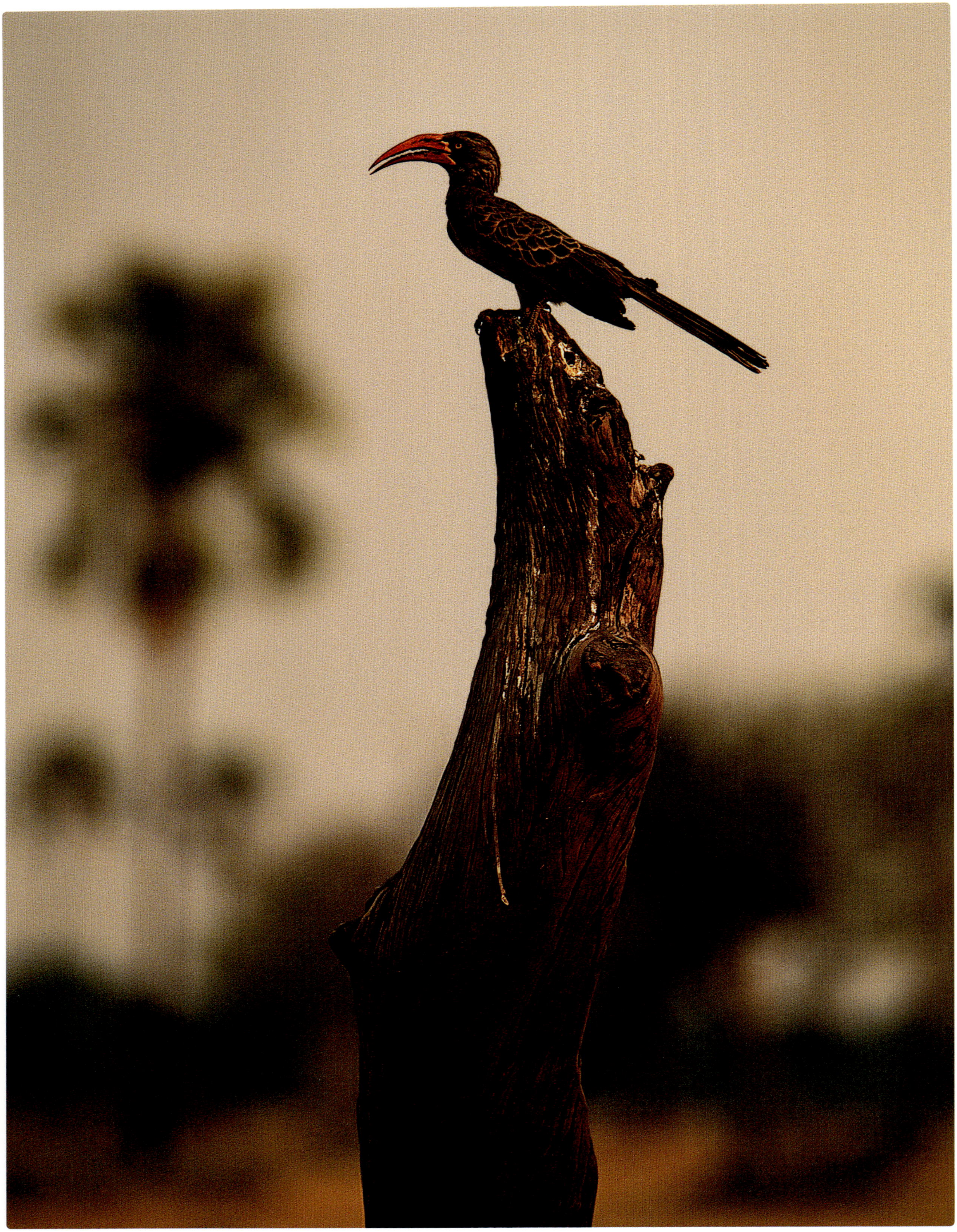

excitement, and gives you an idea of how Gulliver must have felt among the giants. Surrounded on all sides by waving grass, you could be just a few steps from a buffalo, zebra, or elephant. The animals seem to find it reassuring to be hidden by the long grass in the heart of the immense plain. Nature provides a host of clues for the ranger to follow which could be quite impossible to detect from inside a vehicle. An experienced guide will be able to tell you from the state of the flattened grass and the temperature and content of their dung how recently a herd of elephants passed by. He can follow the trace of the dung beetles that collect balls of droppings to roll back home to feed their larvae, or point out angrily chattering squirrels leaping from branch to branch in a dead tree suffocated by the embrace of a strangler fig —and the lionesses sleeping off their latest meal in its shade. But apart from such sightings, which are generally relatively few and far between, walking is an excellent way to appreciate features of life on the savanna that tourists driving round in air-conditioned minibuses simply miss—the elegantly curving branches of a tree, the scents and textures of the plants, the scuttling insects. Trees have a language all their own. The trees of southern Africa tell tales of thirst, searing heat, and the struggle to survive, written in the very shape of their twisted branches. Many species of tree have their own secrets and have given rise to local superstitions and legends. The marula tree can produce as many as seventy thousand fruits that are extremely rich in vitamin C. Elephants are driven crazy by the enticing smell of these fruits and have been known to try and uproot the whole tree to get at fruit hanging from the uppermost branches. They have also been known to get drunk on the fermenting fruits. The locals make a kind of beer from the root of the confetti tree, which is said to be a powerful aphrodisiac. The confetti tree is a thorn bush that gets its name from the vast numbers of tiny cream-colored flowers that cover it in the fall. The mopororo or rain tree is not used as a food source, but it is home to large colonies of tiny insects known as froghoppers, which feed on the shoots and young leaves and then excrete sugary water that drips from the leaves, giving the tree its name.

The early morning breeze starts blowing along the bed of the Luangwa at six A.M., when the light is just beginning to show the outlines of the trees and filter through the branches. It brings with it the delicate scent of wild jasmine as it plays in the sturdy branches of the thousand-year-old baobab. The tree's soft wood is full of nooks and crannies that are home to birds and genets, while leopards can sometimes be seen sleeping in the branches. Squirrels love the tasty fruits of the croton tree, whose seeds have anti-malarial properties. In the plains you may also see ebony trees, famous for their heavy dark wood, sausage trees, much loved by hippos—the locals use sausage tree trunks for their canoes—and candle acacias that lions occasionally climb to rest in.

To make the most of a stay in the magical realm of Tafika, you must take your time. Spend an afternoon just sitting at the foot of a tree, studying the pattern of the branches and leaves, watching the insects scurrying on its roots. Look out for the zebras camouflaged in the long grass, their stripes making them extremely hard to distinguish against the rippling grass. The private reserve has now organized a three-day walk taking visitors round the three camps —Tafika Main Camp, Chikoko, and Crocodile—enabling them to see the best of the park by day and by night.

FACING PAGE:
Many species of hornbill (pictured, a Bradfield's hornbill) live in the arid, tree-dotted savanna. Their clumsy appearance and their characteristic call make them the clowns of the African plains.

TREES HAVE A LANGUAGE ALL THEIR OWN. THE TREES OF SOUTHERN AFRICA TELL TALES OF THIRST, SEARING HEAT, AND THE STRUGGLE TO SURVIVE, WRITTEN IN THE VERY SHAPE OF THEIR TWISTED BRANCHES. MANY SPECIES OF TREE HAVE THEIR OWN SECRETS AND HAVE GIVEN RISE TO LOCAL SUPERSTITIONS AND LEGENDS.

This walking tour has proved such a success that the reserve's owner, John Coppinger, has set up a similar arrangement in the heart of North Luangwa Park. Here, the wilderness is even more untouched than in Tafika. Mwaleshi is paradise on earth, so isolated that there is not even a road leading to it. Since Norman Carr launched the first walking safaris in Zambia in the 1950s, a number of similar outfits have been set up by the owners of private reserves, including Robin Pope, who built the famous Tena Tena Lodge. This lodge is very basic, consisting of just six tents set up in a circle in a grove of sausage trees, not far from the river where the hippos like to wallow. Every so often, the waters of the river burst their banks, washing away great clumps of earth, which means the fragile tents are at greater risk of flooding every year.

There are a number of other camps in the vicinity. Derek Shenton's Kaingo Camp lies in the shade of a copse of ebony and mahogany trees on the banks of the Luangwa. The Mfuwe camp is one of very few in the region to go beyond the basic provision of huts made of straw and branches. It offers eighteen suites built of pink brick and wood imported from Mozambique, built on piles so that the hippos and crocodiles come and feed almost at the very foot of the large, airy buildings. The camp includes a swimming pool, reading room, and conference room. Most of these camps, however luxurious, are forced to close during the rainy season, December to April.

THE LOWER ZAMBEZI PARK WAS OPENED FOR TOURISTS IN 1989 BY THE FAMILY OF THE CURRENT MANAGING DIRECTOR, GRANT CUMINGS. DESPITE THE LACK OF ACCOMMODATION, A VISIT HERE IS WELL WORTH YOUR WHILE, AS THERE IS A FABULOUS RANGE OF WILDLIFE, PARTICULARLY DURING THE DRY SEASON WHEN THIRSTY ANIMALS FLOCK TO THE BANKS OF THE ZAMBEZI.

While the South Luangwa Park has a range of accommodation, all the Lower Zambezi National Park has to offer is the small tent camp of Chiawa. The Lower Zambezi Park was opened for tourists in 1989 by the family of the current managing director, Grant Cumings. Despite the lack of accommodation, a visit here is well worth your while, as there is a fabulous range of wildlife, particularly during the dry season when thirsty animals flock to the banks of the Zambezi. The southern part of the park has another attraction that is just as big a draw as the wildlife: the Zambezi Falls. More and more tourists are coming to visit the falls from this side of the border, no doubt because of the political upheaval in Zimbabwe on the other side of the border. Although Zimbabwe was the first to realize the full potential of the site as a tourist destination, Zambia has now caught up and has a range of excellent hotels within easy reach of the falls. Alongside a number of charming family-run hotels on the banks of the Tongabezi and Sindabezi rivers, the large international hotel chains have recently moved into the region. Visitors to the cozy, elegant River Club Hotel, for example, stay in comfortable individual suites discreetly tucked away beneath the ebony and acacia trees overlooking the Zambezi. The suites are open on all sides—all that comes between you and the African night is your mosquito net. Then there is the Zambezi Sun, the prestigious flagship hotel belonging to the Sun International chain, and the exceptional Royal Livingstone, which has superb air-conditioned rooms, a first-class restaurant, and direct private access to the falls. A family of monkeys has taken up residence in the grounds and it is delightful to watch their antics as you breakfast on the terrace. Some tourists might prefer to give up a little luxury in favor of the great historic interest and old-fashioned charm of the Hotel Victoria, just across the border in Zimbabwe. All of these hotels offer a range of activities for tourists, including early-morning elephant rides in the Mosi-oa-Tunya Park and unforgettable picnics on one of the tiny islands that dot the river, just a stone's throw from the falls—and the crocodiles.

Zambia has a third park open to tourists. The Kafue National Park has everything from primeval forest to wetlands, savannas, and mighty rivers. The park, measuring some 86,490 square miles (224,000 square kilometers), is famous for its lions, which have learned to imitate leopards by climbing trees to sleep in the branches during the rainy season. They are not alone in having adapted their behavior to the cycle of the rains. Edward Smythe, owner of a tiny camp in the park, dismantles his huts every year as the rains begin, only to put them back up when the dry season returns. As soon as the floodwaters recede on the Busanga plain, he puts up his four huts: three straw-roofed shelters for guests to sleep in, and a canvas-roofed canteen. He will only accept guests who are prepared to sacrifice the luxury of modern hotels for a taste of the real Africa. Life in his camp is tough, but visitors come away with an idea of what life was like for the first settlers.

Over the last few years, the Zambian authorities, along with other southern African governments, have come to realize that the natural world is their most precious resource. They are making serious efforts to safeguard it for future generations. However, the political and economic crises that have periodically rocked the country since independence in 1964 have left little room for a real development strategy to emerge. Deforestation and massive erosion are serious issues that the government has been slow to deal with, although the progressive privatization of nationally owned lands since the 1990s has gradually halted the process. The peasant farmers who make up much of the population are nonetheless faced with regular droughts, galloping inflation, and political instability, although to a far lesser extent, it must be said, than in neighboring Zimbabwe.

Judging by recent estimates of the animal population, Zambia's poor farmers are not the only ones suffering from the difficult economic climate. It seems the only way that the very poorest Zambians can survive is still by hunting wild animals, while others have latched onto the illegal trade in animal body parts. A few decades ago, Zambia boasted a population of a hundred thousand elephants. Today, three-quarters of these beautiful animals have been killed by poachers. The fate of the black rhino is even worse. The entire population has been wiped out. Not a single black rhino survives in Zambia today.

FACING PAGE:
Some people prefer traveling on the upper Zambezi by canoe or dugout to feel closer to the animals, but a cruise on the African Queen is doubtless the most comfortable and elegant way to watch the crocodiles and elephants.

FOLLOWING PAGES:
Flying over Victoria Falls, whether in a helicopter, hot-air balloon, biplane, or microlight, is a majestic experience. Only from the air can you get a true idea of the gigantic size of the river, the winding gorges, and the vastness of the falls themselves. In the foreground, the Rainbow Falls. As in the Okavango delta, taxi-planes are the most practical way to travel. This unfortunately means that safaris in Zambia are not noticeably cheaper than elsewhere, even though the accommodation is generally more basic than in other safari destinations.

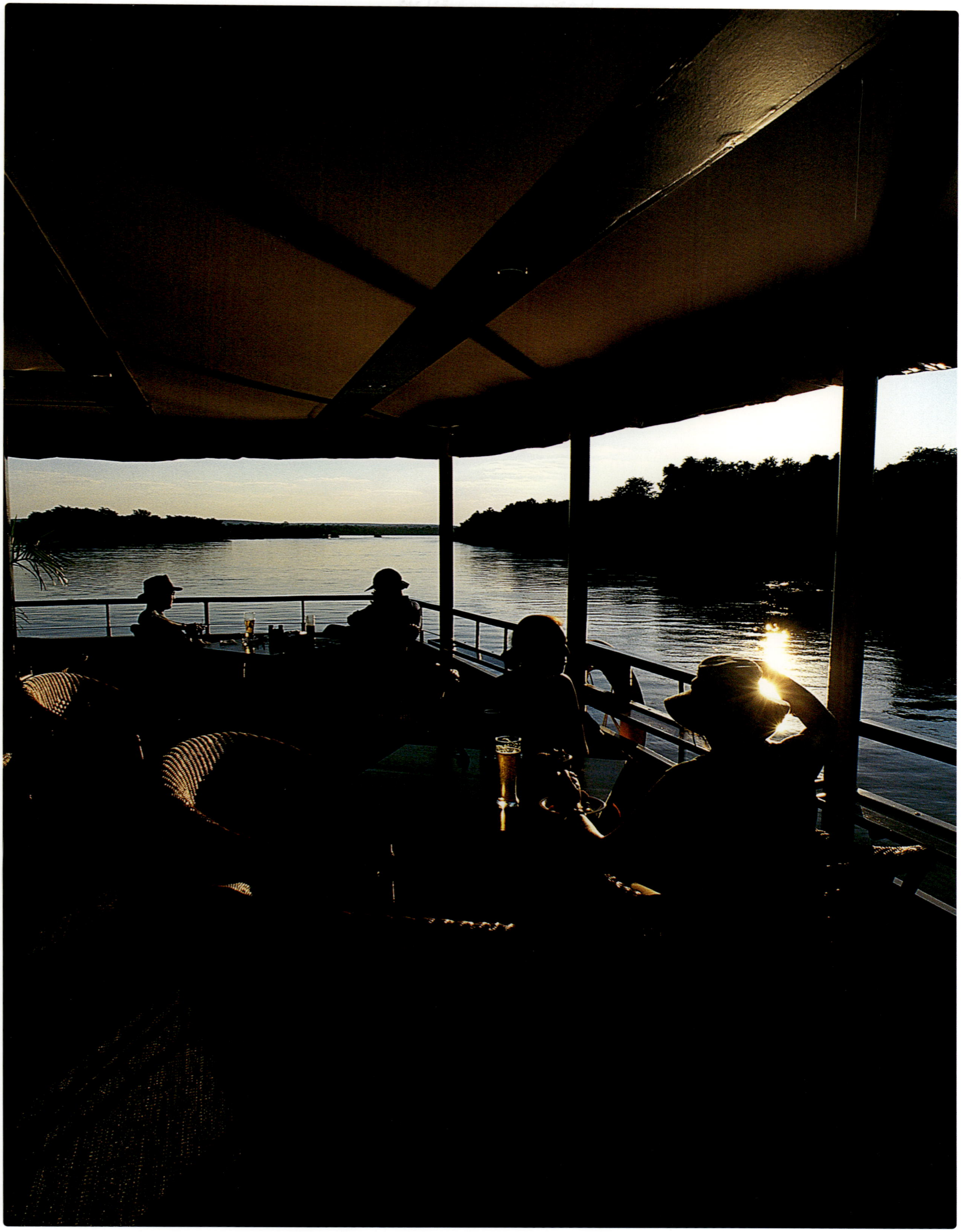

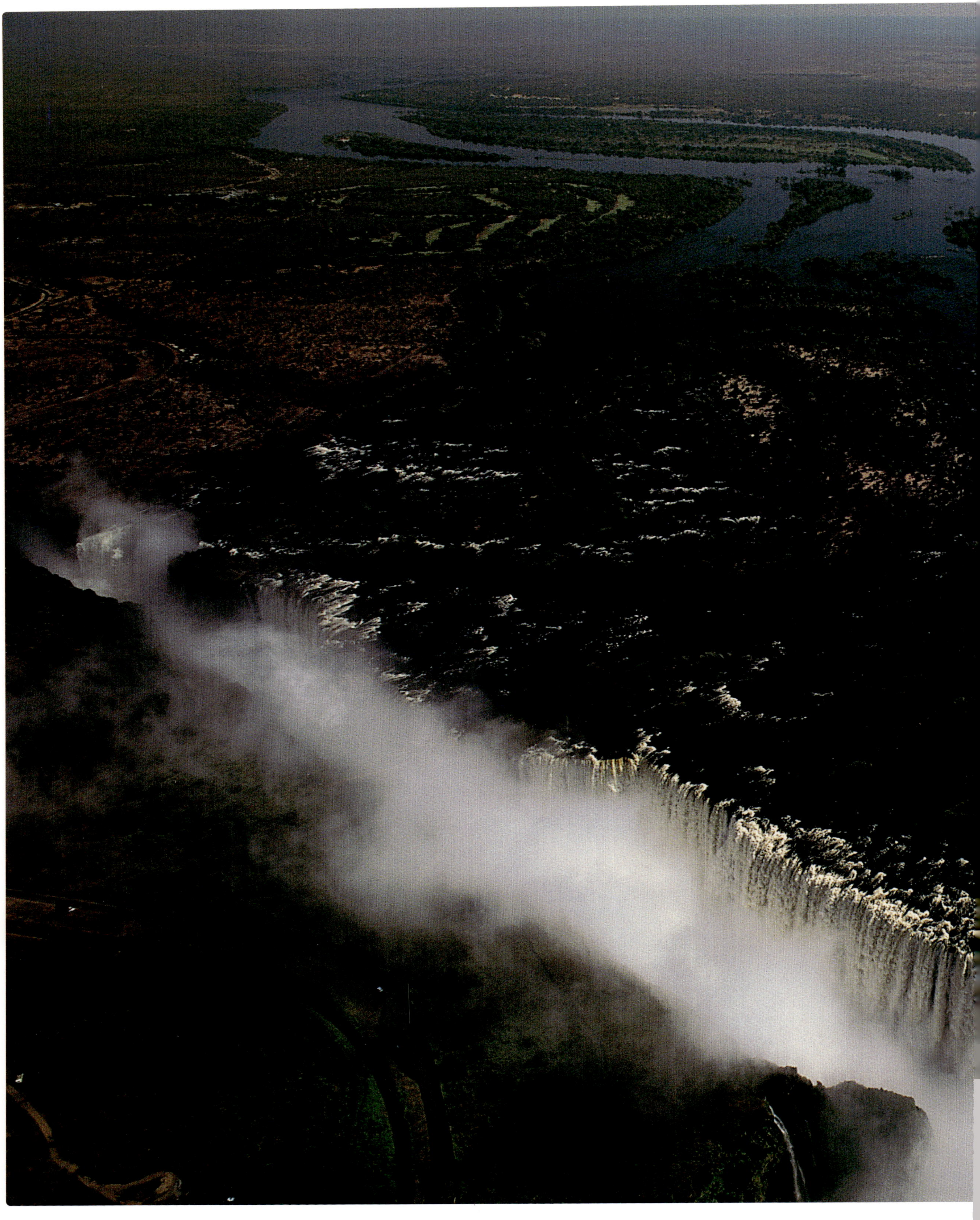

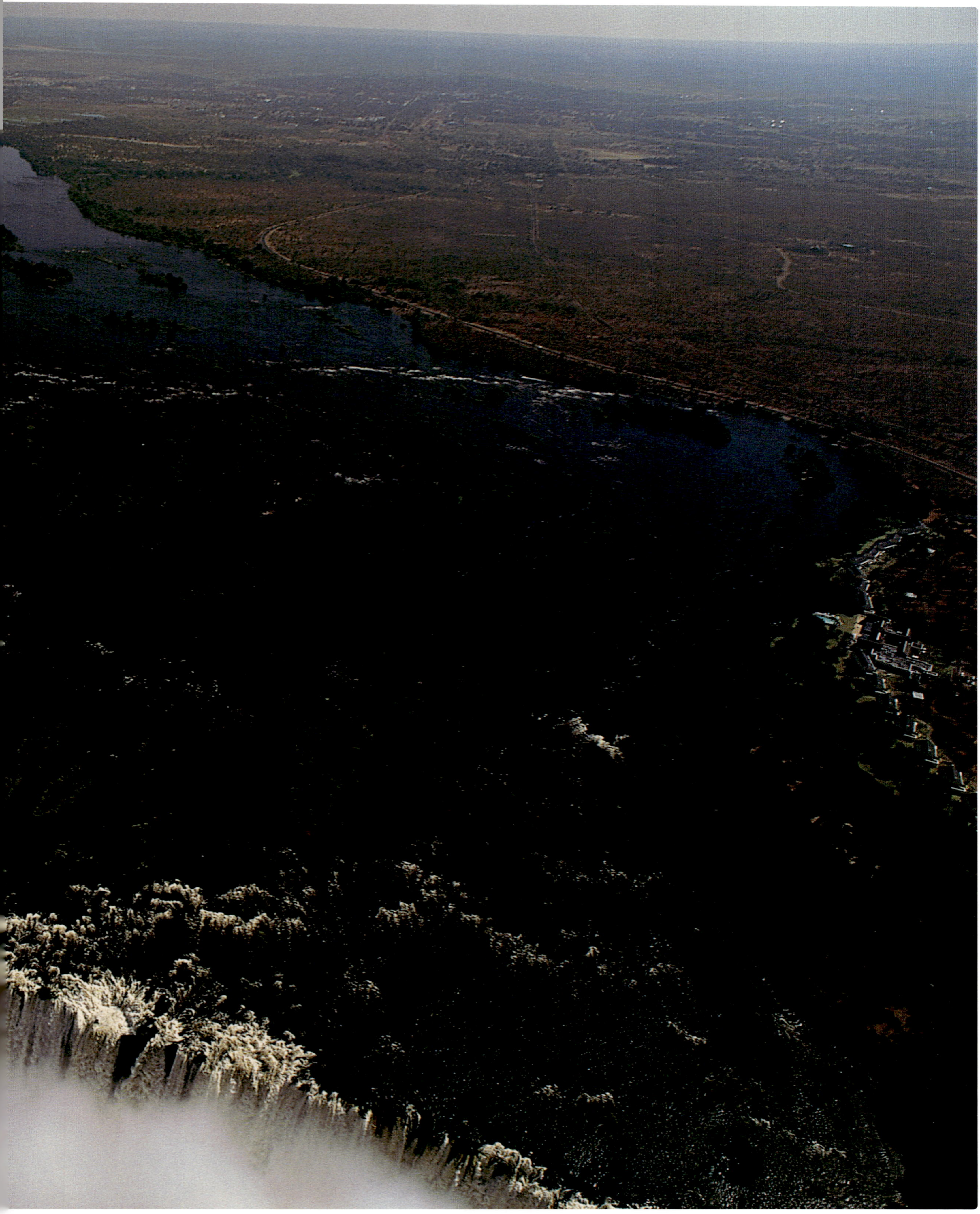

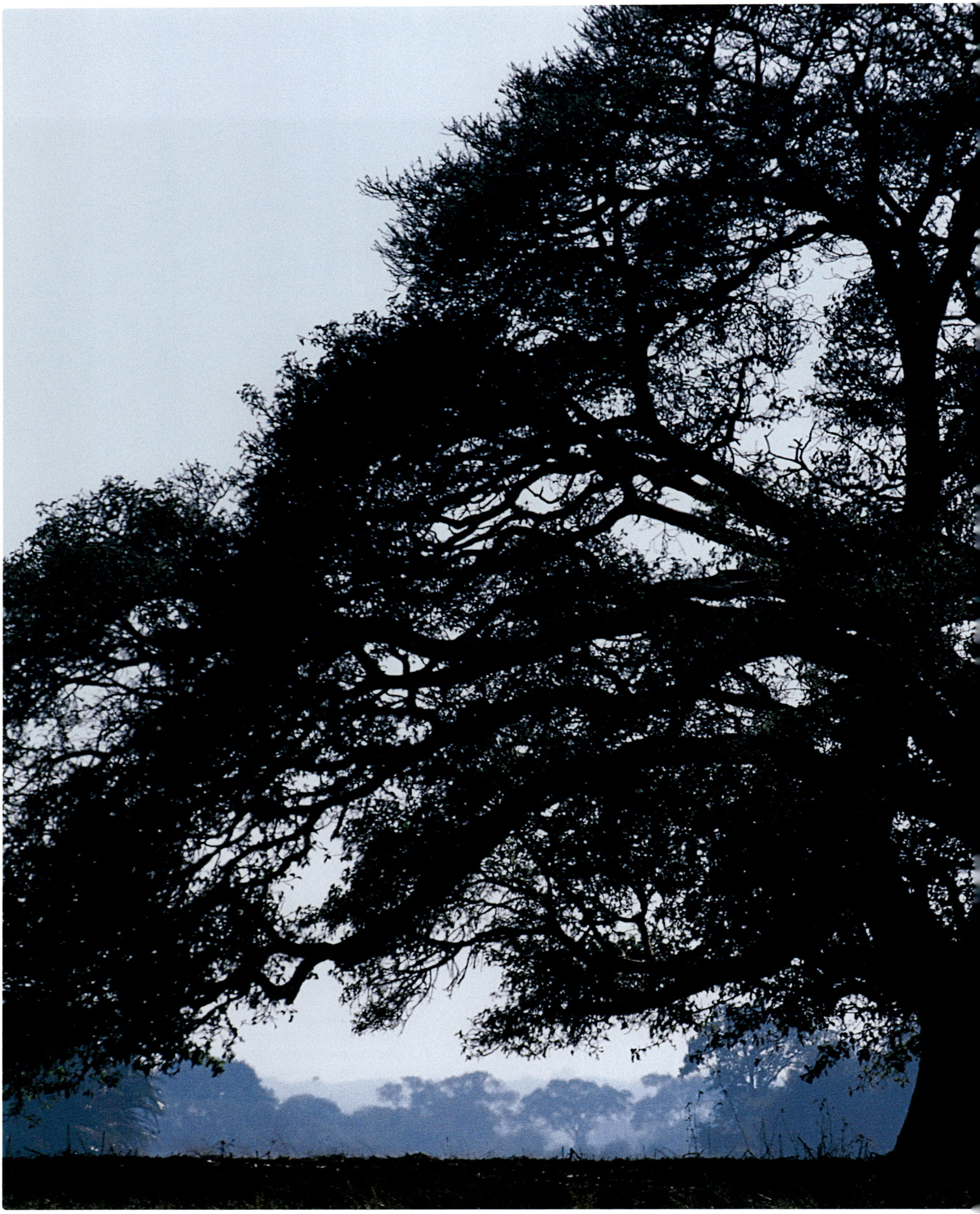

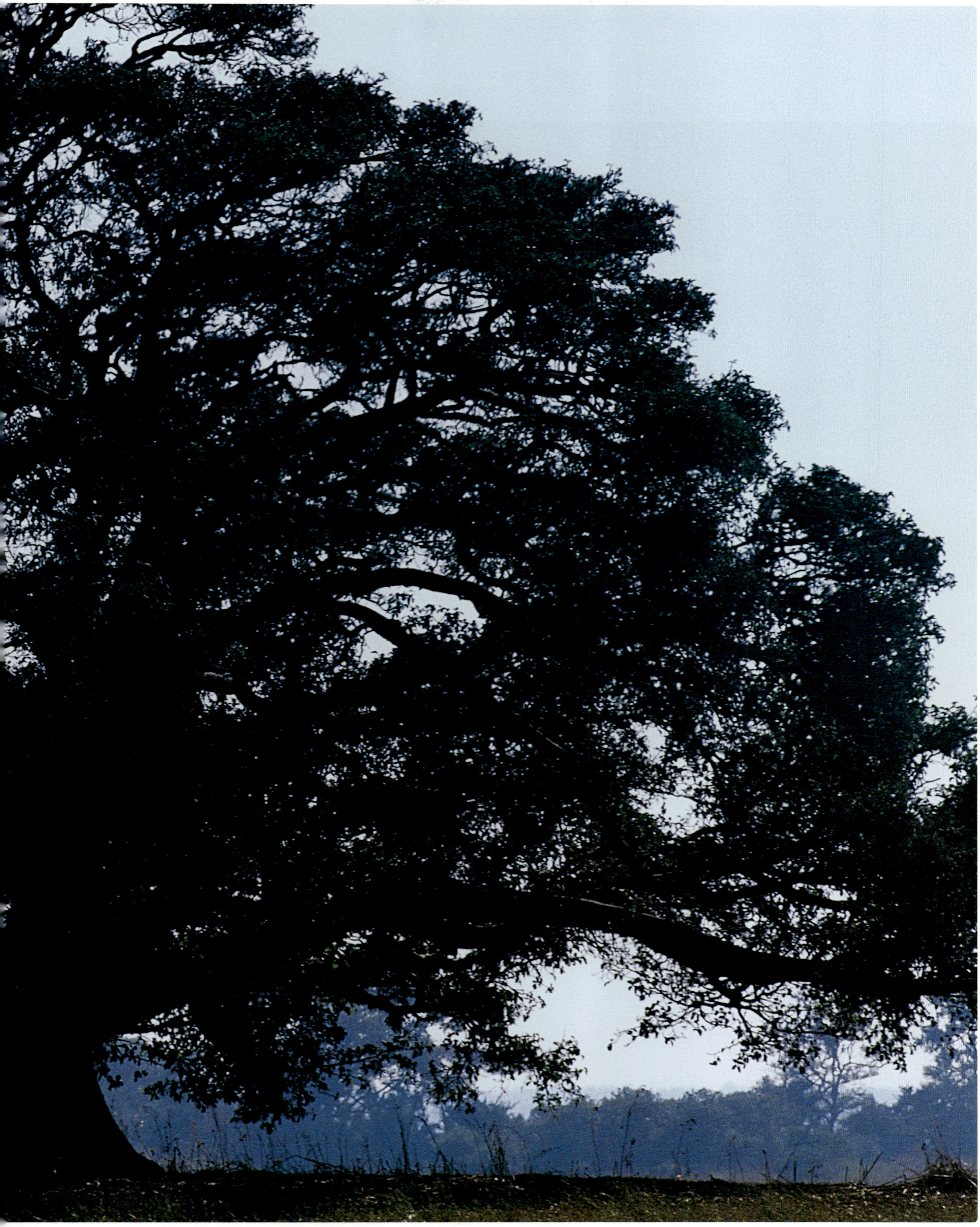

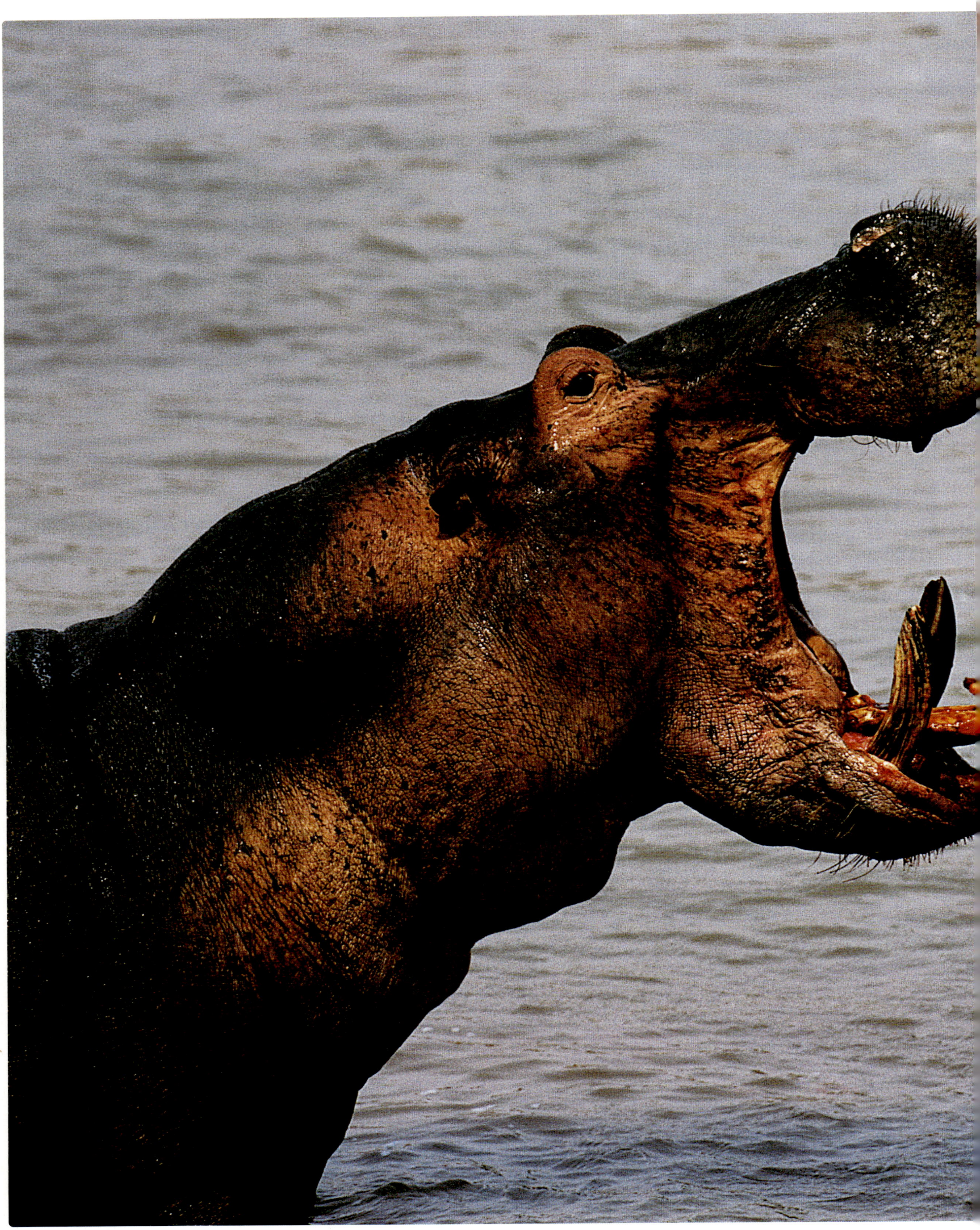

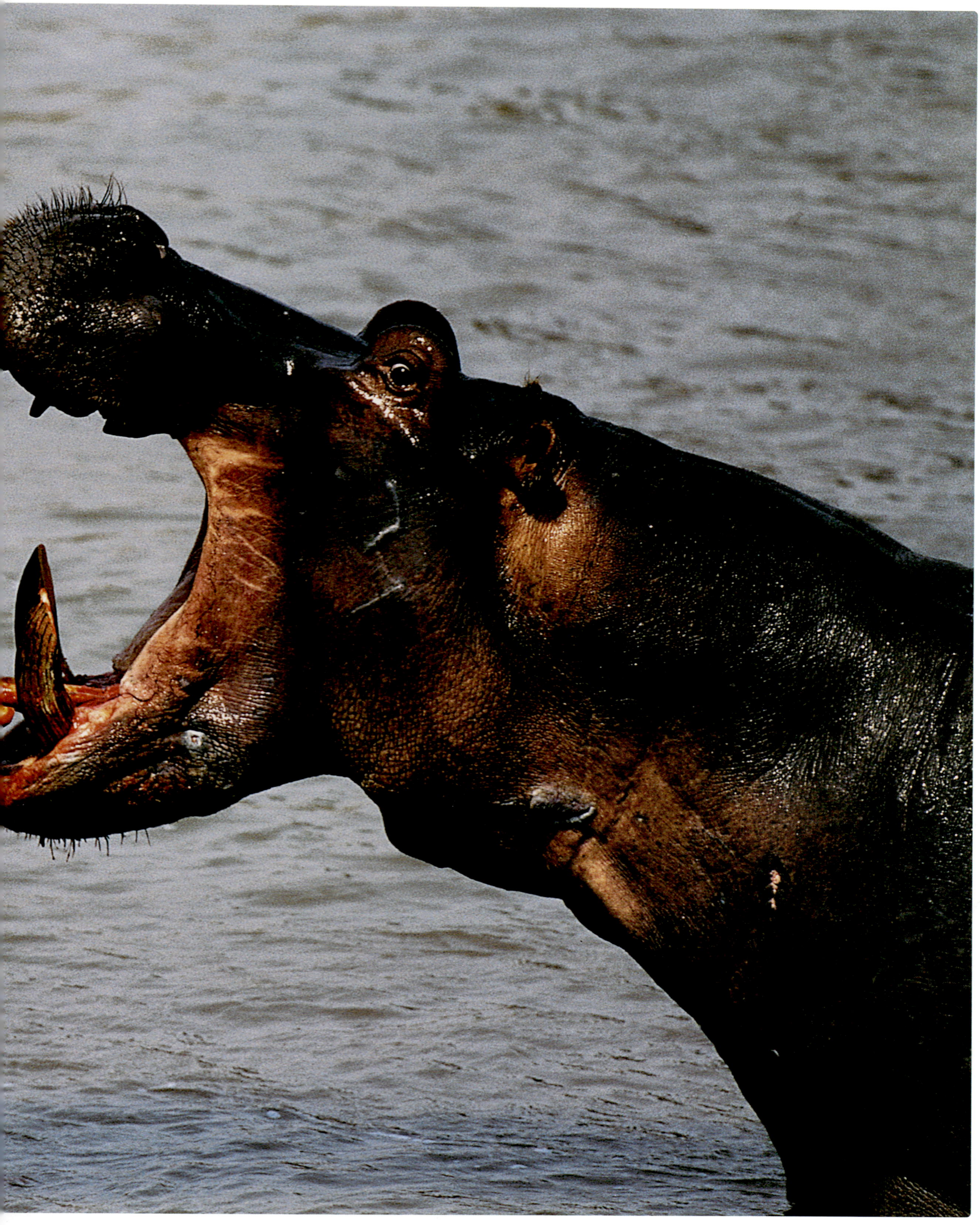

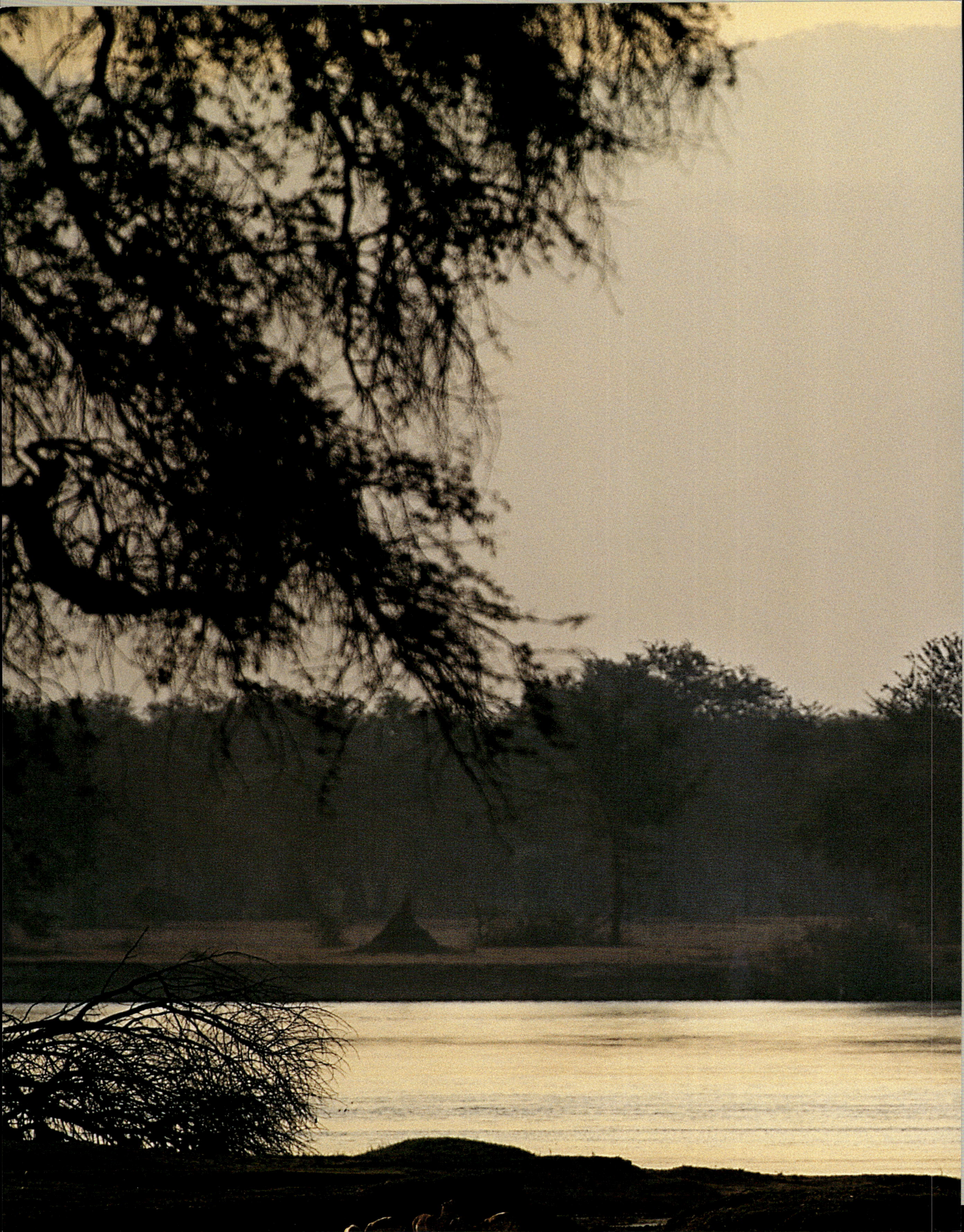

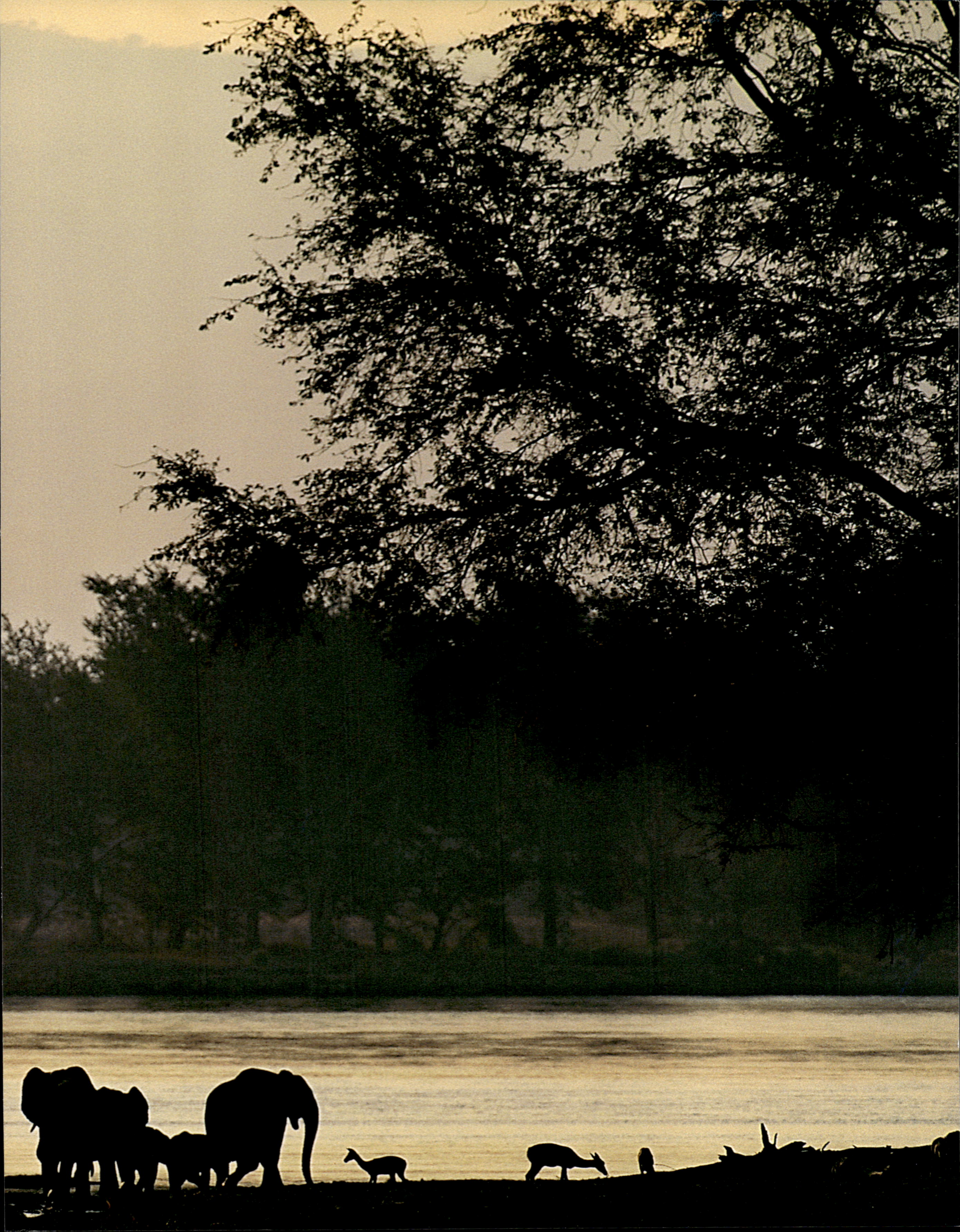

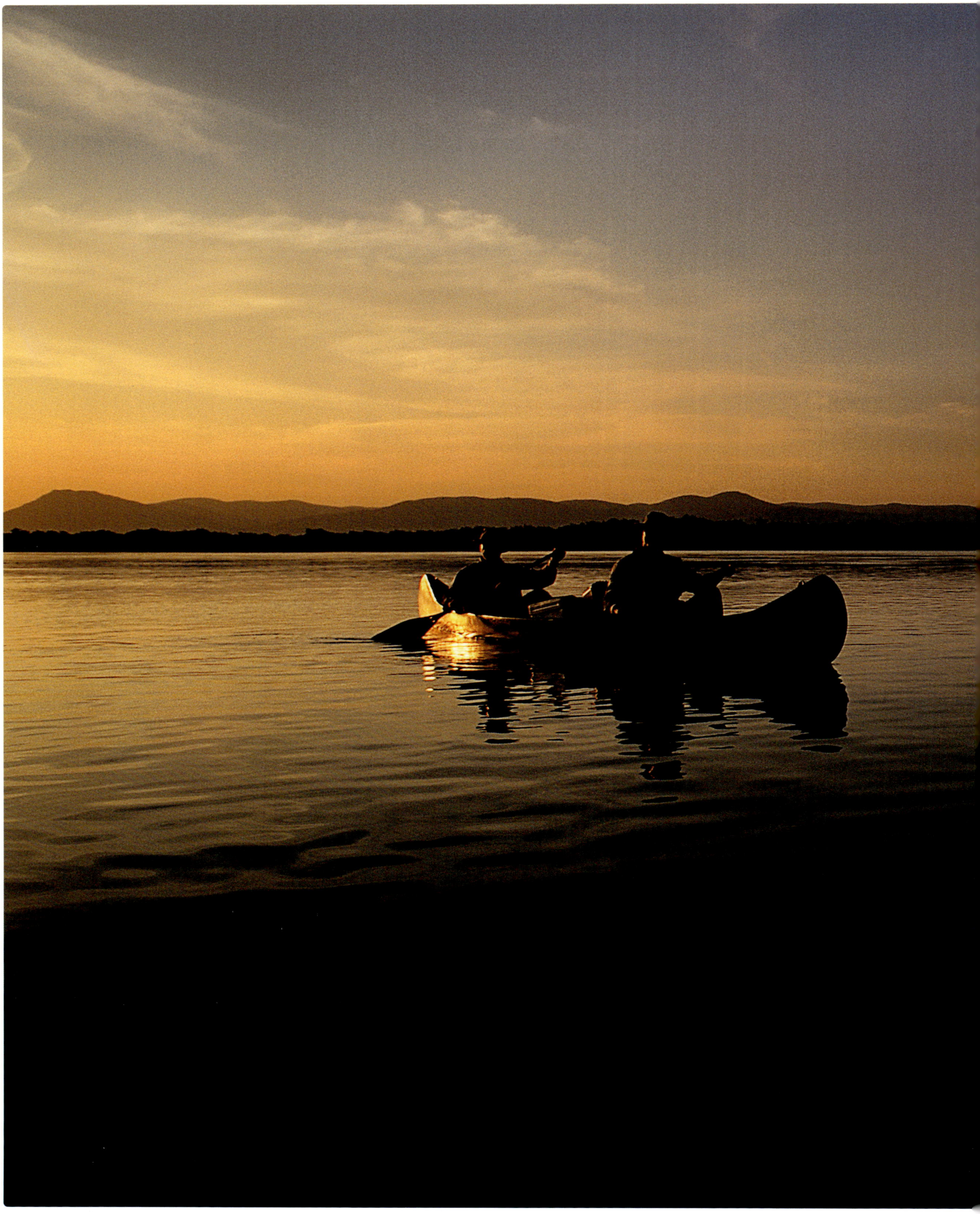

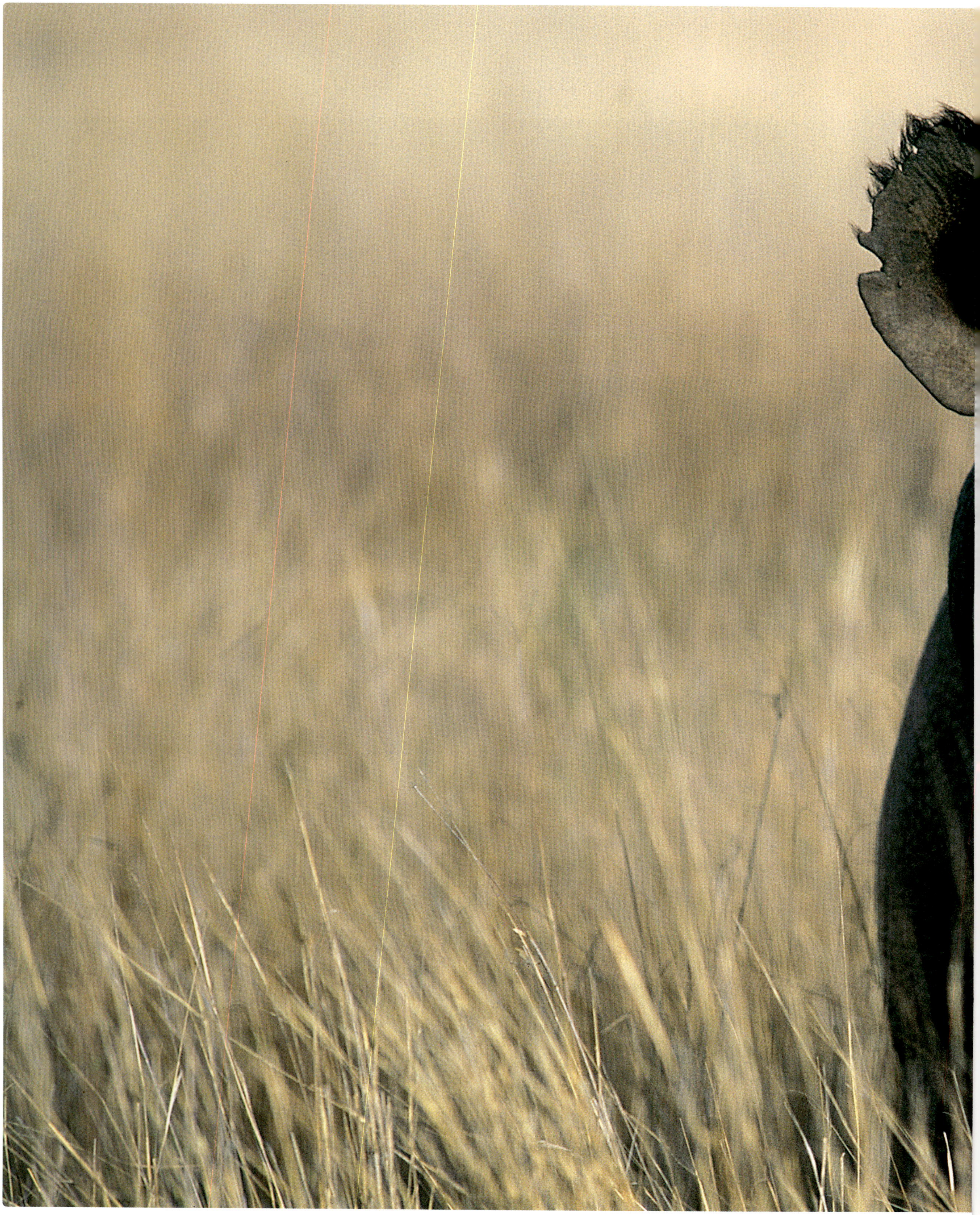

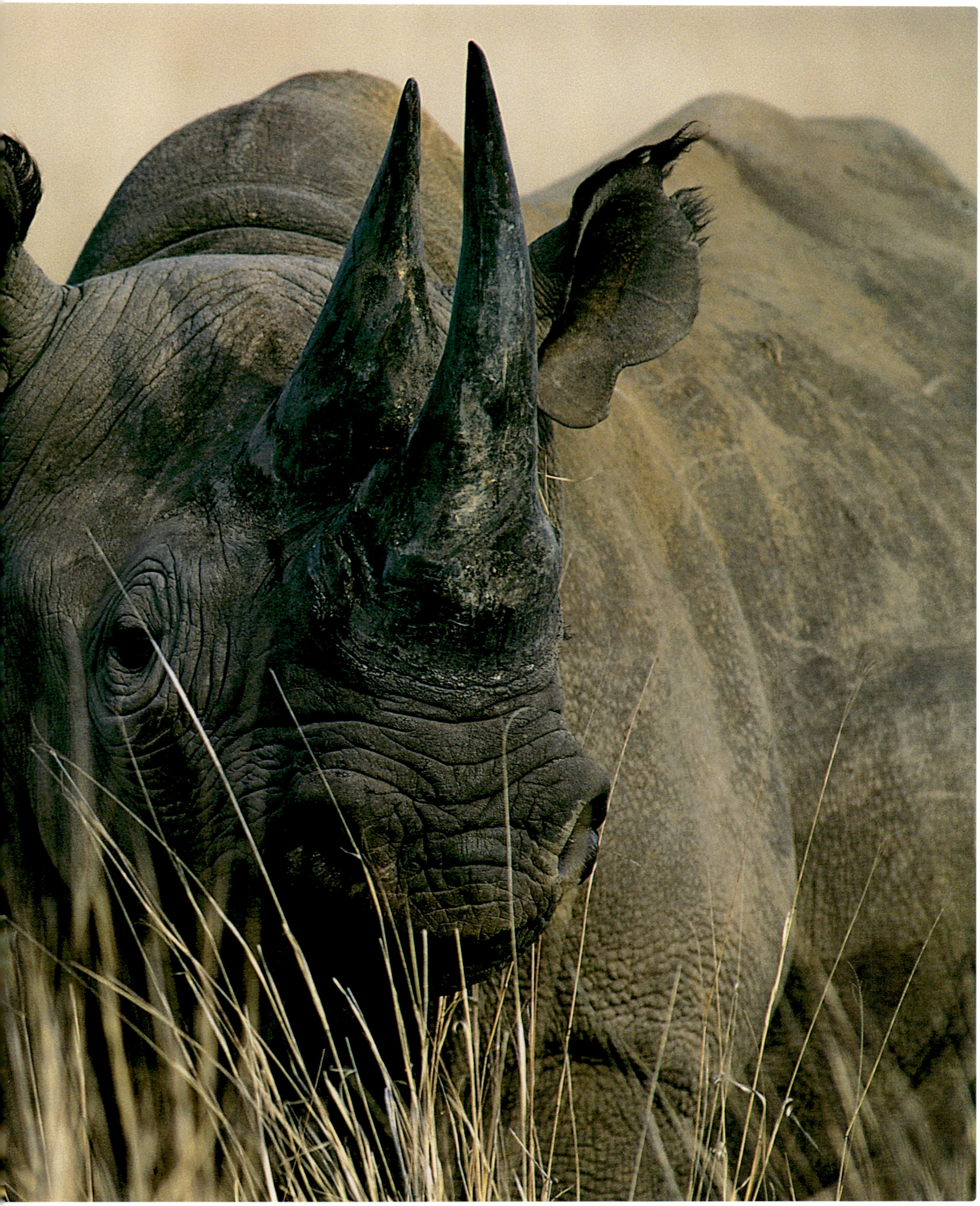

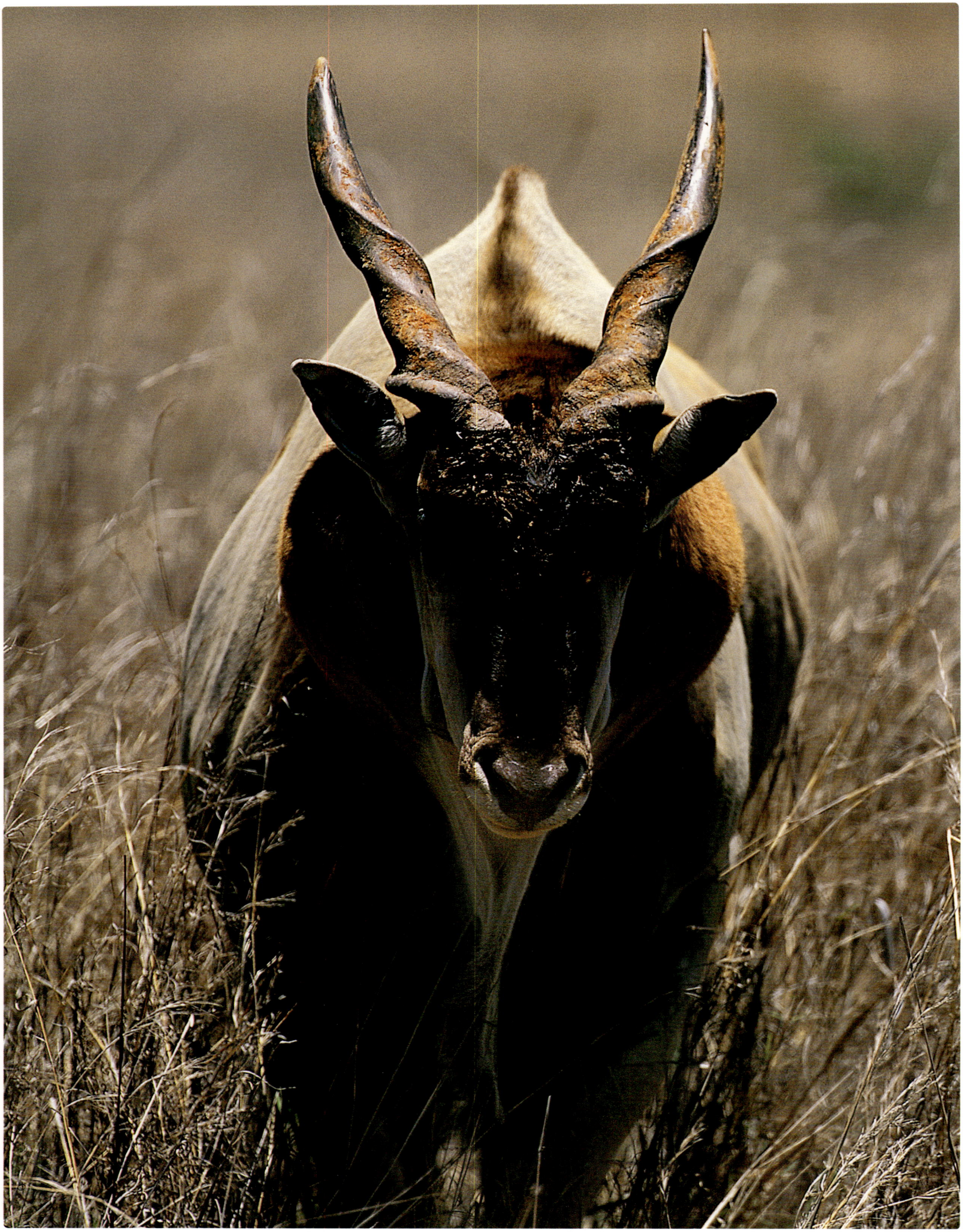

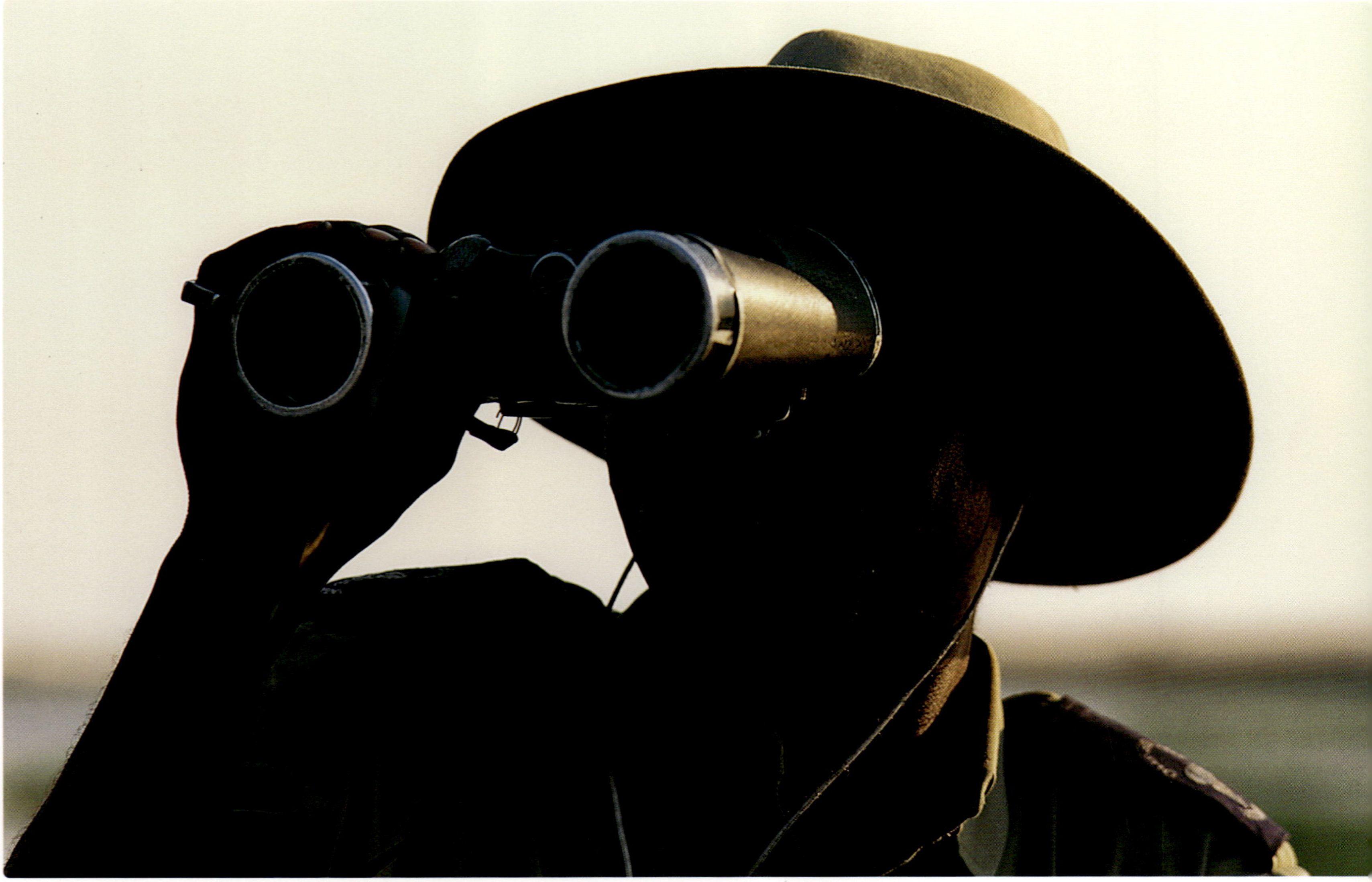

FACING PAGE:

Many private farms that were actively engaged in wildlife protection programs have been despoiled by Mugabe's henchmen, who have killed animals such as this superb eland in order to sell their meat.

ABOVE:

The key to a successful safari is having an excellent guide or ranger who can point out animal spoor and explain how the animals interact with the environment. Doug is a real expert. I was only able to take many of these photographs thanks to his skill in tracking rare and timid creatures.

FACING PAGE:

During the breeding season, which lasts just a few days, lions mate some 160 times. As with all cats, the lioness ovulates as a reaction to the painful withdrawal of the male's barbed penis.

FOLLOWING PAGES:

As night falls over the bush, civets, genets, pangolins, porcupines, leopards, and lions waken for the night's activities. A night game drive will show you an entirely different side of the savanna.

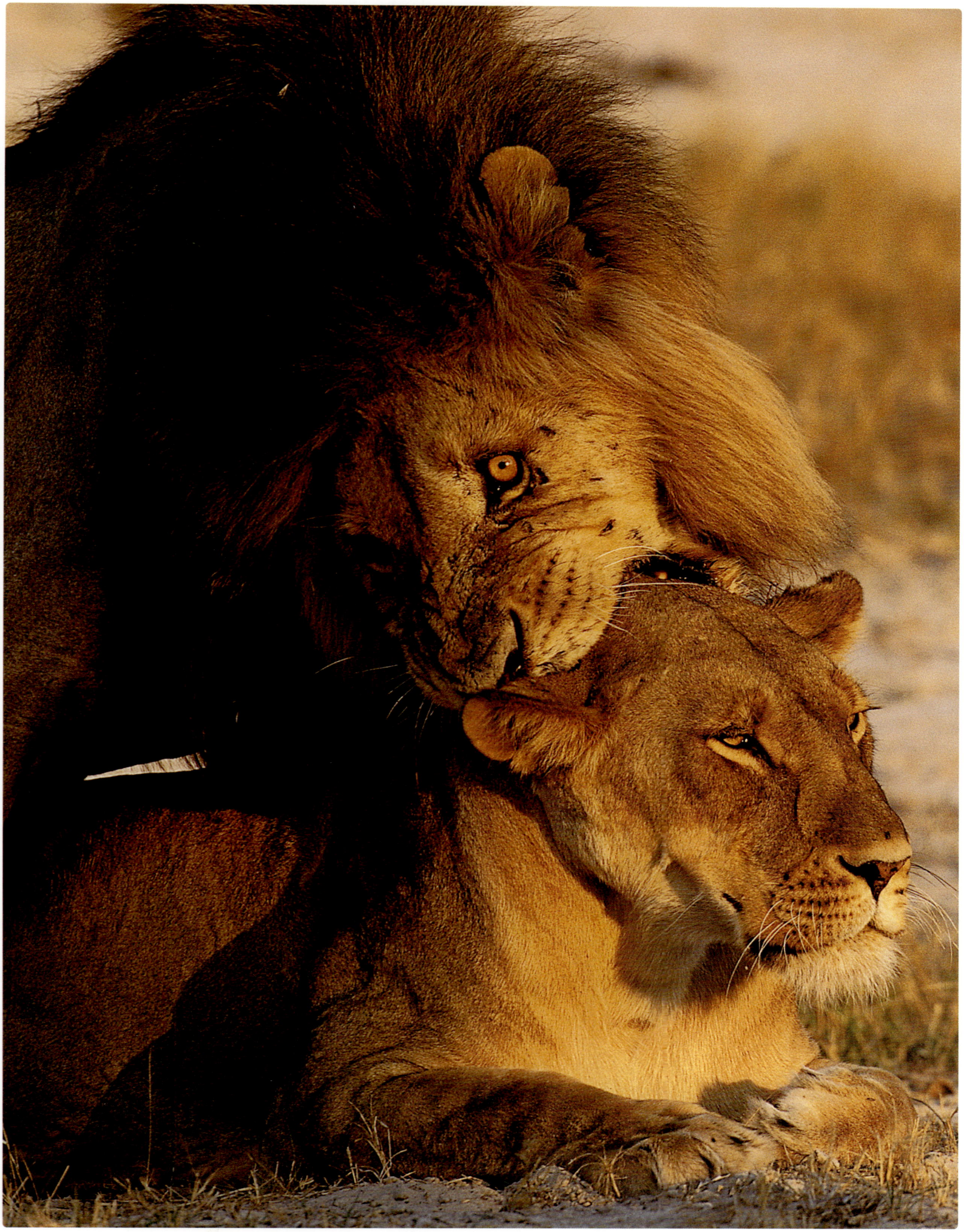

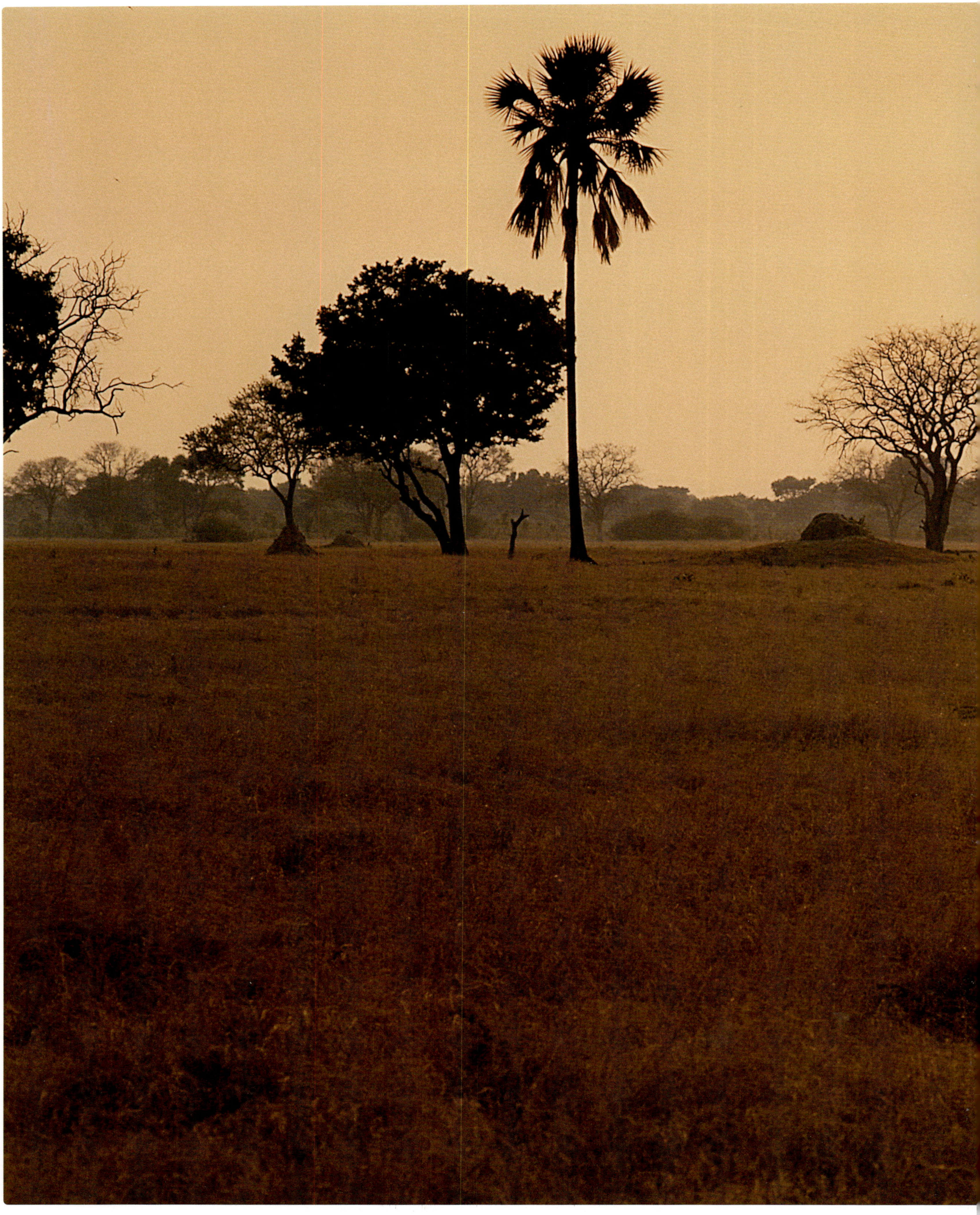

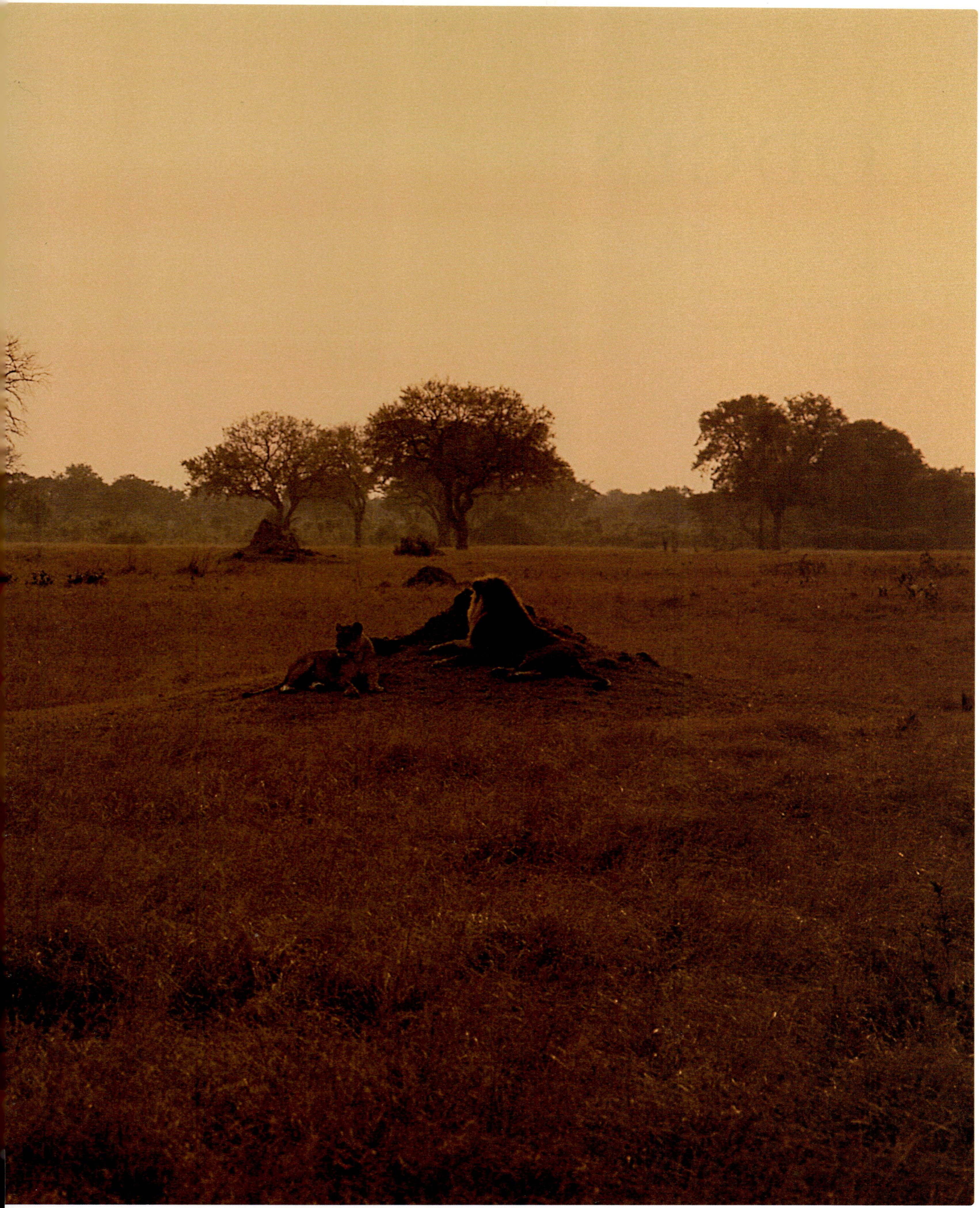